Healing
Depression

"Catherine's simple and practical approach to healing yourself from depression through nutrition and the body-mind connection helps us to get our lives back on track. This is a much-needed book for everyone who suffers from depression in any form. Thank you, Catherine, for sharing your life with us."

— Elizabeth Barhydt
Co-Author, *Self-Help for Stress and Pain* and *Learning Blocks and Self-Help for Kids: Improving Performance and Building Self-Esteem*

"Catherine Carrigan has opened the door for millions of people who suffer from depression, with a highly readable, useful book based on her own experiences with the disease. Catherine has done her research well and includes practical alternatives which everyone can explore to find what works for them. I will recommend the book to my students and clients."

— Paul E. Dennison, Ph.D.
President, Educational Kinesiology Foundation, Co-Author, *Brain Gym Teacher's Edition*

"Many people, including health professionals, believe that serious depressions can be treated only by powerful drugs, electroshock, and various forms of psychological and behavioral therapies. *Healing Depression* is a personal road map for sufferers that lays out the other routes toward healing. Written by a woman who has been there, this book offers new hope for people who find themselves constantly struggling to attain happiness."

— Melvyn R. Werbach, M.D.
author, *Nutritional Influences on Mental Illness*

"The story told by Catherine Carrigan is one of hope, where so many people now suffering don't have hope. It has insights and resources that can make the difference between just being alive and making the commitment to take charge of your life and be your own primary care provider. It will help you be able to utilize the specialists in the health care field to your own best advantage. Read this book and regain your hope and maybe even your zest for living."

— John F. Thie, D.C.

    author, *Touch for Health;* founding chairman, International College of Applied Kinesiology

"This is a wonderful book that can really help people who are depressed. This is a book with heart and facts combined. If you're suffering from depression, this book will give you the hope you need and the way out. You'll see a light at the end of your long tunnel."

— Jerry V. Teplitz, J.D., Ph.D.

    author, *Switched-On Living*

"Catherine Carrigan's unique book should be read and digested by people with depression and the professionals and families who care for them. Comprehensive, yet concise. Interesting, practical, and timely. It provides readers with an in-depth look at many of the causes of depression and what can be done to overcome them. I highly recommend this book."

— William G. Crook, M.D.

    author, *The Yeast Connection and the Woman* and *The Yeast Connection Handbook*

"Catherine Carrigan has written one heart-filled comprehensive book for helping people who suffer from depression. As a body-oriented psychotherapist and muscular therapist, I found her book to be fantastic and a source of hope for mankind. It offers a wealth of useful information for people to incorporate into their lives about how to create wellness. This book is a much-needed, long-overdue guide that I feel will help a great number of people—those who suffer with depression as well as the psychotherapists who counsel/treat people who suffer from depression. I urge my colleagues to read this book with open mind, heart, and spirit. You will realize and receive its powerfulness, the holistic approach to healing depression. I recommend this book for both my clients and my colleagues."

— Denise Borrelli, Ph.D., L.M.H.C., A.T.R., L.M.T.
Director of Education and Mass. Chapter President,
The American Massage Therapy Association;
Adjunct Professor, Springfield College Graduate
School of Art Psychotherapy

"Catherine Carrigan explores the causes of depression, understanding that it has different origins in different people and that multiple aspects must be explored to uncover those factors needed for recovery. Her book stands as a holistic self-help manual that the reader can use to begin to understand the chemical origins of depression.... Ms. Carrigan has been through the fires; she has walked the walk and now is ready to talk the talk. Her experiences, both her triumphs and her failures in finding her way back to health, are enlightening and encouraging and give a ray of sunshine for weary travelers with depression to use as a guide in their own quests."

— Paul A. Goldberg, M.H.H., D.C.
Professor of Clinical Nutrition and Gastroenterology
Director, The Goldberg Clinic, Marietta, GA

Healing Depression

A Holistic Guide

Catherine Carrigan

With a Foreword by Abram Hoffer, M.D., Ph.D., FRCP(C)

MARLOWE & COMPANY
NEW YORK

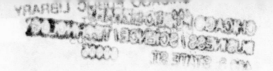

Published by
Marlowe & Company
841 Broadway, 4th Floor
New York, NY 10003

Library of Congress Cataloging-in-Publication Data

Carrigan, Catherine
Healing depression : a holistic guide : 38 questions and proven
answers to help you evaluate a wide range of treatment options / by
Catherine Carrigan.
    p.   cm.
Previously pub. with subtitle: A guide to making intelligent choices
about treating depression (Santa Fe, NM : Heartsfire Books. © 1997).
Includes bibliographical references and index.
ISBN 1-56924-656-4 (alk.paper)
1.   Depression, Mental—Treatment.   I. Title.
[RC537.C2763 1999]
616.85'2706—dc21   99-29136
                                                                 CIP

Manufactured in the United States of America
Distributed by Publishers Group West

With gratitude:

To all the courageous souls around the world who have told me how this book has improved their lives, despite all those who told them these teachings would never work. Let us establish a new paradigm: Mental illness can be healed! I dedicate this book to my husband, Henry Edmunds, and to my readers. I pray that all those who read it may find their own way into the light.

Contents

If there is a disease more appalling and devastating to patients and their families than depression, I have yet to run across it. Even schizophrenic patients—the most tragic sufferers—suffer most excruciatingly when they are depressed. Unfortunately, those who have not suffered deep depression cannot understand what is going on. They equate the mood with the occasional moments when they have been sad, or have grieved over the loss of something or some relationship. But there is no comparison. The great psychoanalyst Dr. Karl Menninger compared this difficulty in grasping the nature of depression to the predicament of a fish in a school of fish in the ocean. That fish has been hooked by a fishing line and is struggling mightily to escape. None of the other fish can see the line and they do not understand why their colleague is so agitated and disturbed. Many of my patients have told me they would sooner lose an arm than go through another bout of depression.

The only way to really know what depression is like is to have one. I do not recommend that anyone should do so. Over forty years ago I took some adrenochrome as part of our research into the causes of schizophrenia. I suffered a two-week depression with powerful paranoid features. Only when the depression suddenly lifted did I become aware of what had happened to me. I have never forgotten the experience. I am therefore very sensitive to the need to have books such as this one appear so that others can benefit by reading about it and not by having to suffer through it on their own. They will then know what they should do if they should become depressed and will be better at supporting their friends and relatives if they should suffer depression.

But Miss Carrigan does more than describe her depression. She also outlines in an interesting way what she did for herself with a lot of help from others and provides a guide for other depressed people to follow. The description of her descent and recovery from her mood disorder is followed by the guide which comprises most of the book. I am pleased by her unusual way of presenting her program. In six sections she has listed thirty-eight questions which she then answers in detail.

In the Medical Connection section are listed all the physical and physiological factors which can produce deep depression. Those factors include environmental allergies, which are a common cause of depression. This statement is as surprising for psychiatrists as it was for me when I first realized the truth of it more than thirty years ago. I had observed that nearly two-thirds of my depressed patients had histories of allergic reactions going back to their childhoods. I mentioned this to a colleague who did not believe me. I challenged him to review his own cases of depression; he did so and confirmed the observation. How many psychiatrists know that the antidepressants started out as antihistamines? These factors are the substance of orthomolecular psychiatry and have yet to find their way into the medical curricula or their textbooks. But they are very real and most important. I could not practice psychiatry without attention to these factors.

In this book stress is honored by a section of its own. Stress by itself may or may not *cause* depression but when a person is depressed ordinary stressors become intolerable.

A major treatment section details the importance of nutrition and the use of nutrients, vitamins, minerals and others. She is describing the modern vitamins-as-treatment paradigm in contrast to the outmoded and limited old vitamins-as-prevention-only paradigm.

Finally, since there can be no feeling of depression without a mind, she gives proper attention to the mind. That is not to say that psychotherapy alone or any of the hundreds of different forms of psychotherapy, group or individual, have ever been shown to be effective in treating depression. It is the total program as described in this valuable book which will bring almost all people out of depression. Antidepressant drugs will have to be used in many cases, but they are adjuncts to the rest of the program and should be eliminated as soon as—but as carefully as—possible.

I have become more and more convinced that personal accounts such as this are of the utmost importance in educating people about the ravages of diseases such as depression. These personal accounts, labeled "anecdotes" by the unthinking, are more helpful than the dry-as-dust clinical accounts which still occasionally appear in the psychiatric books.

No course in the understanding or treatment of depression can be adequate unless this book and other similar books are part of the prescribed reading material.

ABRAM HOFFER, M.D., Ph.D., FRCP(C)
Editor, *The Journal of Orthomolecular Medicine*

Why have I written this book?

I am sharing my story because I believe there are literally millions of others who are searching for a better way not just to manage their depression but to finally be able to eliminate it. If you are currently suffering from depression, I humbly offer this story to you, and I hold out this hope: You can heal your mind, as surely as you can heal a broken leg.

I am not a doctor. I have never been to medical school. I have no training in psychotherapy, psychiatry, counseling, or suicide prevention. What I do have is something I would not now trade for anything: a lifelong experience battling, and at last overcoming, chronic depression.

For eighteen years I took the very best pills, followed the advice of countless well-meaning psychiatrists, and spent untold hours talking out the complexities of a difficult life. Despite the amount of money, time, and effort devoted to my mental health, I never knew what it meant to be mentally balanced until I was forced, by ill health, to find this alternative path.

For whom is this book written?

I am writing this book for all those who suffer depression, whether that depression be of the short-term or long-term variety. Although there is a difference between chronic depression and the short-term varieties, my research has found that much of what happens in the mind and body is the same. I believe, therefore, that anyone who is depressed, for whatever reasons, will be able to benefit from this book.

If you have been under the treatment of a conventional psychiatrist, appreciate what he or she has to offer you, but do not easily accept the idea that you are doomed to choose between only two options, drugs or depression.

Do not easily accept a psychiatric diagnosis until you and your doctors have made a thorough examination to see if your poor spirits may have physical causes, especially if you are in poor health in addition to being depressed.

Depression is truly a disease that affects mind, body, and spirit. The way of healing I will show you is not new. It has been around most of this century, in some form or fashion. Nor is it easy. But if you believe you deserve to be happy, deserve to finally free yourself from the stigma of mental illness, and are born to thrive and be healthy, then open your heart and mind, find health care professionals who are willing to support you, and prepare to act with courage. Do not be ashamed. Believe only that you were meant for something better, that is yet to come.

At my worst, when I was depressed, I felt cut off from the rest of society. Because of that isolation, I often felt friendless and alone. I have been helped, and I remember. I remember what it was like to suffer from excruciating depression. As you read this book, remember that I have been there too, and that I sit here now, in a time that is now past, to speak to you, my reader, my unmet friend.

A word on drug withdrawal

My own process of withdrawing from psychiatric medication took about nine months. Even this slow and careful approach, with the guidance of a psychiatrist and other medical doctors and nutritionists, was plenty challenging.

I was very clear that my goal was to be happy, healthy, and balanced, and that going cold-turkey—simply throwing away my pills, firing my psychiatrist, and hoping for the best—would not be the best approach. I understood that I was not just allowing my body to clear itself of foreign chemicals. I was also rebuilding my spirit on the deepest level possible.

This book should not be used as an excuse for rash behavior, nor should it be substituted for appropriate medical guidance. If you truly want to achieve a free and easy spirit without drugs, do so under the direction of a qualified health care professional.

A talk with a friend

At times, as I've struggled with the research and the writing, I've remembered the words of a friend and advisor: "Just think of what it would be like for you to help even one person overcome what you had to go through." That thought has kept me going. Perhaps you are that person. Perhaps I have been destined to contribute to your life by telling you my story and inspiring you to take the steps necessary to regain the happiness that belongs to you. Perhaps you are now ready to act on my words of inspiration.

If you came to see me on any given day, you might arrive late in the morning, after I had finished a round of yoga or gone to the gym to put my clients through their paces. Or perhaps you'd arrive mid-afternoon, pulling up in the driveway to my home in the Atlanta suburbs while the sun was beginning to cast long shadows in the pines. I'd probably notice your arrival from my upstairs office and open a window and yell down, "Are you the one who's come to talk about depression? Open the front door and come on in."

You can imagine yourself climbing up our long white staircase to the upstairs office where I do my writing. You might pull up an old straw-seat chair and look out past my computer toward the roses down below in the garden. I love roses—I love all flowers in general—and as a gardener I have carefully placed my favorites where I can ponder them as I muse over some difficult line from the upstairs window.

I seldom dress up to write—usually you'd find me in some old cotton leotard with a pair of parachute pants and a faded aerobics sweatshirt on top. I always sit in my grandmother's gray velvet chair, propped up by a few faded cushions. I am incredibly sentimental, and this chair, though too heavy and too unwieldy to be very practical, reminds me of all the love lavished on me as the only granddaughter of a charming old couple.

If you came for a visit and sat next to me at my desk, I'd offer you a glass of water or maybe some hot herb tea, depending on the season. And we could talk.

After you'd told me about yourself, and I looked you in your eyes, I would begin to tell my story. I would tell you why I enjoy my work as a personal trainer. Even though I have never made a fortune at it, I take great pride in helping my clients be much healthier. I train women who have Chronic Fatigue Syndrome, who have fevers every day and digestive disorders, and others with insomnia or slipped disks who haven't exercised in years. On the other end of the scale, I train women who run marathons, or who've broken their wrists parachuting out of airplanes.

When I'm not working as a trainer, I'm usually up here in my messy office, writing either a play or some kind of nonfiction article for a magazine. For more than ten years, I worked as a journalist as the senior business writer for various newspapers, the last stint at a newspaper in Nashville. For ten years I was a stringer for *The New York Times*. My last what I call "real" job was as the editorial director for a health care marketing company.

I am the daughter and sister of two medical doctors, but I never thought I would end up having anything to do with helping people be healthier. My work as a personal trainer and even the research that resulted in this book arose out of a passionate search for my own health. I am thirty-eight years old, and for eighteen of my thirty-eight years—nearly half my life—I was diagnosed as a manic depressive. Technically, I was diagnosed as bipolar II, the most common "brand" of manic depression, if you will, and one that means, essentially, that you swing from periods of elevated mood (hypomania) to periods of normalcy and (in my case) abject and incapacitating depression.

In 1994, I became ill with Chronic Fatigue Syndrome. Although Chronic Fatigue Syndrome is a horrible illness, I am grateful to have finally become so ill that a number of underlying physical ailments were brought to light so I could have the opportunity to rebuild my mind and body in the healthiest way possible.

What you are about to hear is the result of eighteen years' experience on psychiatric drugs plus one year withdrawing from those drugs and another year recovering from the effects of those drugs, along with a lifetime of reading everything I could get my hands on to help myself and others like me. I may not be a doctor, but I have lived and breathed every word of this book.

According to the National Institute of Mental Health, there are, in fact, millions of others like me. About 11 percent of the population suffers from a mood disorder every year. The total yearly cost of treating depression has been estimated at about $44 billion, about 28 percent of which goes for the direct cost of medical care and drug treatment. Seventeen percent of that cost is associated with the 18,000 suicides that occur every year, and 55 percent is attributed to absenteeism and lowered productivity.[1]

According to the *Harvard Mental Health Letter*, depressed people suffer more than those with most chronic physical illnesses.[2] Among serious illnesses, only advanced coronary artery disease results in more days spent in bed. Only arthritis causes more chronic pain. About 60 percent of people with major depression report significantly decreased social contacts, 75 percent report experiencing a severe financial loss in the last six months, 70 percent are experiencing financial strain, and 75 percent experience chronic limitations in both job and physical functioning.[3] In the long run, the social cost of depression is in the same range as the cost of AIDS, cancer, or heart disease, although, with the exception of suicide, its consequences are usually less dramatic.

A significant number—about 12 percent—of those who develop depression will have a chronic, unremitting course. As in my case, chronic depression usually takes its toll over the course of a lifetime, beginning in the early years. Although it might seem more logical for depression to be an illness of those who had lost hope, of the aged, in fact it is more prevalent among the young, who may never have developed hope to begin with. About 70 percent of depressed persons are under forty-five.[4]

Those who suffer from this crushing, relentless disease are more prone to suicide, which is the eighth leading cause of death in the United States. In 1993 and 1994, suicide accounted for more deaths in the United States than AIDS. If you are an average American, the likelihood of your attempting suicide is about 0.9 percent, or a little less than one in 100. The lifetime attempt rate for patients with major depressive disorder is 17 percent. For those with bipolar disorder, however, it's 28 percent. That means better than one in four feel so terrible they have not only thought seriously about suicide but made at least an attempt to end their suffering in the most final way. It has been estimated that between 50 and 80 percent of completed suicides in the United States occur in patients with mood disorders.[5]

Worldwide, the incidence of depression is increasing, and if you really talk to people, if you really get intimate, you'll find more and more who are turning to drugs as a way out of their suffering. So why would I be troubled by that trend? After all, if the risk of suicide is so high among those with mood disorders, drugs seem a good way to preserve the lives of those who are suffering.

I have to tell you I am deeply troubled by what I have found in my research. When your psychiatrist or your general practitioner hands out your first prescription for an antidepressant, he or she is not likely to tell you that researchers such as Ronald F. Bourne, Ph.D., at the Department of Medicinal Chemistry at the University of Mississippi, have found that chronic antidepressant treatment leads to a decrease in the number of brain receptors for serotonin.[6] Nor will your pharmacist likely tell you that when you receive the printout of "general precautions." So what's the big deal? The big deal is that you need the neurotransmitter serotonin in order *not* to be depressed!

I am not advocating banishment of all drugs. Using drugs to heal depression is often like putting a person with a broken leg in a cast. The cast is a benefit because the person can actually walk again on crutches, and the leg is permitted to heal while leaning on those crutches. Ultimately, however, if the cast is never taken off, the muscles will atrophy and the person may lose the use of his limb, plus create a host of other imbalances.

If the use of drugs is prolonged, as it was in my case, then the imbalances can go on to create a whole host of other illnesses. To use another analogy, this would be like trying to stop a flood by installing drains in a lake. You may keep the waters from rising, but end up with nothing left—no tranquil spot of idyllic reflection, no place to raise a harvest of fish to feed yourself or future generations. If you take antidepressants over a long period of time, you may find yourself feeling very depleted—mentally, physically, and spiritually.

For the moment, I won't go into a major discussion of the side effects of antidepressants. But I will tell you that 47 percent of those who go on lithium—which is not technically an antidepressant, but a mood stabilizer and the leading drug of choice for treatment of manic depression—47 percent discontinue its use against medical advice because of adverse side effects.[7] That's a lot of people who have given up faith in the standard treatment without necessarily having a better alternative.

But there are alternatives, found in an unconventional approach which holistically heals the suffering body and mind.

My life of mental illness

I was hospitalized for manic depression at the age of twenty, but that is not the first time I was ever in serious emotional trouble. In fact, as I look back over the fabric of my life, I can't detect at what point emotional instability began to unravel the threads that were supposed to hold me together.

Inside myself, I knew there was no logical reason for the turmoil I experienced on a daily basis. I wished I could be optimistic and just look on the bright side, but there was frequently little logical connection between the severity of my moods and what was or was not happening around me. Other people were always telling me to "Cheer up" or "Put a smile on your face." I always wished my solution were so simple.

Once, at college, I remember bursting into tears in the middle of a restaurant where I was having lunch with my two best friends in the whole world. They were doing their best to love me, to boost me up. I remember it was a beautiful, sunny day, and the two people whom I admired most were telling me what a great writer I was and what a great future I had in store for me. For some reason, the more my friends talked about my brilliant future, the more terrified I became. Emotion flooded through my body so violently that I could not eat, could not think, could not stop sobbing. I could not imagine the future at all because the present was so terribly frightening. I did not know how I could live through the next day, let alone years to come.

Most days, when I was depressed, I just felt a serious lack of energy and connectedness. On medium-bad days I walked around in a quiet state of desperation. When the depression was really bad, well, it was really bad. The worst days I hallucinated and heard voices, usually encouraging me to kill myself. Whether my depression was really, really bad, somewhat bad, mildly bad, or just kind of bad, I was not much fun to be around.

Meanwhile, during these formative years, I went from one state of sickliness to another. As a little girl, I had constant earaches, to the point where I had my ears operated on at age six and my tonsils taken out shortly afterwards. At seven, I was so allergic to bug bites that I developed, all over my legs, scabs that had to be washed regularly with antibiotic soap. Part of my wardrobe had to include a handkerchief because I was seemingly allergic to everything and spent a good part of most days sneezing. At fifteen, I became anorexic, dropping to a low of 85 pounds, but mostly hovering around 90. Then I flip-flopped to the other extreme. Three years after my low of 85, I weighed about 150.

Being young, without much judgment of my own, around this fat phase I began sexual activity. So, naturally, I did what so many other college coeds were doing and started on the Pill. This made my moods much worse, and my crying jags became real emotional upheavals, especially before my period. To top things off, although I was never much of a drinker, there was alcohol, which only made my depression much worse. And, although I was smart enough to avoid hard drugs, which seemed to make even the most stable of my friends more weird than I could usually handle, I did smoke some marijuana. Had I been less liberal I might have had better health.

Psychologists and psychiatrists of various backgrounds and experience levels and with different degrees of caring came and went in my life until about the time I had what's commonly referred to as a nervous breakdown. In case you've never had the pleasure of having a nervous breakdown, you may not realize that in such a state one doesn't really eat or sleep or have any concept of the passage of time. It's like being dropped down a well without a rope. There isn't any beginning or end. You don't really know where you are or have any clue how to get out—a very frightening experience.

At that time, after my first nervous breakdown, a psychiatrist put me on Valium. I felt drugged and suppressed, yet the feelings of hopelessness and unpredictable days of anxiety continued. Instinctively, I knew that particular drug was totally wrong for me. Finally, after two months, I decided to stop taking Valium every day. I got tired of my family asking me, every time I felt depressed, "Did you take your pill?" Off Valium, I didn't feel much better and I didn't feel much worse, but at least I could think for myself again. I remember driving by my favorite park one summer afternoon and seeing details, such as the light flickering on the leaves, that seemed to have totally escaped me when I was so heavily sedated.

Even after I no longer took Valium every day, I continued to turn occasionally to that little yellow pill out of fear, whenever I felt really bad—after all, I did not know any other alternative and I was still very much unbalanced. I suffered from a chronically upset stomach, recurrent colds and yeast infections, and the constant fear in the back of my mind that I might have another nervous breakdown and lose further touch with time, reality, or other people. Four months later, it came. I was hospitalized after threatening to kill myself.

I remember the mental hospital very well. It was next to a river, not a bad place as these sort of institutions go, and was surrounded by a large wooded area where I was able to take long walks once the doctors determined I was an acceptable risk. Although the people there were all well-intentioned, I still shudder when I think of the place. The whole memory seems slightly blurred, like an old motion picture that has been slowed down and faded out. Were it any sharper, it might hurt too much.

Of course, at that time, no one bothered to ask whether my crazy college diet, or the fact that I had a yeast infection, might be contributing to my suicidal depression. During my research in later years, I spoke with Dr. William Crook, the author of *The Yeast Connection* books. He told me about a patient of his who had been able to get out of a mental hospital after going on a yeast-free diet.

What would my life have been like if I had known then what I know now? I might have avoided a psychiatric label, might have been able to avoid so much shame, and most of all might have avoided untold thousands of dollars spent on psychiatric bills and an immeasurable amount of abject suffering. Maybe I wasn't ready for this approach, as I was when I got sick in my late thirties. I am grateful to have found it at all, frankly, and that the rest of my life will be almost indescribably better.

One thing was sure, though: when I went into the mental hospital in 1981, drugs were the most important solution and nutrition wasn't even discussed. That first night in the mental hospital, the nurses gave me new medications in a paper cup. When I woke the next morning, my vision was so blurry I could barely see across the room. Perhaps that's why my memories of that place are so fuzzy. I was so dizzy I could hardly stand up. I later learned I had been placed on lithium and antidepressants.

It was there, in the mental hospital, that the psychiatrist who admitted me told me I was a manic depressive. I didn't really know what that meant, but the way he told me, it seemed like I was a very bad person who should be very ashamed of herself. After ten days of incarceration, I vowed I would never put myself in the position of being hospitalized again, no matter how bad I felt.

In the years that followed, although I continued to suffer so excruciatingly that at times I could think of little but suicide, I survived—which is partly my point. Truthfully, I cannot tell you that I believe psychiatric medications serve no purpose. I believe most doctors who prescribe them, and most patients who take them, are acting in good faith. They think they are following the best solution, often responding to what feels like a crisis situation.

At first the drugs did manage to give me a more even temperament. I was very grateful for them. I was so grateful for lithium, in fact, that I was afraid I would not be able to live a day without it. I followed my doctor's protocols to the letter. I never missed a pill because I was terrified of what would happen if I missed even a single dose. Every major event in my life—the job changes, moves to new cities, insurance changes, even the marriage that brought me to Atlanta—was carefully choreographed so I would never be without my lithium or antidepressants.

Yet during all those eighteen years of medication—three on various other psychiatric drugs and fifteen on lithium and antidepressants—and endless psychotherapy, I continued to face, on a more or less regular and repeated basis, times when I could think of little else but suicide. At those times, I was terrified not just of the depression but of myself. I was terrified that some uncontrollable element of my nature would again cause me the pain and humiliation I remembered from my hospitalization.

Not to mention the worry—I had so much to worry about. Would I ever be able to pass myself off as "normal"? There was always someone—a new in-law, a new friend, even old friends who eventually discovered my scarlet letter—ready to snub me for suffering from an illness they didn't understand.

When I married, I worried whether I'd pass on my disease to any child I might conceive—if I could even have one. I worried about the chance that a fetus conceived while I was taking lithium might develop a fatal heart defect. And, I had to wonder, would I outlive the usefulness of my lithium? There were few long-term studies, at least none anyone wanted to talk with me about. The doctors did sometimes check my blood levels and monitor my side effects, asking me vague questions regarding kidney function and my thyroid gland. No one could tell me what lithium might eventually do to my kidneys. Every time I passed a dialysis center, I wondered if I might end up inside.

Most of all, I was ashamed of not being able to lick my illness. When I was fat, I could lose weight. If I had been an alcoholic or a drug addict, I could conquer my addiction. For most of my life, there seemed no way, however, to overcome my particular brand of affliction, and it didn't matter how many biographies I read of famous artists or well-loved writers or movie stars who suffered the same way.

Friends sometimes speculated that my ability to write was the gift behind my instability, as if I could not be creative unless I was also mentally ill. My standard reply: "It's not worth it. Nothing is worth this much suffering."

I was like the condemned man in the Greek myth, fated to forever keep rolling the rock up the hill, only to have it roll back and flatten me, time after time. Sometimes an unpleasant life event would coincide with these bad moods, and sometimes I could find no logical reason for having gone off the deep end. I got very tired of being repeatedly flattened by that heavy stone, no matter how carefully I choreographed my life or how scrupulously I followed each doctor's exact instructions. I excelled at my schoolwork, at various jobs as a newspaper reporter, and as a fledgling playwright, and yet there was always my mental illness to humble me to the last degree.

The climb out of darkness

I have now been totally off all psychiatric medication for more than two years, and off all antidepressants for two and a half years with no relapse. Most patients who relapse do so within five months or less. And in my former life as a mentally ill person, I had what the psychiatrists call "episodes" at least four times a year, especially around the changing of the seasons and of course during those all-star stress marathons, Christmas and Thanksgiving.

I began the actual process of withdrawal from medication in October 1994, and with each decrease in dosage, my physical symptoms dramatically improved.

I began to withdraw for four reasons. The first was the diagnosis of Chronic Fatigue Syndrome. My physical symptoms included (but were not limited to) persistent, debilitating fatigue, swollen lymph nodes, chronic sore throat, recurrent colds and infections, and mild fever and yet consistently low underarm body temperature. My hands and feet were constantly cold, and my hands were so stiff that if I wrote three pages with a pen instead of a computer, my knuckles and joints would be sore the next day—which really freaked me out, being a writer. I also had problems with incredibly low heart rate—my heart rate walking down the hall at high noon one day was 36 beats per minute—and I had very low blood pressure. Mentally I was so tired I could not think. I spent a good part of every day sitting in a corner chair in my living room reading books about wellness. Being that sick gave me the motivation to do whatever it took to be productive again.

It has been interesting to read that a few researchers now believe that depression may actually begin with a virus. There are many theories of the exact origins of manic depression, of course, including a theory that the disease is linked to specific inheritable genes. There are many similarities between chronic depression and Chronic Fatigue Syndrome, and although there are significant differences, I will leave that debate to the experts. But I do believe that strengthening the immune system, the body's physiological mechanisms for withstanding and overcoming all disease, is a crucial component to healing both afflictions.

The second reason I went off my medicine: The doctor who diagnosed me with Chronic Fatigue Syndrome explained that one of the antidepressants I had been taking had a chemical makeup similar to an antihistamine. I had not outgrown my severe allergies, and by the time I was thirty, despite the fact that I exercised at least five times a week, I had asthma so severe I couldn't walk across a flat parking lot without gasping for breath. Five years later, when I developed Chronic Fatigue Syndrome, the doctor explained that because of the special kind of testing he does, he could not measure the severity of my allergies or put me on appropriate allergy shots until I cleared my body of the antidepressant.

Third, the doctor who diagnosed me with Chronic Fatigue Syndrome also explained that the lithium was probably destroying my thyroid. One of the main risks associated with long-term lithium use is hypothyroidism, a disease that causes low body temperature, cold hands and feet, fatigue, and depression. Essentially, then, long-term lithium use can cause the very key symptom it's supposed to alleviate—namely, depression—plus a whole world of other hurts.

Fourth, at that time my goal was to be able to conceive a healthy child, and I could not be assured of doing that if I stayed on lithium.

Nine months after I began the long, arduous process of withdrawal from lithium and antidepressants, I went to see an endocrinologist. He found goiters on my thyroid and told me I had Hashimoto's thyroiditis. Hashimoto's is an autoimmune disease in which the body develops antibodies to its own thyroid, causing a person to be alternatively hypo (too little) and then hyper (too much) thyroid, like slowing down and then speeding up a train.

I learned that classic manic-depressive illness—technically bipolar I, swinging between extreme highs and lows—is equally common in men and women. However, the malignant variant of treatment-resistant rapid cycling is more predominant in women and is significantly associated with Grade I hypothyroidism.[8]

A recent National Institute of Mental Health ten-year study of bipolar disorder indicated, "The use of lithium and other drugs in the first five years did not affect the frequency of mania and depression in the last five years."[9] Lithium works best in initial treatments for those who suffer from the classic features of a manic and hypomanic state than those with psychotic, dysphoric, mixed, or rapid-cycling features.[10] As you shall see, I question whether those with these more frequent cycles are truly mentally ill or whether they may have fundamental, organic imbalances, such as food allergies or environmental sensitivities, that are causing the rapid swings.

When the endocrinologist told me I had Hashimoto's, the first words out of my mouth were, "Is that what caused my manic depression?" I never received an answer. Hashimoto's disease, you see, can cause many of the same psychological symptoms and is sometimes misdiagnosed as manic depression.

Five months after I took my last dose of lithium and eleven months after I began thyroid replacement therapy, I went back to the endocrinologist and the goiters were gone.

I no longer have to suffer the other terrible side effects of lithium. During most of my twenties and early thirties, my hands shook like a little old lady's. I became used to the shaking, but people frequently asked if I was nervous; in fact, I was just shaking from the lithium. Also, I am no longer putting my kidneys at risk, and if I conceive a child, that child will no longer be highly likely to develop a fatal heart defect due to lithium.

To assuage the fears of some of the naysayers in my family, I went to a very nice, old-fashioned psychiatrist. He agreed, as did the endocrinologist, that I was doing the right thing, and he offered to field the inquiries of anyone in the family who might be afraid I was going off the deep end.

Although I am not perfect, I now have what I always wanted—a free and easy spirit without drugs.

I admit that sometimes I get mildly depressed, but when I do, it is nothing like the extremity of what I felt before, nothing to strike terror in my heart. I would say my moods are now normal, with the exception that I have gained a greater appreciation of the negative effects of stress and therefore take whatever steps are necessary to dramatically mitigate whatever might trouble me. I have an entire arsenal of nutritional and behavioral approaches to alleviate whatever suffering life might naturally throw my way. I am now master of my moods, not vice versa.

The gift I offer

From the beginning of my withdrawal from my medication, the importance of the alternative approach I was taking did not escape me. I figured that if what I was doing worked for me—and I was one who suffered so excruciatingly—it would certainly work for many other people if they only knew what to do.

It has been my experience that suffering is an incredible motivator. I once heard an interview on National Public Radio with a prominent pain researcher. He said that people often asked him, "Do you research physical pain or mental pain?" To which he replied, "There's no difference." When I was on drugs, I always did whatever it took to keep mentally balanced because I was terribly afraid of my own pain. When I got sick with Chronic Fatigue Syndrome, I wanted desperately to be able to be writing and working again. I had tremendous "away-from" motivation. I didn't know exactly what I was heading toward, but I knew I no longer wanted to be subject to that kind of slowed-down torture. As I found answers, I came to believe that many other people suffering with the agonizing pain of depression would also be motivated to try a nondrug approach if they only knew for sure, first, that it *would* work, and second, *what to do.*

My withdrawal from lithium and antidepressants was accompanied by a recovery from the symptoms of Chronic Fatigue Syndrome and a spiritual renewal that gives me strength to this day. So I'm better off, for sure, but where am I going, both personally and with this book?

A prescription for spiritual healing

I came to believe that all healing begins or ends with healing the spirit, and that the real path of spiritual healing of depression in particular is indeed a journey that begins with a series of questions that ultimately lead to other questions and, finally, perhaps to answers. No complete answer will be the same for everyone—modern medicine has taught us that we are all biochemically, genetically, and biographically unique. But we are also similar in nature, and with variations share needs and solutions.

The answers do not require you to give up your current patterns forever. Food sensitivities, for example, are often cyclical and may improve as digestion gets better, so you may not need to be on a heavily restricted diet indefinitely. As I became more mentally and physically balanced, the effort I had to make to maintain that level of well-being sharply diminished. My focus was able to shift from a desperate struggle to exist, psychologically and physically, to one of joy, ease, and comfort.

Nevertheless, having gone through this process, my attitude toward my life and my health has changed forever. I will always use these questions to find ways to make myself better and better.

Finding the complete solution for you will often entail a series of experiments, of trial and error—as in life itself—and may entail reconsideration and redirection over a period of years. I am being honest with you when I tell you that there is no instant cure, but every step you take will bring you closer to the light. Too many of us turn to drugs in hopes of instant solutions. Even if psychiatric drugs do provide some measure of relief, you can use the time they buy you to look for more permanent solutions.

I hope I don't discourage you when I speak of the dedication and persistence this goal will require, for I am also telling you the truth when I say that it is possible to use these methods to overcome even the most severe, life-long depression. It is my hope that my story will serve to point you in the right direction and thereby hurry you on your way.

To bring about lasting spiritual healing, to move out of darkness into light, you must find the answers to the following questions, not necessarily in the following order:

Getting Started

1. Do you have a trusting relationship with a health care professional who is capable of directing the care of both your mind and your body?
2. How do your moods correspond with changes in your diet, your menstrual cycle, your physical symptoms, the weather, and other variables?
3. Do you believe you deserve to be well and happy?
4. Are you blocking your own joy?

The Medical Connection

5. Do you have physical health problems that may be contributing to your depression?
6. Are you on any form of medication that may be destabilizing your emotions?
7. Do you have environmental allergies?
8. Are you exposed to chemicals that may contribute to your depression?
9. Do you have toxic metals in your body?
10. Do you have digestive disorders?
11. Do you metabolize carbohydrates normally?
12. Are your amino acid levels adequate and balanced?
13. Do you have food allergies or food sensitivities?
14. Should you try various home tests to identify your food sensitivities?
15. Do you have a yeast infection?
16. Is your thyroid functioning normally?
17. Are you hypoglycemic?
18. Do you need to detoxify your body?

The Stress Connection

19. Do you have high levels of cortisol in your body?
20. Do you need to lower your stress level?

21. Do you have an adequate stress management program and support system?

The Nutrition Connection

22. Are you willing to adopt a healthier diet?
23. Do you need to adopt dietary and lifestyle changes to stabilize your blood sugar?
24. Do you need to psyche yourself to change your eating habits?
25. Are you willing to give up the ten kinds of foods most likely to aggravate depression?
26. Are you willing to eat more of the ten kinds of foods most likely to improve depression?
27. Should you learn to appreciate vegetables?
28. Are you willing to give up antibiotics and other additives in your food?
29. Do you need to rotate your diet?
30. Do you drink enough water and ingest enough salt?

Vitamins, Minerals, and Other Supplements

31. Does your body properly absorb vitamins and minerals?
32. Do you have symptoms that might indicate a deficiency of B vitamins?
33. Are you deficient in Vitamin C?
34. Do you absorb a balanced ratio of calcium and magnesium?

Habits of Mind

35. Do you get enough exercise to relax your mind?
36. Should you learn new techniques to balance your mind and body?
37. Do you think positively to create the reality you want?
38. Have you learned what your depression has to teach you?

I apologize if any of these questions seem technical in nature. I am not trying to make this process any more confusing than it has to be. Many times during my research, sitting in some cold medical library in downtown Atlanta reading fifteen-syllable words out of medical texts, I have felt as though I were translating some far-away language. It is my goal to home in on the crux of each question so you will find it easier to find the right answer for you.

Also, do not be overwhelmed. I always said if someone had told me five years ago that I would make the kind of changes that would lead to such profound healing, I would not have thought myself capable. If someone had bet me I would stop eating sugar, give away my treasured perfume bottles, take up yoga, and start shopping at health food stores, I would have said, "You're crazy!" Take each step a little at a time, notice the rewards, and celebrate your small successes.

If you were here with me now, as we conclude this introduction, I might give you a hug and we'd take a tour of my garden on your way back home. If it were spring or summer or even fall, there would be some glory of nature to appreciate—a bluebird nesting in the box behind my backyard hammock, a flush of daises washing over the bank of my hillside. Even in winter, without flowers, there is a texture and a richness, a boundless wisdom in the way the humblest leaf is put together.

Even in the midst of despair, there is beauty to enrich the spirit and an intelligence that directs the most unconscious drive for life.

It is all here for your benefit.

PART I

GETTING STARTED

1. Do you have a trusting relationship with a health care professional who is capable of directing the care of both your mind and your body?

2. How do your moods correspond with changes in your diet, your menstrual cycle, your physical symptoms, the weather, and other variables?

3. Do you believe you deserve to be well and happy?

4. Are you blocking your own joy?

Question 1. Do you have a trusting relationship with a health care professional who is capable of directing the care of both your mind and your body?

> "...[T]he underlying concept remains that the majority of behavioral problems do not arise from...organic causes but rather from an assortment of conflicts, hostilities, guilt, dependencies, personality immaturities, and so forth. This bias toward philosophical causes has created a situation in which the majority of behavioral problems are not seriously subjected to a differential diagnosis based on a full range of organic causes." — William H. Philpott and Dwight Kalita, Brain Allergies: The Psychonutrient Connection.

As a practicing playwright, I know very well that the person who can describe his childhood as ideal and his current life as easy is the exception, not the rule.

There we have the beginning of the problem: each of us is a collection of neuroses, repressed memories, masks, and dreams. Depression, when it appears, looks like a purely mental disease. Its causes appear on the surface to be rooted in childhood, philosophical attitude, and current state of personal crisis.

Maybe you can look at your life and conclude that your depression is a logical outcome of your present circumstances. Even if that's the case, you may do well to read on.

Depression is a complex disease involving virtually every organ and energy system in the body. It may be genetic. It may have been caused by a virus, as many of the most current researchers believe. It may begin in faulty digestion, or in an imbalance in the structures of the brain that regulate hormones and emotions. It may be caused by an inability to regulate blood sugar or to metabolize carbohydrates or protein. It may be the result of an allergic reaction. It may happen when delicate brain mechanisms are exposed to a toxic chemical.

But even when it occurs as a response to a sudden stressful life event, it changes our body chemistry.

So we begin with the fact that most of us are psychologically flawed and that depression presents a complex clinical mystery worthy of the most dogged medical detective. Add to that a health care system that divides "health care" and "mental health care" and busy doctors who feel red tape takes away from the time they can afford to spend with patients, and it's easy to see why the word *healing* is seldom connected with *mental health care.*

If you are known to have a psychiatric diagnosis, it will be much easier for a medical doctor to brush off your physical complaints as psychosomatic, dash off a prescription for an antidepressant, and hurry off to a patient he or she feels has a "real" problem. It will take a very special health care professional to take the time to figure out the precise factors that are contributing to your depression, be they physical or emotional in nature.

Whatever path brings you here, whether it's a long road or a short one, it's up to you to find a good health care professional who meets the following criteria:

❖ You can talk comfortably with him or her.

❖ He or she is willing to answer your questions, take you seriously, and not brush you off. When I was sick, my father, a busy medical doctor himself, told me that I was exactly the kind of patient most physicians don't like: the kind who asks questions. But it is my observation that patients who take the responsibility to question how they are being treated are often more likely to find answers that actually work. Your physician should be someone who respects your questions.

❖ Most of important of all, that person should be someone—preferably not just a specialist in one area—who is capable of treating the entire mind and body. As an analogy, think of two gardeners with rose bushes. One sort of gardener, finding his bush covered with beetles and blackspot, could spray it repeatedly with insecticides and fungicides, containing but never completely eliminating the problem. A careful gardener, however, would re-examine the conditions he has provided and give the rose bush what it needs to be strong and healthy so insects and diseases don't bother it in the first place.

A recent study of doctors who prescribed antidepressants suggests you may be more likely to get to the bottom of physical factors contributing to your depression if you visit a primary care physician. Primary care physicians diagnose physical disorders—i.e., non-mental disorders—in a majority of the visits in which a depressive disorder is also diagnosed. On the other hand, if you visit a psychiatrist, the chances of medical, non-mental factors being discovered may be less than one in ten.[1]

Why is your choice of doctor so important? Because if your partner in recovery misses the crucial clues that might lead to uncovering the source of your depression, you may end up suffering even more. In *Toxic Psychiatry,* the book critical of his own profession, Dr. Peter Breggin writes:

> If a psychiatrist is faced by a depression that is genuinely hormonal or biochemical in origin, the worst thing he can do is to give the patient psychiatric medications, all of which worsen the biochemical condition of the brain.
>
> Nor can psychiatrists necessarily be trusted to detect such a real disease when it turns up. I'm aware of a malpractice case against several biologically oriented psychiatrists who failed to diagnose a flagrant case of Cushing's disease over many years and instead gave the patient multiple psychiatric hospitalizations, drugs, and electroshock.[2]

In eighteen years on medication, I met with a wide variety of some of the kindest, most well-educated psychiatrists, each of whom had something to contribute to my well-being. However, once I had been labeled manic depressive, the search for any physical contributing factors was over. My care centered solely on drugs and talk therapy. During all those years, I had a number of other health problems that might have provided clues that something larger was amiss than perhaps an unfortunate genetic birthright, a lousy childhood, or a sensitive temperament.

Even if you cannot find a single person who is capable of managing all of your health care, find someone who is willing to be a true partner in your recovery and who cares about you enough to coordinate your care with other professionals.

In the year of my recovery, I visited an allergist, a psychiatrist, an endocrinologist, and a nutritionist, only two of whom felt comfortable consulting with each other. Ideally, a doctor should be able to place his or her ego aside and work in a team with other health professionals.

Value what each doctor has to offer, but do not easily accept a psychiatric diagnosis until you have answered the questions that follow.

Action Plan

Question 1. Do you have a trusting relationship with a health care professional who is capable of directing the care of both your mind and your body?

When you schedule an appointment with a health care professional, explain to the receptionist that you are looking for someone who can treat you from a holistic point of view, encompassing the care of your body, mind, and spirit.

For referrals, you may want to contact:

American Academy of Environmental Medicine
P.O. Box CN1001-8001
Ten East Randolph St.
New Hope, PA 18938
(215) 862-4544

American Holistic Medical Association
4101 Lake Boone Trail, Suite 201
Raleigh, NC 27607
(919) 787-5181

American Preventive Medical Association
459 Walker Road
Great Falls, VA 22066
(703) 759-0662

International College of Applied Kinesiology
6405 Metcalf Ave., Suite 503
Shawnee Mission, KS 66202
(913) 384-5336

International Society for Orthomolecular Medicine
16 Florence Ave.
Toronto, Ontario
Canada M2N 1E9
(416) 733-2117

Consider an appointment your opportunity to interview the doctor, in addition to the other way around. You may want to ask:

1. What is your understanding of depression?
2. Do you see depression as a cause or as a symptom of something else?
3. Are you willing to investigate the possible causes of depression?
4. How would you do that?
5. How will you know when your methods work or don't work?
6. Will you be willing to coordinate my care with other medical doctors or alternative practitioners?
7. How will you handle follow-up questions if I need reassurance or further explanation?

Work out an agreement with your doctor about the last question. Many doctors charge for follow-up questions, or restrict the length of their office visits.

Question 2. How do your moods correspond with changes in your diet, your menstrual cycle, physical symptoms, the weather, and other variables?

> *"The balance of our very physiological well being depends intimately not only on its innate condition but also on all the external reality surrounding it, up to and including the forces of the macrocosm."* — John C. Pierrakos, *Core Energetics.*

Once you have found a health care professional or team of doctors who can coordinate your care, you must be able to provide them with accurate, precise information about which factors seem to influence your moods most predominantly.

It is important that you investigate how the following variables affect your state of mind:

1. What you ate at each meal.
2. Time of each meal.
3. Snacks.
4. What you drank with and between meals.
5. Moods throughout the day.
6. Any physical symptoms, whether or not they seem related to your mental well-being.
7. Menstrual cycles.
8. Weather.
9. Number of hours you slept at night.
10. Number of naps.
11. Any medications you took that day.
12. Amount of alcohol consumed.
13. Number of cigarettes smoked.
14. Kind of exercise and amount of time spent exercising.
15. Important events in your emotional life and how you reacted to them.
16. Overall ranking of how you felt in body and mind.
17. Any other factors that seemed to have had an impact on how you felt emotionally or physically.

18. Optional, if a thyroid condition is suspected: Underarm body temperature. (See Question 16.)

Not only will this information assist your doctors in finding patterns so they can treat you more effectively, it will be the greatest tool you have to persuade yourself to follow a healthier lifestyle.

For example, when I first began investigating these factors, I would wake up in the morning and tell my husband it was going to be a great day. Two hours after eating a breakfast of oatmeal, pears, and cashews, I would feel like throwing myself out of a speeding automobile. It seemed totally crazy at the time, but once I stopped eating oatmeal and all gluten grains in general, I stopped feeling suicidal.

Although I had eaten wheat, oatmeal, and other grains for years, it wasn't until I began paying attention to how different foods affected me that I was able to make the choices that led to a dramatic improvement in my moods.

I also noticed that on the days I spent a lot of time driving, I tended to be more exhausted and discouraged, even when I wasn't driving in a high-stress rush-hour situation. Although I have never been tested for sensitivity to petroleum products, I was able to see over time a pattern that emerged and chose a job where I didn't have to spend as much time on the road.

I also noticed that my moods were worse during heavy pollen and mold seasons, and as I looked back over my life I remember hitting emotional lows in spring and fall, which seemed to indicate an emotional reaction to environmental allergies. Although I can't control the seasons, I can choose to take better care of myself during peak allergy season to compensate for whatever ill effects I might otherwise experience.

Other factors, such as emotional stress, seemed much more obvious, but even in that realm I have used what I have learned to prepare myself or even change the way I choose to react. For example, when I was very sick with Chronic Fatigue Syndrome, I noticed that my physical symptoms would become much worse if I became angry or upset. My recovery quickened when I learned how to make better choices. Rather than exploding or even suppressing my anger, I chose to let more things slide and look for the gift in every seeming disappointment.

I noticed also how even good stress, such as the production of my plays, seemed to translate into a burden. I learned that I need to take time out to relax even during positive experiences in my life.

In centuries past, human cultures were much more attuned to the effects of the cycles of the sun, moon, climate, and even stars. We may be out of touch, but that does not mean that we have stopped being affected by our environment or that there is anything unusual about these factors or that other new ones, such as foreign chemicals or even electromagnetic radiation, determine the quality of our lives.

What this is all about is noticing and developing your own sensitivity to the factors that affect your moods, so you can begin to make choices that are right for you.

Action Plan

Question 2. How do your moods correspond with changes in your diet, your menstrual cycle, physical symptoms, the weather, and other variables?

Acquire a notebook to use as your food, mood, and weather diary. Refer back to the variables in the discussion of Question 2, and every day in the notebook make precise notations about which factors influence your moods. Several companies publish health diaries, but any private notebook will suffice.

If you choose to follow an elimination diet (see Question 14), keep accurate records of that process in your diary, also.

Make sure that you include any factor that may be applicable; there may be variables in your life that I have not listed.

Question 3. Do you believe you deserve to be well and happy?

"Twenty-five years of study has convinced me that if we habitually believe, as does the pessimist, that misfortune is our fault, is enduring, and will undermine everything we do, more of it will befall us than if we believe otherwise." — Martin E.P. Seligman, *Learned Optimism.*

Question 3 may seem too obvious to merit much attention, but I believe it was a key factor in my own recovery from mental illness. Indeed, the will to *not just survive but to thrive,* the motivation to overcome all necessary obstacles, must be switched on before recovery from any disease is possible.

It seemed I had to suffer a great deal before I was able to conclude that I had had enough, and that at last it was time to find love, health, and peace. I had to be convinced that I didn't deserve to waste my life feeling sick and depressed. Something in my very core had to be stirred before I could believe I deserved to be happy.

At times, when I was very sick with Chronic Fatigue Syndrome, I would go to one of my doctors and say, "With everything I'm doing, I don't deserve to be sick like this," to which he would reply, "That's not a very good attitude." In many senses, the doctor was right. None of us deserve to be sick, or to be born to parents who aren't capable of loving us, or to be physically abused, or to have inherited genes predisposing us to mental illness, or to have any number of the possible permutations of human afflictions. In the end, though, it doesn't matter what brought us to this place. What matters is what we choose to do about it.

What I learned from my own recovery is that illness is not a booby prize that lands on those of us who have in some way misbehaved, or even a booby prize at all. Illness, and particularly mental illness with its daily, hourly, relentless challenges, provides each of us with a unique opportunity for personal growth.

Perhaps, as you are reading these words, you are not amused. This, you say, is not the particular challenge you would have chosen for yourself.

The key is to face yourself and face your beliefs. If you believe deep in your heart that you deserve to be well and happy, you will not overlook any possibilities for good health and happiness.

I received a similar message from my mother during the worst period of my life, in my first marriage. I had gone off my lithium and antidepressants for five months to try to conceive a child without subjecting it to the side effects of medication. During that time, I was subject to an incredible array of suicidal moods that made me withdraw from my friends. Those upheavals frightened not only me but also my husband, with whom I already had a very unhealthy relationship. I gained ten pounds, never got pregnant, and was barely stable enough to concentrate on my work. I spent hours at a time crying, immobile, in a corner chair in my living room. I had always had a difficult relationship with my family, and my father wasn't speaking to me. The only support I received, other than from a psychiatrist, was from a weekly group for abused women. During that time, my mother sent me a book, *Happiness Is a Choice*. I thought, when I opened the package, *Yea, right! That's easy for her to say.* I was angry when I received the book, thinking she was trivializing my concerns, but I slowly learned my lesson.

Of course, there are innumerable possible permutations of human suffering, many of which are much worse than anything I ever experienced. One friend who grew up with manic depression can recall being nailed to a fence—literally—by his parents for trying to run away. As an adult he has faced his demons and, like me, has gotten off his medication after following an alternative path to health and balance.

Perhaps your story feels worse. Perhaps it sounds easier. The real question is, are you ready to learn your lesson? Are you ready to claim what happiness life has in store for you?

Nine months after I made up my mind, I left my first husband. I had decided I deserved better. Two months later, the company where I worked fell on hard financial times and asked me to work for free for two months. I refused. I decided at last that I deserved to do what I always wanted to do, which was to write plays. I quit and took up playwriting, working part-time to make ends meet.

It was three years later, after I had met and married a wonderful, kind man who believes in me and my writing, that I faced my next big choice: to be sick with Chronic Fatigue Syndrome or find some way to recover. One doctor explained that the second choice, physical recovery, would require me to go off lithium, on which I had depended for my stability for fifteen years.

One night recently, I received a call from an old friend. Although she had been taking antidepressants, she still felt desperate more often than she would like, and this night was one of her bad times. She had had a fight with her father, with whom she had not spoken for five years before, and she was angry with her husband for not having asked for a raise.

"Let go and find peace in yourself first and then everything around you will improve," I told her. "It may take a while, but when you begin to believe you deserve to be happy, you will show others how to love you by loving yourself. It won't matter who was wrong or right in the past. What can you do right now to calm down? And what can you do tomorrow—what little thing can you do tomorrow to bring joy into your life?"

She had to think. She had thought only of taking care of her children, or worrying about other people and what they were and were not doing. And then she realized she had not been helping anyone by not taking care of herself. She had called me in tears, angry at everyone else in her life. She hung up with a new appreciation of herself.

Too often we believe that taking care of ourselves is a matter of selfish interest. By healing ourselves, by taking responsibility for our emotions, our physical well-being, and our spiritual growth, we can heal a little bit of everyone around us.

To begin the process, we need to believe with a passion that we deserve to be happy. Through this belief, we can become willing to take whatever steps are necessary to arrive at that conclusion.

Action Plan

Question 3. Do you believe you deserve to be well and happy?

Write down your agreement with the following statements. If you totally agree, mark "100 percent." If you feel ambivalent, note on a percentage basis how much you agree or disagree.

I deserve to be happy. I am _____ percent positive about this. I am _____ negative about this.

I deserve to be physically healthy. I am _____ percent positive about this. I am _____ negative about this.

I am guided by a higher power that has my best interests in mind. I am _____ percent positive about this. I am _____ negative about this.

Before you can get well, you must be motivated to do so. If you find that you have any negative beliefs here, investigate where they come from. Is there something you need to forgive yourself for?

Question 4: Are you blocking your own joy?

"The more energy we let flow, the healthier we are. Illness in the system is caused by an imbalance of energy or a blocking of the flow of energy." — Barbara Ann Brennan, *Hands of Light.*

Those of us who seek to rid ourselves of depression seek something that goes by the name of *joy*, but the process of seeking this emotion often seems like trying to meet a cousin on the street whom one has never met and knows only by name.

When I finally finished the long process of withdrawal from my medication, I was at last mentally balanced. I had what I always wanted—a free and easy spirit without drugs. But I had no joy. Friends would tell jokes and the punch lines would whiz right past me. I could not compute. In social situations, I worried that I wasn't coming across very well because I never laughed and seldom smiled. Although I was kindhearted and well-meaning, I was completely devoid of mirth. A friend, a standup comedian, couldn't even make me chuckle, although sometimes I managed to crack a smile. I felt guilty when I was around him, for not appreciating his gift.

And that's just it. I really wasn't. It wasn't that I didn't *want* to enjoy my life. I just didn't know how.

And so, after ridding myself of depression, I began to pursue joy. It was an unusual sort of quest. At first, I realized I had been locked in a serious struggle for too long, a struggle for my health, a struggle to maintain at least the appearance of mental cohesion. It was completely understandable to me that I looked at every moment as a choice between life and death, between sanity or insanity. But I really wanted to be able to laugh.

I rented funny movies, spent time relaxing in the hammock in my backyard, even went to comedy clubs with my husband, who was the only one for a long time who could manage to make me giggle, if only for a moment. And then one day, as I was studying Touch for Health (see Question 36), I began to comprehend the direction I would need to take. In order to assist my personal training clients at the gym, I frequently studied the relationship between the body, physical ailments, and special points that needed to be pressed, feathered, or tapped. I pursued this study regularly so I could remember quickly what to do when faced, for example, with a bad back or a tight quadriceps. In the process of my study, I began to come to a new appreciation of what I had learned about pain. According to what I had seen so many times, pain is caused by blockages along the meridians, or pathways of energy in the body.

Years ago I thought acupressure was total nonsense, but after seeing it work so many times—even with the most skeptical clients—I had become a believer. A new client, someone I'd never met before, would come to me with a headache. I'd hold a few points, and ten minutes later the client would feel fine. Relief always came when these blockages were removed. So balance, and health, was restored when these lines of energy were running smoothly, without obstruction.

As I began to think of joy, I realized that what was true for physical ailments of the body could also be true on a much larger scale for this unrecognized but much-heralded emotion, joy. Joy must come when our energy flows freely throughout the body. The trouble is, too many of us block our own joy. So when it does come—in those fleeting moments when we actually recognize it—we are often willing to shut it off to return to the pain and depression with which we have become all too familiar.

There is no law that says we can't be joyful every day of our lives, but too often we devote ourselves to worrying about what might have been or even what we think we should be doing. We fault others and we fault our-selves, and in so doing we miss the gift that life offers at every moment.

As I began to look at ways I blocked my own joy, I realized that I had spent too much time in fear, afraid to let go of the past, constantly on guard lest some injury might repeat itself. And, again, I saw this pattern on a micro and a macro level in my life. I was afraid of eating the wrong thing, in case I might end up sick or depressed again. I was afraid to go home, in case I might remember what it had been like growing up or in case some predictably unstable relative might fail to value me, as had happened so often in the past.

It wasn't as though I felt that to be joyful I had to go on some exotic vacation, or win the lottery, because even in the few moments of glory in my life—my wedding day, the first production of my plays in New

York—there was always something missing. As I blocked my pain for fear that it might overwhelm me, I also blocked my own joy. Unconditional joy was indeed a distant cousin whom I longed to recognize.

As time went on, I began to see that although I had sometimes felt guilty about the amount of time I had invested in my health, everyone around me had benefited tremendously. As I began to feel more balanced, my family was so much happier. And they weren't just happy for me; there was a certain joy that my recovery had given *them*. I could look into their eyes and see that as I had freed myself from depression, I had freed them too. As I became healthier and learned so many techniques to care for my own mind and body, I saw that I had so much more to offer my clients and my friends.

And so the effort was far from selfish; it was a gift I could now give to everyone. As I became more joyful, I could bring more joy to everyone around me.

As I began to talk with friends about how I cured my own depression, I saw the pattern repeated in endless variations. I saw that many, many people are afraid to let go of what they know. They don't know what they want to replace depression *with*. Many times it seems that they are lost in the same way I had been. They could not recognize joy if it came up to them on the street and hugged them.

As you ponder how you block your own joy, ask yourself to what extent you agree with the following statements:

I deserve the best in life.

I am worthy of love just the way I am.

I love myself unconditionally.

I love others unconditionally.

I deserve _____.

I need to forgive _____.

If I could only forget _____,
I could be happy now.

If I only had _____,
I could be happy now.

There are no right or wrong answers, only a thought process that will help you to see more clearly what you are doing to welcome or discourage joy in your life.

Joy doesn't require special equipment. You already have a heart and mind, and as you unblock the pain hidden in them, you will bring yourself and everyone around you to a higher state of bliss than you ever thought possible.

Action Plan

Question 4. Are you blocking your own joy?

Draw a treasure map:

At the end of a long, dotted line, draw an old chest, like the kind you'd find on a desert island, filled with hidden gold. Now open the chest in your mind. Inside, you will find the priceless treasures you need to feel joyful. Now, on your map, list what these are. These should not be conditions that only the world can give you, such as a million dollars, or even world peace, but what you would need inside yourself, such as unconditional love, and safety, self-acceptance, or a quiet mind.

At the beginning of the map, draw a picture of yourself as you are now, the treasure hunter. Circle the word *START* just above the drawing of you.

> We shall not cease from exploration
> And the end of all our exploring
> Will be to arrive where we started
> And know the place for the first time.
> — T.S. Eliot, *Four Quartets*

You will know you have arrived at joy when you come to the end and realize, to paraphrase the poets, that what you need has been inside you all along.

If the distance from where you are to your treasure chest seems long, what prevents you from finding this treasure *now?*

What can you do to erase the time it seems that it will take, so you can be joyful in the present moment?

PART II

THE MEDICAL CONNECTION

5. Do you have physical health problems that may be contributing to your depression?

6. Are you on any form of medication that may be destabilizing your emotions?

7. Do you have environmental allergies?

8. Are you exposed to chemicals that may contribute to your depression?

9. Do you have toxic metals in your body?

10. Do you have digestive disorders?

11. Do you metabolize carbohydrates normally?

12. Are your amino acid levels adequate and balanced?

13. Do you have food allergies or food sensitivities?

14. Should you try various home tests to identify your food sensitivities?

15. Do you have a yeast infection?

16. Is your thyroid functioning normally?

17. Are you hypoglycemic?

18. Do you need to detoxify your body?

Question 5. Do you have physical health problems that may be contributing to your depression?

"Psychiatric symptoms may be caused by alcohol-related syndromes, degenerative brain diseases, endocrinopathies, traumatic brain damage, collagen diseases, demyelinating brain diseases, seizures, encephalitides, and toxic and metabolic diseases."
— Irl Extein and Mark S. Gold, eds., *Medical Mimics of Psychiatric Disorders.*

With this question, I am not recommending that you become a hypochondriac. What I am recommending is that you look to see if you have any one of a number of physical ailments that have been positively correlated with depression. These physical problems may include, but are by no means limited to:

Candida or yeast infection.
Hypoglycemia.
Thyroid problems and other endocrine disorders. Recent studies suggest that thyroid disorders are the most common physical illnesses that contribute to depression.[1] Other reported cases suggest that treatment of subclinical hypothyroidism may be all that's necessary to cure life-long depression.[2]
Environmental allergies and food allergies.
Amino acid deficiencies.
Electrolyte imbalances.
Vitamin or mineral deficiencies.
Toxic exposure to heavy metals or chemicals.
Cardiopulmonary obstructive disease.
Brain tumors.
Alzheimer's disease.
Strokes and seizures.
Hypertension.
Viral infections.
Diabetes.
Insulin resistance or difficulty metabolizing carbohydrates.
Any chronic illness.

If you are tired in addition to feeling depressed, you will want to ask your doctor to rule out simple, physical factors that may be causing you to feel fatigued. A person may be physically tired and, as a result of constant fatigue, feel like giving up emotionally. These simple, obvious, physical factors may include, but are not limited to:

Anemia
Hypothyroidism
Liver dysfunction
Coeliac disease
Sleep disorders

I cannot overemphasize the importance of this step. What I'm really recommending here is to look deeply and see why your biochemistry is out of balance. If you can correct the fundamental imbalance, then you may no longer need a system of accommodating it, be that drugs, a special diet, or anything else.

It is of course up to your doctor, when he or she makes a psychiatric diagnosis, to rule that your emotional symptoms are "not due to any organic mental disorder" according to the *Diagnostic and Statistical Manual of Mental Disorders*.[3] Studies have shown, however, that many such ailments have escaped notice until depression reaches an advanced stage. And, as one who finally overcame her own chronic depression when many such problems were finally brought to light and corrected, I recommend that you are absolutely certain this step is not overlooked.

In one study of 250 inpatients of a psychiatric service, for example, 12 percent were found to be suffering from physical conditions that were a causative factor for their emotional illness.[4] Doctors who care enough to look often find real, identifiable physical illnesses behind their patients' mental suffering.

In the immortal words of my mother, "Childhood is a vastly overrated experience." If you are chronically depressed, there may be something actually wrong with you other than the usual slings and arrows life shoots your way. Again, I caution: Do not accept a psychiatric label until you have really searched not only your life but also your body to figure out what that something may be.

The conventional medical establishment is already acknowledging that mental illness may be in fact due to a prior medical condition because the recent *DSM-IV* (the latest edition of the American Psychiatric Association's diagnostic manual) has added another category for mood disorders, namely "mood disorders due to a medical condition." That was formerly joined under the name "organic," meaning "associated with a known brain malfunction."[5] I believe that as more becomes understood about the functioning of the brain and, in particular, the way the brain is affected by nutrition, more and more mental illness will be found to have an underlying physical cause.

Scientists are looking for a link between depression and Chronic Fatigue Syndrome, often associated with a virus. An answer may have been suggested at a 1995 international symposium on mental illness. Doctors at the conference sponsored by the Stanley Foundation, the research arm of the National Alliance for the Mentally Ill, furthered the notion that a viral infection could be associated with psychiatric disorders. Dr. Bob Yolken hypothesized that a virus could impair development of the central nervous system, resulting in manic depression.[6]

You may well ask yourself, "Are these processes out of balance because I am depressed? Or am I depressed because my body doesn't follow the usual models?" This is the kind of question that has puzzled the most brilliant researchers in the fields of psychiatry, psychobiology, psychoneuroendocrinology, gastroneuroimmunology, and a host of other highly specialized fields. It's almost a chicken-or-the-egg type question—which came first?

The solutions to many mysteries have yet to unfold. And until the answers do come and are proven on a scientific basis, it's up to those of us who suffer from depression to find the best ways to cope. It may take persistence, and it may take a special doctor to work with you, but there are reams of information already available that may assist you in your goal.

Action Plan

Question 5. Do you have physical health problems that may be contributing to your depression?

If your physician manages to identify factors that are causing you to lose physical or emotional energy, ask him or her to help you identify the cause. For example, if you are depressed because you are tired and your doctor discovers you are anemic, you may have trouble absorbing nutrients from your food, which may be due to a digestive problem caused by parasites or allergy to gluten grains, among other possibilities. If you simply take vitamins to treat the symptoms of anemia, you may not do yourself the favor of eliminating the cause of your depression.

If you feel no fatigue, ask your health care practitioner whether he or she recommends any advanced testing. Some problems may be identified through simple blood tests, while others require detective work on the part of your doctor. In that case, you may want to review Question 1 and make sure you are seeing the right health care professional. You may need the medical equivalent of Sherlock Holmes—with more of a sense of compassion.

Question 6. Are you on any form of medication that may be destabilizing your emotions?

> *"Most medications prescribed in clinical practice are capable of adversely affecting the central nervous system and producing significant changes in the patient's mood, perception, thinking, cognition, and behavior."* — Ghazi Asaad, *Understanding Mental Disorders Due To Medical Conditions or Substance Abuse.*

Before rushing off to find a drug to cure your depression, better look in your medicine cabinet to see if any of the drugs you are already taking may be making you depressed. For example, my emotional upheavals were much worse when I took birth control pills. Even though my psychiatrist at the time knew I was suffering from depression, there was no warning about the effects that the birth control pills would have on my mood. It was only a few physicians later, when I was being admitted to a mental hospital, that a connection was made and I was advised to discontinue them.

That's why it's so important to make your doctor your partner and to include in your discussions, whatever your primary malady, an *accurate* description of what's going on with your mind and your body.

Medications for a wide variety of physical diseases have been found to cause depression. For example, hypertension was the most commonly coded medical diagnosis found in a recent study of primary care doctors who diagnosed patients with depression. Ironically, many of the antihypertensive medications, including clonidine and other medications for heart disease, such as propranolol, procainamide, hydralazine, reserpine, and methyldopa, have long been reported to cause depression.

The following chart lists other medications that may cause depression. The second column lists other possible side effects of the medications:

Anesthetic Medications
Halothane   Anger, tension, fatigue
Isoflurane   Anger, tension, fatigue

Antibiotic Medications
Isoniazid   Auditory and visual hallucinations, catatonia
Cycloserine   Nervousness, irritability, anxiety

Anti-Cancer Medications
Steroids
Decarbazine
Hexamethylamine
Vincristine
Vinblastine   Anxiety
Asparaginase   Personality changes

Antiparkinsonian Agents Hallucinations, paranoid delusions
Levodopa
Carbidopa
Amantadine
Bromocriptine

Cardiovascular Agents
Propranolol
Procainamide
Reserpine
Methyldopa
Hydralazine

Central Stimulants   Hallucinations, paranoid delusions, insomnia
Ritalin
Amphetamines
Pemoline

Hormone Replacements
Premarin   Headaches, dizziness
Provera   Insomnia

Non-steroidal Anti-inflammatory Medications

Indomethacin	Anxiety, agitation, hostility, depersonalization
Sulindac	Anger, combativeness, homicidal feelings, obsessive talking

Over-the-Counter Medications

Phenyl-propanolamine
Antihistamines and decongestants
Ephedrine
Pseudephedrine
Aminophylline
Indocin
Corticosteroids

Psychiatric Medications

Antipsychotics	Oversedation, total muteness, malignant syndrome
Lithium	
Sed/Hypnotics	Oversedation, disinhibition
Disulfiram	Anxiety

Sources: Irl Extein and Mark S. Gold, eds., *Medical Mimics of Psychiatric Disorders*; Ghazi Asaad, *Understanding Mental Disorders Due To Medical Conditions or Substance Abuse*; Ronald Arky, ed., *Physician's Desk Reference.*

There's even a name for this kind of suffering—iatrogenic disease. Disease caused by a physician, however inadvertently.

But while we're talking about drugs as depressants, it's important not to overlook the so-called recreational drugs, especially alcohol, hallucinogens such as LSD and mescaline, phencyclidine (PCP), and cocaine. Although alcohol and many of these drugs initially stimulate the brain, they later can cause sedation and depressive symptoms. One theory is that some people who have chronic yeast infections are unable to tolerate any sort of alcohol because *Candida albicans* releases toxins similar to alcohol that disrupt the function of the central nervous system. Dr. William Crook speaks of several patients who have been accused of drunkenness when in fact they were suffering from yeast overgrowth in their bodies.[1]

Anyone wanting to avoid depression should definitely avoid recreational drugs as well as alcoholic beverages, which depress the central nervous system. One half of suicides are alcohol-related.[2] Dr. Joseph D. Beasley, an expert on alcoholism, says that alcohol exacerbates the potential for violence, indecision, anxiety, panic attacks, and mood swings, as well as causing problems with sleep and sexual performance.

What's less well known is that alcoholics have a higher rate of allergies and food sensitivities than the general population. Often they are sensitive to the foods from which their favorite beverages are derived —potatoes for vodka drinkers; wheat, barley, or corn for the whiskey drinkers; or grapes for those addicted to brandy or wine.[3] "Addressing their allergies is just as important as treating their liver disease," Dr. Beasley observes.[4]

Action Plan

Question 6. Are you on any form of medication that may be destabilizing your emotions?

Make a list:

Medications I take regularly:

Medications I take occasionally:

Consult with your doctor or pharmacist, or go to the library and look up the *Physicians' Desk Reference*, which lists the side effects of common medications. If you are on any drug that lists depression as a possible side effect, ask your health care practitioner if there are any alternative treatments that might be appropriate.

List also:

Alcoholic beverages (kind & how often):

"Recreational drugs" (kind & how often):

Average number of cigarettes per day:

Average number of caffeinated drinks per day:

Question 7. Do you have environmental allergies?

"When a person is exposed on an infrequent basis to some substance, and has an immediate reaction to that substance, then the cause and effect of the allergy is apparent to all.... When the exposure to an allergy-causing substance is constant, however, eventually the acute symptoms will give way to either a period of no symptoms, or to chronic symptoms such as headaches, depression, or arthritis. In other words, the acute symptoms have been suppressed because of the constant nature of the exposure, and the body has reacted by attempting to adapt itself to the problem." — Theron G. Randolph and Ralph W. Moss, *An Alternative Approach To Allergies.*

If your food, mood, and weather diary indicates that your depression deepens in the spring or fall, or is worse at various times of the day, your moods may well be affected by environmental allergies.

Allergies are traditionally defined by a kind of specific reaction the body produces in response to the presence of an allergen, which can be any substance recognized as a foreign invader. In this traditional model, the immune system produces antibodies to the allergen, and these antibodies attach themselves to mast cells, which release histamine, a chemical that causes tearing, itching, and runny noses.

The trouble is that the mast cells that release histamine are not just located in our noses. They are also located in the brain, and the peripheral neural structures are rich in mast cells.[1] Histamine is also a neurotransmitter, a chemical that the central nervous system uses to send messages back and forth to the brain. It has been described as an inhibitory neurotransmitter, and has been found in extremely high levels in the body chemistry of mental patients who are suicidally depressed.[2] So when you have an allergic reaction, not only does your nose know it, but your brain feels the effects as well.

Recent research suggests that the immune systems of some depressed subjects reflect an ongoing inflammatory process throughout the body, complete with higher activation of killer immune cells, both during and after remission.[3] Some researchers have found suppressed immune systems, while others have found overactive immune systems in depressed subjects.[4] Biological psychiatrists, scientists who study the relationship of the body to the mind, have theorized that the different immune states may be related to different kinds of depression.

Given this apparently chronic state of alarm in the immune systems of some of those who tend to become depressed, it follows, then, that a good way to start getting our bodies to heal our minds is by examining the everyday challenges to our immune system, namely environmental allergies.

The trouble is that there are many maladaptive reactions, including reactions that take place in the brain, that fall outside the traditional explanation of the allergic process.

Clinical ecologists, or doctors who take a more comprehensive view of allergies, take into account immediate and chronic reactions, including physical and psychological reactions to anything contacted, ingested, inhaled, or injected. Since the substances that can cause reactions can be literally just about anything, it's easy to see how this whole field of environmental medicine is challenging from many perspectives.

Doesn't it follow that people who are hypersensitive are allergic to life? That seems to match up with most people's definitions of the word "crazy." Skeptics have had plenty of ammunition to launch, belittling those of us who suffer in this way as neurotic, psychosomatic complainers.

Doctors who work closely with highly sensitive patients have recognized the connection between emotional experience and physical symptoms. Dr. Daniel Kinderlehrer, who practices internal and environmental medicine in Newbury, Massachusetts, told the interviewer of one allergy newsletter:

> I came to recognize that many of my sickest, multiply sensitive patients do, in fact, have histories of severe abuse in childhood.
>
> Here's the pattern: It didn't matter how good they were, it didn't matter how hard they tried to avoid being hurt, they still ended up getting hit, beaten, and abused. Such individuals tend to become incredibly withdrawn, feeling worthless, powerless and out of control.

As the nervous system maintains its hypervigilant mode, always looking out for the next attack, it communicates its concerns to the immune system.

The hypervigilant immune system is one that *doesn't feel safe*, and quickly learns to become "trigger happy."[5]

Dr. Kinderlehrer also noted that those who did seem to develop some degree of tolerance to their allergies were those who had done some emotional process work—which is why anyone who undertakes to heal the mind through the body should also be finding ways to face their childhood demons and learn to accept and forgive themselves and others.

While it does follow that people who are chronically depressed seem to get upset about everything, it is also true that susceptibility to allergies can overwhelm the immune system and lead to what's been called cerebral allergies.

Martha Sanbower, a therapist who has worked with environmentally ill patients, has noted that healing the depression of those who are highly allergic won't really begin until proper physical diagnosis, including the identification of allergies, is made. "Body awareness is crucial for these people, and it is necessary to work on this throughout therapy," she wrote in the *Journal of Orthomolecular Medicine*. "It is common for these people to feel obsessed with their bodies for a period of time as they learn to tease apart their physically based reactions from those that have a truly emotional origin. This will eventually allow them to 'step back' from those physical reactions, rather than becoming emotionally overwhelmed by them."[6]

PSYCHOLOGICAL PROBLEMS THAT MAY BE CAUSED BY ALLERGIES

Headaches
Migraine
Vascular
Histamine
Tension
"Emotional"
Muscle spasm

Cerebral Depression
Acute and chronic depression
Drowsiness approaching narcolepsy
Episodic dullness or dreaminess
Learning disorders
Tension-fatigue syndrome
Minimal brain dysfunction

Cerebral Stimulation

Restlessness

Nervousness, anxious, inner
shaky feeling

Jitteriness, tremor

Insomnia

Hyperactivity

Behavior problems

Inappropriate emotional out-
bursts

Uncontrolled anger

Fear, panic

Psychiatric

Feelings of apartness, "spacey"
(unreal)

Floating sensation

Episodic amnesia

Pathologically poor memory

Inability to concentrate

Personality changes, psychoses,
schizophrenia

Autism

Hallucinations

Source: Marshall Mandell and Lynne Waller Scanlon, *Dr. Mandell's 5-Day Allergy Relief System,* pp. 17-20.

As for myself, I am highly allergic to many things I have been tested for—dust, molds, grasses, trees, cats, dogs, and especially ragweed. The first doctor who ever tested me told me he was going to put me in his "Allergy Hall of Fame" because I scored in the top sensitivity in virtually every category. After I began taking shots every week for my allergies, which are not only multiple but severe, I noticed my moods became much more even.

As you are undergoing the process of allergy testing, be sure to make note of how you feel both before and after your shots, even if your doctor does not ask. You may want to take your food, mood, and weather diary along with you to the testing. If you can connect a severe depression with a severe sensitivity to ragweed, for example, you may be able to organize your life to minimize your exposure to it and thereby reduce your chances of being depressed.

Action Plan

Question 7. Do you have environmental allergies?

Make a list:

My known allergies:

Suspected allergies:

Symptoms I have that may be associated with allergies:

Notice whether your symptoms vary with factors such as the climate, weather, seasons, or even locations. Take note of whether you feel different in your home or office or even garden.

Take your notes to your doctor and ask him or her about allergy testing. If you decide to be tested for allergies, make note of any psychological changes that occur during the test.

If you do have multiple allergies, ask your health care practitioner not only about how you can treat your allergy symptoms, but also if he or she needs to evaluate your immune system or determine whether you have a buildup of other toxins in your body. For example, if you have multiple allergies, you may have a weakened immune system, or you may benefit from a detoxification program that will clear not only your allergy symptoms but the causes of other imbalances as well.

Question 8. Are you exposed to chemicals that may contribute to your depression?

"A person suffering from depression is given counseling and medication, but rarely does anyone think to see if that person is being exposed to 1 of the 40 chemicals known to cause depression." — Cynthia Wilson, *Chemical Exposure and Human Health.*

In the emerging field of environmental illness, it is now generally recognized that such common activities as driving down a modern interstate choked with gas fumes may induce a state of depression, depending on the relative strength of a person's immune system, the degree of his or her sensitivity to chemicals, and the combined total of toxic substances he or she is exposed to at any given point in time.

Does this sound like I'm shifting the blame from, say, a lousy childhood to a lousy environment? Partly, yes. It may be no accident that the incidence of depression is increasing worldwide as a wide variety of chemicals are newly invented and dumped into the atmosphere every year.

To arrive at an understanding of the way chemicals can affect the brain, it's important first to comprehend a few concepts that form the basis for environmental medicine.

The first is the concept of a target organ. Everybody understands that standing in a field of wild flowers can make you sneeze. Pollen allergies affect the sinuses, and thus sneezing, which affects the nose, and can even lead to asthma, which affects the lungs. But what if a target organ of these allergies or environmental sensitivities is also your brain?

According to *General and Applied Toxicology*, a standard textbook on chemical exposure, a target organ "may be the most sensitive site of adverse action of a systemically absorbed agent."[1]

Many physicians have believed that something called the *blood brain barrier*, which restricts certain molecules from crossing into sensitive brain tissue, protects our thinking organ from most harmful substances. However, there are parts of the central nervous system that are

not protected by the blood brain barrier, and even those that ai
fooled by stealthy chemicals that are fat soluble or properly ionized.

From this knowledge, various physicians have developed the concept of cerebral allergy, which Dr. William H. Philpott and Dwight G.
Kalita outlined in their book *Brain Allergies: The Psychonutrient Connection*. Simply put, while some individuals may be able to handle toxins, pollens, foods, and chemicals, others may have genetic tendencies,
enzyme deficiencies, malnutrition, infections, or other predispositions
that lead to inflammatory reactions in the brain, sometimes experienced in the form of depression.[2]

The second concept to comprehend is the notion of *total body load*.
We all understand the feeling of "having had enough" in an argument
with our spouse, or of being under so much emotional stress we feel
something has to give. So it is with our physical bodies. Total load is the
sum of all toxic substances in the body which, when an individual's
threshold is reached, will lead to physical or emotional symptoms.[3]

That's why nutrition becomes so important. We may not be able to
control our exposures to chemicals, allergens, electromagnetic radiation, or other environmental substances, but we can choose to lighten
the total load on our bodies by eating well, based on our individual
needs.

Third is the concept of *bipolarity* which, on the face of it, I find strik-
ingly similar to the concept of manic depression in psychology. Just as
in manic depression, a mood can swing from high to low. However,
doctors who practice environmental medicine attribute at least part of
the swings to reactions to exposures to toxic or allergic substances.
Bipolarity "is the abnormal fluctuation of the body characterized by a
stimulating, withdrawal, and depressive reaction as a result of pollutant
stimuli."[4]

Rea explains bipolarity as a two-part response that affects the
immune, enzyme, detoxification, and metabolic systems. "The first
phase involves a stimulatory/withdrawal reaction in which the stimu-
latory response is dominant. The second phase is a depressed reaction
in which immune and enzyme detoxification and metabolic systems
are unable to adequately process their total load."[5]

For example, initially an allergic person may find his mood stimulated by exposure to a chemical or indeed any substance to which he

later becomes sensitive. As he feels stimulated by, for example, milk, he will find himself developing an addiction. It's for that reason that many people who develop sensitivities are surprised to find they are hooked on the very foods that aren't good for their individual constitutions. They eat them all the time because, at least at one point, those particular foods made them feel better.

This stimulated state may be followed by withdrawal as the particular substance, whether it be a chemical or a food to which one is addicted, is removed from the diet. The last stage of adaptation is depression, where the body's metabolic, enzyme, and immune systems become depleted or sustain damage, even temporarily, and are unable to process their total toxic load.[6]

The fourth concept to understand is the concept of *switch phenomenon*, which occurs when sensitivity to any given toxic substance shifts from one target organ, such as the brain, to another, such as the heart or stomach. Also, what may cause us to feel great one day may make us feel depressed as exposure continues over long periods of time.

THE SWITCH PHENOMENON

Severity of Reaction	Type of Reaction
4+	Manic
3+	Hypomanic, toxic
2+	Agitated
1+	High
Zero	Even keel
1-	Localized responses, e.g., rhinosinusitis, headache, PMS
2-	Systemic responses, vasculitis, phlebitis
3-	Aphasia, brain fag
4-	Depression

Source: William J. Rea, *Chemical Sensitivity*, p. 35.

The fifth concept to comprehend is the fact that each of us is an individual—biologically, psychologically, spiritually. Empirically, we can see this in our own households. Brothers and sisters may be brought up in the same family and end up with not only slightly different physiognomy but entirely different outlooks on life. Although depression has many symptoms that cross all walks of life, age groups, and sexes, the way it manifests itself in my body may be entirely different than the way it shows up in yours. Two-time Nobel Prize winner and prominent vitamin researcher Linus Pauling explained:

> It is estimated…that a human being has a complement of one hundred thousand genes, each of which serves some function, such as controlling the synthesis of an enzyme. The number of characteristics that can be variable, because of a difference in the nature of a particular gene, is presumably somewhere near one hundred thousand rather than only five hundred; and accordingly we reach the conclusion that no single human being on earth is normal (within the range that includes 95 percent of all human beings) with respect to all characteristics.[7]

Chemicals that have been observed to cause depression of the central nervous system include:

Acetaldehyde
Acetylene tetrabromide
sec-Amyl acetate
Benzene
Benzyl alcohol
Benzyl chloride
2-Butoxyethanol
n-Butyl acetate
sec-Butyl acetate
tert-Butyl acetate
Camphor
Carbon tetrachloride
Chlorobenzene
Chloroform
beta-Chloroprene
Cumene
Cyclohexane
Diacetone alcohol
1,1-Dichloroethane
1,2-Dichloroethylene
Dichloromonofluoromethane
2,4 Dichlorophenol
Dichlorotetrafluoroethane
Dimethylaniline
Dinitrotoluenes
2-Ethoxyethyl acetate
Ethyl benzene
Ethyl bromide
Ethyl chloride
Ethyl ether
Ethyl formate
Ethyl mercaptan
Ethyl silicate
Ethylene dichloride

Ethylene glycol	Methyl iodide
Ethylene glycol dinitrate	Methyl methacrylate
Formaldehyde	alpha-Methyl styrene
Formic acid	Methylal
Glycidol	Nicotine
Hexchloroethane	Nitromethane
n-Hexane	Octane
Hexone	n-Pentane
Hydrazine	Propane
Isoamyl acetate	n-Propyl alcohol
Isobutyl alcohol	Propylene oxide
Isophorone	Pyridine
Isopropyl acetate	Styrene
Isopropyl alcohol	Sulfuryl fluoride
Isopropyl ether	1,1,2,2-Tetrachloroethane
Linalyl alcohol	Toluene
Mesityl oxide	1,1,1-Trichloroethane
Methyl n-amyl ketone	1,1,2-Trichloroethane
Methyl alcohol	Trichloroethylene
Methylchloride	1,2,3 Trichloropropane
Methyl formate	

Source: Cynthia Wilson, *Chemical Exposure and Human Health.*

While many of these chemicals may sound foreign to you, you may recognize some of them as common ingredients in tobacco smoke, gas fumes, pesticides, perfumes, and many cleaning products that you are exposed to on a regular basis.

Different occupations may expose you to different chemicals that may be taxing your system, but you don't necessarily have to work in an industrial plant to be exposed. Anyone who drives to work may be exposed to petroleum products from car exhausts, and new cars may release toxic gases from new carpet and vinyl. Office workers are regularly exposed to copy machines and chemically-treated paper. Whether your office is old or new, you may suffer from something called "sick building syndrome," which occurs when poor ventilation traps toxins inside and causes a plethora of health problems.

How would you know if you are being exposed to chemicals that affect your moods? One way to begin is to go back to your food, mood, and weather diary. Notice whether you feel better at work or outdoors, at the seaside or in clear mountain air. I noticed that I would feel shaky, tired, and weak and my handwriting would even become erratic after our lawn service would come to treat our grass with herbicides and pesticides. As a result, I recommended that we switch to organic garden alternatives whenever possible. Doctors who specialize in environmental medicine may be able to work further to determine if you are exposed to toxic substances.

Most doctors, including many allergists and other professionals who call themselves experts in environmental medicine, do not know how to test for chemical sensitivity. Furthermore, unlike allergies to environmental substances such as dust, mold, trees, and grass, there is no known effective way to desensitize a person to chemicals. Most doctors who are aware of the problem, therefore, recommend that sensitive individuals minimize their exposure and advise that the best way to reduce symptoms is to avoid man-made chemicals as much as possible.

And it's also why some doctors who treat patients for depression recommend a program to detoxify the body.[8] Such a program may include fasting or the IV administration of massive doses of ascorbic acid with other vitamins and minerals, followed by a maintenance diet of organic foods.

In addition to detoxifying your body, you should also consider cleaning up your environment. This task may include the kind of work I like least—cleaning, dusting, mopping, polishing, etc., etc., on a weekly or even daily basis—and it could include bringing in plants or special filters that help clear your indoor air. The topic of environmental cleanliness goes beyond the scope of this book. However, many excellent books are currently available on this topic, including The E.I. Syndrome by Dr. Sherry Rogers. Dr. Rogers recommends that because we spend about one-third of our lives sleeping, we ought to make our bedroom an oasis. This room should be free not only from the usual grime that accumulates in the course of daily living but also from chemical toxins and electromagnetic radiation, as well as environmental allergens such as dusts and molds.[9]

Action Plan

Question 8. Are you exposed to chemicals that may contribute to your depression?

1. Make a list:

Chemicals to which I am regularly exposed:

In my home

In the workplace

In my car

Other

Notice whether you feel different in various locations, such as your home, your office, or the great outdoors.

2. Stop wearing perfume and other scented personal products, including deodorant. This step is important because 95 percent of the chem-

icals used in fragrances are synthetic compounds derived from petro-leum.[10] As much as possible, switch to organic products, and notice whether you feel different.

3. If you feel chemicals may play a large factor in your depression, you may want to refer to any of Sherry A. Rogers' excellent books on the subject, especially *The E.I. Syndrome: An Rx For Environmental Illness*, or contact the American Academy of Environmental Medicine, (303) 622-9755, for a referral to a physician near you.

Also helpful is the Human Ecology Action League (H.E.A.L.), P.O. Box 29629, Atlanta, GA 30359, (404) 248-1898. In addition to publishing a newsletter, *The Human Ecologist*, which covers (among other things) how the environment affects the human nervous system, H.E.A.L. sells numerous information sheets about multiple chemical sensitivity, including bibliographies of books and resource lists of companies that sell organic products, as well as tips on how to clear your environment, how to dispose of hazardous waste in your home, natural gas appli-ances, and water treatment, etc.

4. Procedures for testing may vary, but one medical doctor who tests for chemicals, Adrienne Buffaloe of New York, NY, checks serum levels of suspected chemicals, and may perform a fat biopsy, since chemicals are frequently stored in the body's fat cells. She also uses a brain SPECT scan calibrated for chemical sensitivity to check for classic patterns of cerebral blood flow and brain neuron function aberrations. If she finds a pattern of toxicity, Dr. Buffaloe recommends not only avoiding chemicals, but also supporting the liver to assist in detoxification, and a heat treatment that mobilizes chemicals from fat deposits.[11] Begin by asking your health care provider if such tests are necessary for you.

Question 9. Do you have toxic metals in your body?

"Some people have spoken to psychiatrists for years, with little visible progress. After amalgam removal (of mercury tooth fillings), they are far more capable of addressing and processing their problems to completion." — Hal A. Huggins, *It's All in Your Head.*

Historians have theorized that one of the reasons the Roman empire declined was as a result of contamination from lead pipes. A hundred years from now, future historians may reckon that one of the reasons depression increased so rapidly in our society was as a result of widespread exposure to toxic metals.

Few of us ever consider the quantity of potentially toxic metals with which we come into contact on a daily basis. Toxic metals are in the fillings in our teeth, in the aluminum pots in which we cook, and in the city water we drink on a daily basis. We can also be exposed to toxic metals in our workplace, in household and gardening chemicals, in cosmetics, and even in medications.[1]

Even after I had been on a health-supporting diet for a year and a half and had had numerous IVs to remove toxic metals from my body, I still had extremely high levels of aluminum and tin, as well as moderate amounts of a number of other heavy metals. Although aluminum has often been discussed as a possible factor in Alzheimer's disease, it has also been proposed as a possible cause of suicidal thoughts.[2]

In his book *Brain Allergies*, Dr. William H. Philpott described heavy metal toxicity as one of the key elements to be considered in diagnosis of mental problems, along with nutritional deficiencies or excesses, reactions to foods, chemicals, inhalants, microorganisms and their toxins, and finally what he called "learned responses to life experiences."[3]

Heavy metals are also associated with a wide range of physical ailments. Here are some of the key metals to ask your doctor about, and mental symptoms associated with toxic buildup of each:

Aluminum—Depression, dementia, suicidal thoughts, Alzheimer's disease

Bismuth—Difficulty with memory, hallucinations

Mercury—Depression, psychotic behavior, sometimes diagnosed as schizophrenia

Cadmium—Increased sensitivity to pain

Lead—Hyperactivity, fatigue, psychotic behavior, sometimes diagnosed as schizophrenia

Copper—Hyperactivity, depression, postpartum psychosis, dementia, autism, PMS, insomnia, senility

Sources: Hal A. Huggins, *It's All in Your Head;* H. Richard Casdorph and Morton Walker, *Toxic Metal Syndrome: How Metal Poisonings Can Affect Your Brain;* Pat Lazarus, *Healing the Mind the Natural Way,* p. 95; and Syd Baumel, *Dealing with Depression Naturally,* pp. 24-25.

Removal of mercury amalgam fillings has become a subject of controversy within the dental profession. After a workshop on the biocompatibility of metals in dentistry, the American Dental Association acknowledged that mercury is released from amalgam fillings. However, in an official position statement, the A.D.A. said, "Allergic reactions to mercury and other constituents of amalgam…are extremely rare. The association between allergies and oral *lichen planus* requires further investigation. Finally, dental amalgam, which has been used extensively for more than 100 years, has an exemplary record of safety and benefit to the dental patient."[4]

Replacing amalgam fillings may not necessarily be the best option. Aside from the cost—which can reach up into the thousands of dollars—the process may be painful, may result in the loss of teeth, and may expose a patient to yet more mercury during the removal process. Yet one study of twenty-two patients with multiple, severe sensitivities showed a 63 percent improvement in symptoms when fillings were removed. "The more sensitive patient is the one most likely to note any lessening of metabolic load, however small," noted the study's author, Alfred V. Zamm.[5]

I myself have not had my fillings replaced, and friends who have gone through the ordeal have had mixed results. My doctor recommends that I avoid chewing gum, as he argues that long periods of chewing release mercury into the body.

Action Plan

Question 9. Do you have toxic metals in your body?

1. Ask your doctor about tests to see if you have toxic metals in your body. As with testing for toxic chemicals, many physicians are not trained to test for toxic metal buildup. If you have symptoms that may indicate toxicity, ask your health care provider whether he or she would recommend hair analysis or a blood serum profile.

2. If you have mercury amalgam fillings in your teeth, consult with your dentist to find out about tests to determine if you are sensitive to mercury, and about other tests to determine what other materials might be compatible with you to replace them. If your dentist recommends removal, get a detailed description ahead of time and ask how you will be protected from further mercury exposure while the procedure is taking place.

3. If you do have toxic metals in your body, ask your doctor how he or she would recommend getting rid of them, including procedures for detoxification, which may include chelation therapy, a special diet, or supplements. (See Question 18.)

4. Reduce your exposure to heavy metals by avoiding aluminum pots and pans and switching to bottled or other purified water from which heavy metals have been removed.

Question 10. Do you have digestive disorders?

"It is my conviction that diagnoses such as 'schizophrenic,' 'manic depressive' and other psychotic, neurotic, or psychosomatic labels are relatively meaningless and tend only to aggravate the illness. It is the underlying organic cause that is important. We should be diagnosing paranoia caused by wheat allergy, dissociation as a manifestation of sensitivity to eggs, catatonia as a manifestation of mold or hydrocarbon allergy, and so forth, according to people's specific reactions to individual foods, chemicals, and inhalants." — William H. Philpott and Dwight K. Kalita, *Brain Allergies: The Psychonutrient Connection.*

If you think you're not really crazy, your gut feelings may be more right than you could have ever imagined. The cause of your depression may reside not so much in your head as in your gastrointestinal tract, including:

Difficulty absorbing vitamins and minerals from foods.
Food allergies or sensitivities.
Yeast overgrowth.
Leaky gut syndrome, which often results from yeast overgrowth and results in food sensitivities.
Difficulty absorbing and utilizing amino acids from proteins.
Difficulty metabolizing carbohydrates.

Whether your depression has lasted thirty years or three months, you may find the most effective relief by:

Asking your doctor about tests to find out if your body is absorbing the nutrients you need for proper brain function.
Avoiding those substances that may cause your brain and/or your gut to become inflamed.
Asking your doctor whether a program of detoxification would help to rejuvenate your digestion.

re we go on to examine each of these digestive disorders in detail, it's important to understand why digestion is so crucial to the process of maintaining balanced emotions.

Although we think of our brains and our guts being miles apart, and even of one being superior to the other, our "gut feelings" have been shown to be more intricately intertwined with our finer thinking than previously thought.

Recent research takes this picture even further. In a new field of medicine called neurogastroenterology, scientists are finding that we literally have two brains—one in our heads, the other in our guts. Nearly every substance that helps run and control the brain has turned up in the gastrointestinal tract. Major neurotransmitters such as serotonin, dopamine, glutamate, norepinephrine, and nitric oxide are there too. In fact, when researchers bothered to count, they found that the gut contains 100 million neurons—more than the spinal cord has.[1]

To improve your digestion, you need to consider your:

Liver, which metabolizes proteins, carbohydrates, and fats; manufactures bile; and detoxifies the body. Eastern medicine has
long recognized the importance of a properly functioning liver
to overcoming depression. Toxic substances that the liver cannot clear may interfere with the midbrain, where emotions are
processed.

Gallbladder, which aids the digestion of fats, where many chemicals are often stored, and keeps the small intestine free from
harmful microorganisms.

Stomach, which produces gastric juices essential for digestion.

Pancreas, which produces enzymes essential for digestion and
assists in stabilizing blood sugar.

Small intestine, where the greatest absorption of nutrients occur.

Large intestine or colon, which concentrates and excretes wastes.

In a book I mentioned earlier, called *Brain Allergies,* published in 1980, a year before I was hospitalized for manic depression, Dr. William H. Philpott described how a degenerative disease process beginning with faulty digestion could result in a garden variety of mental disorders.

For example, people who are sensitive to wheat or gluten, the protein in wheat, often have trouble taking in B vitamins, which are important for maintaining a calm, positive outlook. If you are sensitive to gluten, you may be eating lots of pasta, bread, and bagels that contain B vitamins, but your body won't be able to make much use of vitamins, or calcium or iron.[2] If we aren't absorbing the nutrients we need, we simply can't supply the brain with the raw materials necessary to maintain proper emotional balance.

Food sensitivities affect our two brains—the one in the head and the other in the intestines—in other ways as well. During allergic reactions the body releases histamine, which Dr. Philpott found could set off inflammatory reactions not only in the colon but also in the brain. Another nutritionally-oriented physician, Dr. Carl C. Pfeiffer, has found that high histamine levels are a common characteristic of patients with chronic depression.[3]

The trouble with *Candida albicans* and other yeasts that can populate the gastrointestinal tract is that these yeasts emit lots of nasty byproducts, including acetaldehyde, alcohol, and carbon monoxide, all of which play havoc with the proper functioning of the brain.[4] One theory has it that if *Candida* and other yeasts populate out of control, they may perforate the lining of your intestinal walls, causing undigested food particles to leak into the blood stream. When that happens, your immune system recognizes these food particles as foreign invaders and you may develop food allergies or sensitivities.[5]

Research over the last thirty years has found that many depressed people do not metabolize carbohydrates or the amino acids in proteins at a normal rate.[6] In fact, these metabolic disorders are so common that a test for a deficiency in at least one amino acid, GABA, may be the closest thing they've ever arrived at for a blood test to prove predisposition to mood disorders.[7]

One recent study found a high degree of correlation between a common digestive disorder, irritable bowel syndrome (IBS) and depression. Doctors found that 57.69 percent of those with what's called double depression—major depression plus morbid anxiety—had irritable bowel syndrome, versus 2.5 percent in a group of "psychiatrically normal" controls.[8] Thus by taking care of the brain in the gut we may be able to lessen the severity of reactions in the brain in our heads.

Action Plan

Question 10. Do you have digestive disorders?

1. From your food, mood, and weather diary, compile a list of your common digestive problems, which may include:

Constipation
Gas
Diarrhea
Indigestion
Heartburn

Notice whether any of these symptoms correspond with unfavorable changes in your mood.

2. Ask your health care provider about tests that examine for:

Parasites
Infection, including bacteria, yeasts, and fungi
Malabsorption
Digestion efficiency, including tests for the digestion of
    carbohydrates and fats
Coeliac disease

Question 11. Do you metabolize carbohydrates normally?

*"Patients with schizophrenic, manic-depressive and involu-
tional psychoses do not utilize carbohydrate at a normal
rate.... The metabolic disorder is not specific in that it does
not distinguish any one of these psychoses from the others."*
— Harold Edwin Himwich, *Biochemistry, Schizophrenias
and Affective Illnesses.*

After I had been on a yeast-free, sugar-free diet for well over a year, I
was still having digestive problems and my doctor could not understand why. A simple gastrointestinal test showed I was not digesting
carbohydrates.

I made further amendments to my diet, which brought about further improvements in my mental and physical well-being. I cut out
most carbohydrates such as breads, pastas, and potatoes, and even a lot
of starchy vegetables in favor of a higher-protein diet and more vegetables. Thankfully, the doctor said I could still eat some fruit because fruit
is digested quickly.

As I made these changes, I found I had more energy and fewer cravings for food. And, when I researched the subject, I found that medical
scientists had been making the connection between carbohydrate metabolic disorders and psychological problems since well before I was born.[1]

Not everyone who gets depressed will have this metabolic disorder.
However, in patients with schizophrenia or manic depression, adrenal
corticoid use, deficiency of the B vitamin thiamine, liver disease, and
epinephrine injection all make the biochemical disorder worse, and
reportedly all but the epinephrine injection make the psychological
problems worse also.

In addition, biochemicals released during stress also aggravate the
metabolic disorder and the mental disturbance. As I researched this
subject, I could see how a person could perhaps inherit a metabolic
disorder that would ultimately set off a downturn in emotions when
aggravated by prolonged emotional upset, starvation, or lack of sleep.[2]

Metabolic disorders themselves are fairly common in this country.
Researchers who study weight loss claim about 25 percent of the

population is what they term "insulin resistant." In that case, too much insulin in the blood results in increased hunger and craving for carbohydrate-rich food, increased fat storage in cells, and a decreased ability to remove fat from fat cells.[3] It is estimated that about 75 percent of overweight people are insulin resistant.

Several mood disturbances have been associated with cravings for carbohydrates. These disorders include seasonal affective disorder, or SAD, the kind of depression that occurs in winter; premenstrual syndrome, or PMS; and carbohydrate-craving obesity, or CCO.[4]

All three mood disturbances include depression, inability to concentrate, and episodic bursts of overeating. It now appears that these disorders are affected by disturbances in melatonin, a hormone that affects mood and energy levels, as well as the neurotransmitter serotonin, which regulates a person's appetite.[5]

The theory is that if you eat carbohydrates when you are depressed, you are unconsciously trying to self-medicate, because carbohydrate consumption boosts the levels of the calming neurotransmitter, serotonin.

One way to find out if you have a carbohydrate metabolic disorder is to ask your doctor about gastrointestinal tests. You can also try a high-protein, low-carbohydrate diet and see if your mood improves.

Action Plan

Question 11. Do you metabolize carbohydrates normally?

1. Switch to a high-protein, low-carbohydrate diet (see Question 26) for one week. Notice if your mood improves.

2. You may also want to experiment with food combining, and see if there are any improvements in your mood or gastrointestinal symptoms. To do so, avoid eating proteins and carbohydrates together (i.e., avoid combinations such as steak and potatoes or pasta with meatballs). Eat proteins and non-starchy vegetables together, without carbohydrates. Cut back on fats, which inhibit the digestion of protein. Eat carbohydrates and vegetables together at another meal. Eat fruit by itself on an empty stomach. Melons are best eaten as a separate meal from other fruits. Don't drink liquids with or immediately following a meal.[6]

3. Ask your health care provider about tests to determine whether you are digesting carbohydrates. If you are not digesting carbohydrates, you also may want to check whether the unhealthy environment in your gut has led to a yeast overgrowth.

Question 12. Are your amino acid levels adequate and balanced?

"Despite the difficulty of demonstrating that a particular biochemical measure is a true genetic trait marker for vulnerability for development of an illness, the accumulated data suggest that low plasma GABA may represent a biological marker of vulnerability for development of various mood disorders."
— *Clinical Chemistry.*

About the time my doctor was discovering that my body was not digesting carbohydrates, I underwent another series of tests to see if I was absorbing proteins properly. Blood work showed I did not even show up in the low end of the normal range of six amino acids, the basic building blocks of proteins.

Amino acids have been used for years in the treatment of depression. The reason is that amino acids are not only the building blocks of protein, but also the building blocks of neurotransmitters, the chemical messengers the brain uses to communicate with nerve cells throughout the body. Without the amino acids phenylalanine and tyrosine, for example, your brain can't make the adrenaline or noradrenalin you need to respond to stress.[1]

Recent research has turned up important trends in amino acid absorption, in patients with both depression and manic depression. One study of patients with major depression, for example, found levels of five large neutral amino acids—tyrosine, phenylalanine, leucine, isoleucine, and valine—to be significantly lower than the levels found in normal individuals.[2] Another study of people with manic depression found there might be abnormalities in the metabolism of tryptophan and tyrosine, and that these levels remained unchanged even when they were being treated for their illness with lithium.[3]

Perhaps the most exciting recent discovery was about gamma-aminobutyric acid, a supposedly nonessential amino acid formed from glutamic acid. Amino acids are classified as essential if the body can't manufacture them on its own. Taken with the B vitamins niacinamide and inositol, GABA prevents anxiety messages from reaching the motor centers of the brain. In simple terms, GABA acts as a tranquilizer.

One study found that GABA levels were significantly lower in about one-third of patients with major depression and also low in patients with mania and those with manic depression who were depressed. In addition, low levels of GABA may be a common inherited trait in families with mood disorders, which has led to speculation that testing for low levels of GABA could show who might be vulnerable to developing mood disorders.[4]

Although tryptophan is the building block for serotonin, low levels of which has been found to be a biochemical predictor of likelihood to commit suicide,[5] the U.S. Food and Drug Administration took it off the market in 1989 because certain individuals developed massive toxic reactions to it.[6] In massive doses, tryptophan can cause undesirable perceptual and mood changes.[7] However, it can be absorbed in moderate amounts from food, the best sources of which include pineapple, turkey, chicken, yogurt, bananas, and unripened cheese.[8]

According to Dr. Priscilla Slagle, author of *The Way Up From Down*, other alternatives to tryptophan supplementation include magnesium, a mineral that promotes relaxation; and the amino acids taurine and glycine, which calm the nervous system; as well as the B vitamins niacin and niacinamide.[9]

Two other authors recommend DL-phenylalanine (DLPA). Robert Erdman, author of *The Amino Revolution*, argues that DLPA is the most effective amino acid for treating depression because it prevents the breakdown of endorphins, the body's natural painkillers.[10] Dr. Arnold Fox, author of *DLPA To End Chronic Pain and Depression*, recommends consulting with a qualified physician to supplement with this amino acid as part of a complete lifestyle adjustment, including improving your nutrition, exercise, and use of visualization and affirmations.[11]

Before you decide to try supplementing your diet with amino acids, ask your doctor to perform blood tests to check your individual levels. Supplementation without complete knowledge of your individual biochemistry could lead to further imbalances in your body.

Even without supplementation, however, you may try including more protein in your diet. If you do have shortages of amino acids, you may have digestive disorders that are preventing their proper absorption. If that's the case, you will want to ask your doctor how you should go about improving your digestion.

Action Plan

Question 12. Are your amino acid levels adequate and balanced?

1. Ask your health care provider about blood tests to determine your amino acid levels. If you are deficient, ask him or her to explain how the deficiency may have been affecting your moods.

2. If your doctor recommends amino acid supplements, ask him or her how long you need to take them. In the meantime, if there is a deficiency, ask your doctor to investigate further and determine if there is a reason, such as a digestive disorder, why you are not properly absorbing proteins.

Question 13. Do you have food allergies or food sensitivities?

"No one is suggesting that the mental hospitals are full of food-sensitive individuals who simply need an elimination diet to set them free from their illnesses.... Less serious forms of mental illness, such as depression and anxiety, are commonly reported among those with food intolerance, usually accompanied by some physical symptoms.... In many cases, it was the physical symptoms alone that were the target of the treatment, and both physician and patient were pleasantly surprised at the change in mood that occurred simultaneously." — Jonathan Brostoff and Linda Gamlin, *The Complete Guide To Food Allergy and Intolerance.*

There's no telling who started the argument. Was it the Greek Lucretius in the first century B.C., who observed, "What is good to one, is to others bitter poison"?[1] Or was it the seventeenth century's Richard Burton, who observed in *Anatomy of Melancholy* that "Milk and all that comes from milk increase melancholy"?[2] Or was it the early pioneers of clinical ecology who, in the 1920s in America, just as the medical establishment was beginning to accept the theories of Freud, began to stir things up by saying that mental illness was *not* all in one's head but maybe, more specifically, related to what one put in one's mouth?

It may sound far-fetched, but some of the most conventional scientists have recognized for years that food sensitivities may be playing a huge role in a myriad of health complaints. In one particularly dry tome, *Nutritional Toxicology*, researchers from the National Heart, Lung, and Blood Institute noted, "It has been suggested that the primary care physician should suspect a sensitivity to food in those patients who are resistant to various types of therapy but insist that something is wrong with them. A variety of symptoms are often common in these individuals, including fatigue, headaches, irritability, depression, and/or anxiety."[3]

The incidence of strict food allergy in the overall population is less than about one percent.[4] However, researchers have well established that a wide range of reactions fall under the general classification of food sensitivity. These include reactions that involve the immune system, those that don't involve the immune system, sensitivities that occur as a result of illness or drug therapy, and metabolic disorders.[5]

A wide variety of other mechanisms may cause problems. Consuming foods high in histamine, such as certain types of fish, may cause reactions.[6] People who are allergic to strawberries fall into the category of those suffering from what's called an anaphylactoid reaction, where histamine is spontaneously released without the intervention of specific immune modulating cells. Some individuals may lack the enzymes to digest dairy products, or the protein component of wheat, rye, barley, and oats, or even fava beans. Other so-called idiosyncratic reactions, where the mechanism that causes problems is not clearly understood, have been documented in individuals consuming chocolate, FD&C Yellow No. 5 (tartrazine), sulfites, food colorings, sugar, and MSG.[7]

Food sensitivities may develop after some predisposing condition, such as an illness or drug therapy. Illnesses that are known to have caused food sensitivity include Crohn's disease, ulcerative colitis, cystic fibrosis, and bacterial or viral gastroenteritis.

In fact, digestive disorders may play a major role in the development of food sensitivities. What appears to be a food allergy may in fact be an "enterometabolic disorder," meaning that something in the intestinal tract produces a toxic reaction in the body.[8] These toxic reactions could come from the metabolic debris of unfriendly bacteria living in the intestinal tract, or they could be caused by specific food or environmental toxins. For this reason, your food sensitivities may improve if you get to the bottom of any digestive disorders.

Individuals taking monoamine oxidase inhibiting drugs, used in antidepressants and in the treatment of Parkinson's disease, have also been found to develop food sensitivities,[9] especially to wine, aged cheese, chocolate, fermented foods, and yeast.[10]

Much of the recent research surrounding food sensitivity and behavior problems has focused on children, and doctors who tried to make these links have met with plenty of skepticism. As one professor of child health put it, "Children with behavior disorders often temporarily improve for a few weeks when given a diet which avoids food additives, but this appears to be a placebo effect."[11]

But the concept of food sensitivity is definitely an idea worth pondering, especially when we become adults and can monitor for ourselves how we react to various foods and make intelligent choices in our own best interest. Dr. Alan R. Gaby, research director of Baltimore-based Consumers for Nutrition Action, believes that "millions of Americans suffer from unrecognized food allergies, which can cause (or worsen) a wide range of physical and emotional disorders."[12] Dr. Abram Hoffer, a pioneer in the use of nutrients to treat mental illnesses, has gone so far as to estimate that 75 percent of all depressions are caused by food allergies.[13]

Another compelling reason to get to the bottom of your food sensitivities: While you may not be able to control your exposure to other toxic substances that may be affecting your central nervous system and therefore your moods, such as the smog-filled highway on which you drive to work, or the pesticides your neighbors spray on their yard, you can always reduce the total load on your immune system by cleaning up your diet.

The entire subject of food sensitivity is controversial within the medical profession. To qualify as being truly allergic to food, you must have antibodies to those foods in your blood. Individuals with this rare kind of Type I food allergy may be so exquisitely sensitive that they suffer symptoms from kissing the lips of a person who is eating the offending food.

Other immune complex reactions may take between 4 to 6 hours and 48 hours—and often 72 to 96 hours—to show up since it can take days for food to move through the GI system.[14] At least one expert, Dr. Sherry Rogers, believes most cerebral reactions—including depression, hyperactivity, migraine, and fatigue—are more immediate and usually occur within minutes to hours of ingestion.[15] However, others have noted that delayed reactions may take days to show up, long after you have forgotten what you ate.[16] As a result, how you feel today may well be a function of what you ate yesterday or the day before.

Symptoms of Food Sensitivity
Headaches, including migraines
Fatigue, memory loss, anxiety, and hyperactivity
Depression and schizophrenia
Recurrent mouth ulcers
Muscle and joint aches, rheumatoid arthritis

Vomiting, nausea, stomach ulcers, duodenal ulcers
Diarrhea, irritable bowel syndrome, constipation, gas, bloating,
    Crohn's disease
Water retention, kidney problems
Constant runny or congested nose, asthma
Irregular heart beat, inflammation of the capillaries
Itchy eyes, eczema, rashes, hives

Source: Jonathan Brostoff and Linda Gamlin, *The Complete Guide To Food Allergy and Intolerance.*

You may have inherited some food sensitivity, as is sometimes the case with intolerance to dairy products, due to a lack of the enzyme lactase, which is used to digest milk. Other food sensitivities develop with age. Although infants may be able to digest dairy products, the enzyme lactase in many cases disappears in early childhood.[17]

In other cases, food sensitivities develop as a result of "leaky gut syndrome," where undigested food particles escape into the bloodstream. According to Jeffrey Bland, a leading researcher on the subject, leaky gut may result from a variety of factors, including:

A poor quality diet high in fats and sugars that leads to the thinning of the mucus membrane lining;
Drug and medication use, particularly non-steroidal anti-inflammatory drugs that cause gut inflammation;
Habitual alcohol consumption;
Psychological stress;
Exposure to environmental toxins; and
Growth of parasitic bacteria in the stomach, such as salmonella, clostridia, certain forms of E. coli, or parasitic infections such as giardia, ameiosis, and others.[18]

If you suspect you may have food sensitivities, there are several alternatives from which you may choose to identify them. Each of these methods has its own advantages and disadvantages:

Blood tests your doctor can order for you. These include the radioallergosorbent test or RAST test, which checks for antibodies to food in your blood.

Advantages:

Your health insurance may cover this test.

It's fast.

It's persuasive. A traditional health care provider may be more easily persuaded to work with you on your nutrition if you can use a blood test to prove your food allergies.

Disadvantages:

A RAST test will not identify all kinds of food sensitivities, which can involve any number of non-immune mechanisms.

Without health insurance, it's expensive. You may spend hundreds or even thousands of dollars.

Applied Kinesiology. A health care practitioner trained in Applied Kinesiology can use muscle checking to demonstrate how key organs—especially your spleen, liver, heart, and stomach—are affected either positively or adversely by individual food constituents.

Advantages:

It's fast.

If you consult an applied kinesiologist, the visit is generally cheaper than a blood test for food allergies.

A kinesiologist can advise you about which foods your body reacts to most favorably.

Disadvantages:

This method is highly unreliable to evaluate food allergies.

Many conventional health insurance companies will not pay for alternative health care providers.

An elimination diet you can follow yourself.

Advantages:

It's cheap.

Disadvantages:

You may spend weeks or months sorting out all your food sensitivities.

It requires careful note-taking, including keeping records not only of the kind of foods ingested but the amounts, time, and other aggravating factors, such as stress, illness, or medication.

See Question 2 for more information on keeping a food, mood, and weather diary.

The Coca pulse test championed by Dr. Arthur Coca. This method is based on the premise that allergic reactions will produce variations in your pulse rate. For more information on how to use this method, see Question 14.

Advantages:

It's cheap.

Disadvantages:

If you smoke, you must stop smoking while you use this method to get accurate results.

You may take weeks or months to sort out all your food sensitivities.

This method requires careful note-taking.

Other allergic reactions may affect your heart rate.

None of these methods can be relied upon as 100 percent accurate because your emotional reactions to food may be influenced by the following factors:

It may take hours or even days for a meal to move through your intestinal tract and produce symptoms.

Some food reactions require the simultaneous presence of another stress factor, such as exertion, histamine, or aspirin.[19]

After a period of avoidance, you may not respond again to a damaging food for several doses, or indeed ever again.[20] The good news is that also means you may be able to overcome your food sensitivities and eventually return to a more normal diet.

Seasons of the year, menstrual cycle, and infections may also influence your results.[21]

False negatives may occur when the dose is not large enough or not repeated often enough.

To be absolutely certain, you may want to completely avoid a food and all other foods in its food family (See Question 14 and Question 29 on rotating your diet for further explanation of food families) for at least three weeks. Then reintroduce that particular food and see how you react.

Action Plan

Question 13. Do you have food allergies or food sensitivities?

Ask your health professional about which test would be appropriate for you to determine food sensitivity.

Meanwhile, keep a log in your food, mood, and health diary of psychological symptoms that tend to recur when you consume common food allergens.

What I notice when I eat wheat:

What I notice when I eat corn:

What I notice when I eat eggs:

What I notice when I eat dairy products:

Other foods that tend to make me depressed:

Question 14. Should you try various home tests to identify your food sensitivities?

"The pulse-dietary tests should be made the first step in the examination of every patient being studied for mental defects." — Arthur F. Coca, *The Pulse Test.*

If you're curious to see how food affects your moods, there are two techniques that you may try at home to prove to yourself and perhaps also to your doctor how vulnerable you are. These include an elimination diet and the Coca pulse test, which has been around since 1956.

Elimination Diets. On the face of it, an elimination diet is pretty simple. Cut a suspect food out of your diet for at least a week, ideally three weeks, and then eat it again and see how you react afterwards. And by cutting it out, I mean don't eat that food in any shape or form. If you're testing for sensitivity to milk, for example, don't consume dairy products in *any* form and don't eat any foods with milk, butter, cream, cheese, yogurt, whey, or casein, a protein in cow's milk. Then when you make the challenge, preferably eat that food alone in its purest form.

You can make your elimination diet a complex affair or it can be as simple as that.

To start the job, you need to keep a food, mood, and weather diary (see Question 2). You need to keep copious notes when you're following an elimination diet because there are three main reasons your moods may improve under this regimen.

First, you may be intolerant to the food you've avoided.

Second, your initial mood after eating a particular food may be a coincidence. If you keep a good diary, you will be able to note what other factors may have played a role, so you can go back and repeat the challenge until you feel confident about making an objective evaluation.

And third, if you improve, it may simply be a placebo effect. If that's the case, keeping notes will help you to arrive at the conclusion that you don't need to be as restrictive.

As you're keeping track, write down not just what you ate, but also how much. Studies of people who are intolerant to dairy products, for example, have found that many can tolerate as much as a glass of milk a day without symptoms. On the other hand, those who have a true food allergy may develop symptoms after being exposed to even minute traces. Patients with celiac disease (intolerance to gluten grains common to schizophrenics) may have to follow the strictest diet to eliminate not only wheat but rye, barley, oats, spelt, kamut, and additives derived from wheat such as MSG.

Physicians who run clinics to help people with multiple chemical sensitivities sometimes ask their patients to fast for a period of days before beginning an elimination diet, with the idea that the body needs to clear itself of preexisting toxins before an accurate food test can be initiated. Others use a primitive diet restricted to only one food, such as boiled rice, noodles, or white potatoes, or a so-called "caveman" diet free of common allergens.

Such drastic measures may not be necessary, however, if you are willing to keep good records to discuss with your doctor.

Dr. Sherry Rogers, an expert on environmental illness, has pointed out that the amount of effort you put into your elimination diet will have a direct effect on your recovery. "Obviously, people who first fast and then rotate rarely or infrequently eaten (less than once a week) foods get better quicker than those who try the shotgun approach."[1]

As you're adding suspect foods back into your diet, try adding no more than one a day so you can monitor your symptoms. If you are unsure of your reactions, go back to a basic diet clear of common allergens such as wheat, dairy, eggs, and corn. Start over, challenging each suspect ingredient one at a time.

As you're writing down your symptoms, write down what's happening not only with your mind but also with your body. Doctors who deal with sensitive patients note that their symptoms may alternate between psychological and physical complaints. After one exposure, for example, you may have an asthma attack, while after another you just feel mildly depressed. Dr. Rogers says the most common symptoms of food sensitivity are fatigue and depression for which there is no logical cause.[2]

If you do find yourself feeling depressed, make a note whether or not there is some reason to feel that way and, if so, how you have reacted in the past to similar circumstances. You may have been discouraged after work before, for example, but did you feel more discouraged, downright depressed, after coming home and eating several pieces of wheat bread?

As you're going through your elimination diet, remember that it's not a life sentence. If you feel bad, return to a basic yeast-free, sugar-free diet and give yourself a break. If you try to figure out your food sensitivities without professional help, it may take time.

FOODS TO AVOID IF YOU SUSPECT YOU'RE SENSITIVE TO WHEAT OR GLUTEN GRAINS:

Barley
Rye
Oatmeal
Spelt
Breads
Bagels
Crackers
Cereal
Pretzels
Whiskey
Breaded fish and vegetables
Gravies
Hot dogs
Cookies
Candy
Pasta
Cereals
Ice cream
Pudding
Meat loaf
Processed cheese
MSG
Bouillon cubes

FOODS TO AVOID IF YOU SUSPECT YOU'RE SENSITIVE TO MILK:

Casein
Whey
Yogurt
Butter
Bread
Cakes
Puddings
Ice cream
Mashed potatoes
Sherbet
Salad dressing
Margarine
Donuts
Scrambled eggs
Soup
Cheese
Breads
Coffee whitener
Sausages
Vinegar
Cream
Chocolate
Cocoa
Whipped toppings
Cookies
Custard
Cold cuts

FOODS TO AVOID IF YOU SUSPECT YOU'RE SENSITIVE TO CORN:

Popcorn
Cereal
Corn oil
Margarine
Processed foods
Bologna
Sausage
Some vitamin pills (check ingredient list)
Cornstarch
Modified food starch
Dextrin
Corn syrup
Maltodextrins
Dextrose
Lactic acid
Inositol
Sorbitol
Mannitol
Glusonic acid
Hydrol
Caramel color
Alcohol
Food in waxed paper cartons

Carbonated beverages
Sweetened fruit juices
Instant tea or coffee
Canned or frozen fruits
Cold cuts
Ham
Hot dogs
Jams and jellies
Canned vegetables
Catsup
Peanut butter
Chewing gum
MSG
Distilled vinegar
Many vitamins and medications
Grits
Colas
Gummed labels
Gelatin desserts
Gin
Ginger ale
Graham crackers
Whiskies, Scotch, bourbon, brandy, wine

FOODS TO AVOID IF YOU SUSPECT YOU'RE SENSITIVE TO EGGS:

Bread
Cakes
Sherbet
Beer
Eggnog
Pretzels
Waffles
Meringues

Cookies
Ice cream
Donuts
Pasta
Bouillon
Noodle soup
Mayonnaise
Root beer

Sources: Frederick Speer, *Food Allergy*; Doris J. Rapp, *Is This Your Child: Discovering and Treating Unrecognized Allergies*.

The Coca Pulse Test. This test can be used in conjunction with an elimination diet, or you can use it by itself to notice if you are experiencing reactions to what you're eating. In his book *The Pulse Test,* Dr. Coca recommended the following procedure:

1. If you smoke, stop using cigarettes or cigars while performing this test because tobacco affects the heart rate and may skew your results.
2. Count your pulse before each meal for 60 seconds. There are two easy places on the body to count your pulse. One, the carotid artery, is found by placing two fingers on your neck about two inches below your ear lobe. The other is found at your wrist just below your thumb.
3. Count your pulse three times after every meal at half-hour intervals.
4. Count again before you go to sleep and when you first wake up in the morning.
5. Record everything you eat at every meal.
6. Continue these records for two or three days with your usual meals. Then, on the third or fourth day after you've compiled a record of your average pulse reactions, begin making single food tests for two or more whole foods. Eat a small portion of a different single food every hour. Count your pulse just before eating and again a half hour later. Don't test any food to which you already know you're allergic.
7. Review the results with your health care professional. If your pulse does not change after eating any given food, you are probably not sensitive to it. Pulse rates that are more than 6 beats above the estimated normal daily maximum should not be blamed on a recently eaten food but on other allergies or reactions. Larger increases in your pulse rate may indicate food intolerance.

Dr. Coca, the medical director of one of the largest drug companies in the country, noted that he had been able to help patients eliminate their depression with this simple, cheap technique. "The use of the procedure of psychoanalysis would seem to represent a modern refinement of our old acquaintance—symptomatic treatment," he wrote in 1956. "Moreover, it is reasonable to assume that nearly all of those patients who are now being treated with that method are in need of the new antiallergic treatment with which their chances of permanent recovery seem excellent."[3]

Action Plan

Question 14. Should you try various home tests to identify your food sensitivities?

If your food, mood, and health diary indicates a possible connection between your moods and common food sensitivities, pick the one you most suspect and eliminate it completely from your diet. If you believe you may have food sensitivities and don't know where to start, begin by eliminating wheat, all products containing wheat, and other gluten grains for at least three weeks.

How I felt before the elimination diet:

How I feel now:

Question 15. Do you have a yeast infection?

"Depression and manic depression, like Chronic Fatigue Syndrome, MS and other disorders...can develop from many different causes. These include genetic factors, nutritional deficiencies, endocrine disturbances, viral infections, chemical sensitivities and toxicities and psychologic stress or trauma. I do not want you (or anyone) to think I'm saying that Candida albicans is the cause of depression. Yet, if you suffer from depression and/or any other disabling disorder and give a history of:
- *repeated or prolonged courses of antibiotic drugs*
- *persistent digestive symptoms*
- *and/or recurrent vaginal yeast infections—*

a comprehensive treatment program which features oral antifungal medications and a special diet may enable you to change your life." — William G. Crook, *The Yeast Connection and The Woman.*

The biggest revelation during the course of routine allergy testing came the day I was injected with *Candida albicans*, a common yeast. I remember walking in to the doctor's office, glad to see the lady who was measuring my allergies. I was eager to discuss our favorite mutual obsession: gardening. I had brought with me three flower catalogues, heavily marked with ink to indicate my favorite species. Although I started the test laughing and bragging about my horticultural excesses, within minutes of being exposed to a highly diluted drop of *Candida*, perhaps generously described as the size of a pin prick, I wanted to cry.

At first, my depression seemed almost logical. I was watching a cute little three-year-old boy and mulling over my own previous inability to have children. I might never have children, I began to think. I had been too sick, taken too many drugs for too many years—and there I was, in the doctor's office yet again. As I sat and stared as the boy pawed his mother for further attention, my eyes were welling with tears when I realized—it must have been the *Candida* that made me feel so suddenly tired, so manifestly depressed. I noticed the rest of my body. My hands were tingling. My jaw felt stiff. I was tired.

If that's how I overreacted to the tiniest amount of *Candida*, I wondered, what about all the other times I had thought I was logically despondent over some real-life event, when in fact I was simply having an allergic reaction to *Candida*? Even if my reactions to feel sad seemed logical, would my depressions have been as severe if I hadn't been allergic to the yeast with which I was so profoundly infected?

Just as common substances such as dust and pollen can overwhelm our immune systems, *Candida*—another common substance—can wreak havoc with our equilibrium. Many excellent books have been written on the subject, so I will do my best to summarize the salient points with regards to depression.

The yeast called *Candida albicans* inhabits the mouth and gastrointestinal tracts of 30-50 percent of normal individuals.[1] In addition, there are many relatives of *Candida* that wreak similar havoc. In balance, these yeasts are among the millions of microorganisms living alongside the healthy bacteria in the intestines that synthesize vitamins and assist the immune system.

Problems begin to occur when antibiotics, steroids, sugar, and oral contraceptives upset the equilibrium of normal gut flora, killing off the healthy microbes, and paving the way for an overgrowth of *Candida*. When this happens, the byproducts of *Candida* travel to the four corners of the body and begin to create many unpleasant symptoms.

Infections of *Candida albicans* and other yeast species have been reported in virtually every tissue, including the central nervous system.[2] *Candida* has been found colonizing the brains of diagnosed schizophrenic patients and has been implicated in cases of severe psychopathology.[3] Some experts liken the experience to being taken over by a foreign intelligence. Exhausted, confused, debilitated with thoughts of low self-esteem, your mind does not feel like your own.

There are about eighty toxic byproducts of *Candida*,[4] including carbon monoxide, alcohol, steroids, and acetaldehyde, a substance also found in smog, cigarette smoke, and alcoholic beverages.[5] As these byproducts travel to the brain, they can upset the delicate balance of the mechanisms that regulate hormones and emotions. They also impair the body's ability to clear itself of other toxins, thereby leading to increased sensitivity to chemicals in the environment.

Many who are overwhelmed by *Candida* toxins can't tolerate alco-

holic beverages because their systems are already overloaded with alcohol. In fact, there have been documented cases where individuals have
been presumed to be intoxicated when in fact they were merely suffering from a yeast overgrowth.

As if it weren't enough to unleash these toxic chemicals inside the
body, *Candida* has been shown to suppress the immune system,
increasing susceptibility to viruses and to autoimmune diseases, in
which the body begins to attack itself. It has also been implicated in a
wide range of systemic diseases, including arthritis, irritable bowel syndrome, and asthma, as well as multiple endocrine disorders including
hypothyroidism.[6]

How severely you will be affected by *Candida* greatly depends on
how healthy you are to begin with—and that's part of the reason why
rebuilding a healthy emotional outlook depends on taking better care
of your body. The most virulent of the *Candida* species, *Candida albicans*, is able to invade and damage tissues only when host defenses are
impaired.[7]

Key Factors That Have Been Linked To an Overgrowth of *Candida*

Prolonged use of antibiotics
Junk food diets devoid of important nutrients
High-sugar, high-yeast diets
Use of birth control pills or steroids
Chemical exposure
Lowered immune resistance as a result of viral and bacterial
    infections and stress
Pregnancy
Environmental exposure to mold

Symptoms Linked To Yeast Overgrowth

Depression
Hyperactivity
Anxiety
PMS
Irregular periods, painful menstruation
Intestinal problems, including gas, irritable bowel syndrome, col-
    itis, diarrhea, constipation, and nausea

Arthritis
Heart irregularities, including rapid heartbeat, irregular pulse,
   low or high blood pressure, and chest pains
Thyroid disorders, endocrine imbalances
Vaginal yeast infections, infertility
Loss of sex drive
Food allergies and food addictions
Fatigue, dizziness, confusion, blurred vision, and poor memory
Alcoholism
Fungus infections
Low blood sugar
Increased sensitivity to chemicals
Asthma, bronchitis, earaches, sinusitis, and sore throats
Headaches
Muscle aches and weakness
Acne, hives, and rashes
Immune deficiency, autoimmune diseases
Bladder and kidney problems

Sources: John Parks Trowbridge and Morton Walker, *The Yeast Syndrome*; and William G.
Crook, *The Yeast Connection*.

In addition to suffering from the side effects of the toxins, you may
also be allergic to the *Candida*, which is often like living in a filthy
house and being severely sensitive to dust mites. Check with your
physician about two kinds of laboratory tests—both for yeast overgrowth and for allergy to yeast. In addition, you may want to try a
yeast-free, sugar-free diet on your own and see for yourself if your
depression improves.

Action Plan

Question 15. Do you have a yeast infection?

1. List any symptoms you have that may indicate a yeast overgrowth:

2. If your symptoms indicate a high probability of yeast overgrowth, there may be no need to order expensive tests, and you may want to go ahead and try a yeast-free diet (see Questions 25 and 26) and see if your mood improves.

3. If you have multiple symptoms of yeast overgrowth, consult with your doctor to see whether medical tests are appropriate. These may include tests of oral, vaginal, and gastrointestinal yeasts. If your overgrowth is significant, you may want to ask about medication to kill off the yeasts, such as Nystatin.

4. Ask your doctor about a test to see if you are allergic to *Candida*. If you are, ask about allergy shots to reduce your sensitivity.

Question 16. Is your thyroid functioning normally?

"...thyroid dysfunction is by far the most likely condition to present as depression to the psychiatrist." — Irl Extein and Mark S. Gold, *Medical Mimics of Psychiatric Disorders.*

When I was finally seen by an endocrinologist after sixteen years of lithium therapy, he diagnosed me with Hashimoto's thyroiditis, a condition that alternates between under- and then overproduction of thyroid hormone. By that point, I was no longer surprised. I knew by then that the conventional doctors I had seen had missed too many of the crucial points of my personal medical history. Even months before I saw the endocrinologist, three doctors had told me there was nothing wrong with my thyroid. It was only after looking at my blood tests over a period of time and seeing the fluctuation that a doctor made the correct diagnosis.

So what's the big deal? Why would some obscure medical diagnosis have mattered? Because Hashimoto's is frequently misdiagnosed as—you guessed it—manic depression.

Patients with Hashimoto's and either hypo- or hyperthyroid conditions have been known to display the full range of psychiatric symptoms, including psychoses. Seeing things. Hearing things. The fact is, you don't have to be mentally ill to bear the brunt of acute psychological suffering. Women in particular are more vulnerable to hypothyroidism[1] and thus are at higher risk for developing the thoughts and feelings associated with depression.

Did I have Hashimoto's disease all my life? Or did lithium, which is known to gradually destroy the thyroid function of about one-third of patients who take it regularly, ultimately do me in? I may never be able to find the answers to these questions, but I now know enough to warn others what to look for. So how do you rule out thyroid disease? For starters, look to see if you have any of the symptoms.

SYMPTOMS OF HYPOTHYROIDISM

Physical Symptoms
Hair loss
Yellow-orange discoloration
   of skin, particularly on the
   palms of hands
Excess weight
Muscle weakness
Dry skin
Intolerance to cold
Recurrent infections
Drooping, swollen eyes
Constipation

Mental Symptoms
Depression
Fatigue
Loss of appetite

Sources: M. Sara Rosenthal, *The Thyroid Sourcebook*; and W.M.G. Tunbridge, *Thyroid Disease: The Facts.*

You may ask your doctor about tests to see if your thyroid level is in the normal range, but be persistent if your tests look normal and you still don't feel well. Experts who have studied the link between depression and thyroid abnormalities say that some people are simply exquisitely sensitive to thyroid imbalances, and that "routine" testing may identify only about 10 percent of these patients.[2] Depression may simply be the first sign of hypothyroidism.

Aside from the blood tests your doctor may order to check the levels of thyroid hormones, you can perform a simple underarm temperature test. Get a basal body temperature thermometer, the kind used to track body temperature for ovulation, the kind that is well calibrated. Instead of placing the thermometer in your mouth, put it under your arm first thing in the morning before you get out of bed and keep it there for ten minutes. For women, start your measurements the second day of menstruation. If you take your temperature in the middle of your cycle, your results may be skewed when your temperature rises during ovulation. Keep the record for at least five days. If your underarm temperature is consistently below 97.4 degrees, you may have a problem with low thyroid function, which could well be an underlying cause of your depression. Normal underarm temperature should be between 97.8 and 98.2 degrees.[3]

Now let's look at why the thyroid, a butterfly-shaped gland in the neck, should make such a difference to our sense of psychological balance.

The thyroid is part of the endocrine system, which also includes the hypothalamus, a bundle of nerve cells and fibers in the middle of the brain, also known as the limbic system, which controls our emotions. The pituitary gland, located behind the bridge of the nose, has been called the master gland. The adrenal glands, located atop the kidneys, manage our response to stress and to changes in our blood sugar levels.

For starters, the hormones these organs secrete regulate body temperature, metabolism, sleep, sex drive, appetite, and water balance. So the very structures that control unconscious body processes are also believed to regulate the ups and downs we feel every day.

Hypothyroidism can slow down our overall metabolism, making us feel fatigued and depressed and leading to further imbalances in the endocrine system.

Action Plan

Question 16. Is your thyroid functioning normally?

1. List here any symptoms you have that may indicate hypothyroidism:

2. Take your underarm body temperature for a week, first thing in the morning, upon rising. List the results:

3. Ask your health care professional about medical tests for your thyroid function, including tests to see if you may have Hashimoto's, the autoimmune thyroid disease.

Question 17. Are you hypoglycemic?

"It is of great relief to the patient who feels he is 'going mad,' or states that he is 'unable to cope any more,' to be told that there is not a nervous breakdown round the corner, nor is his personality breaking up owing to some hidden subconscious mental conflict. What is happening is probably due to an imbalance in his metabolism involving an insufficient supply of fuel to the nervous system (i.e. low blood sugar) which in the majority of cases is easy to treat and often completely reversible." — Martin L. Bud, *Low Blood Sugar (Hypoglycemia): The 20th Century Epidemic?*

Until I went on a yeast-free diet and eliminated the foods to which I was sensitive, I was so hypoglycemic that my life seemed to revolve around eating. As a newspaper reporter, I can remember halting important interviews to ask for something to eat. Sometimes I felt the symptoms of low blood sugar—the shakiness, brain fog, and confusion—even if my stomach wasn't growling, or even if I had just eaten two or three hours before. My husband quickly learned to drop everything and head for the nearest chow line if I even hinted at being hungry—better that than to deal with a wife who was irritable, jumpy, or unpredictable.

Of course, as a person who always took responsibility for my health, I did my best to combat the hypoglycemia with what I thought, at the time, was a proper diet. I ate protein and/or took protein supplements, particularly at breakfast. I never skipped meals and frequently broke my meals down into small, healthy snacks. I tried to eat a lot of fiber to tide me over from meal to meal. I avoided coffee because the caffeine, which stimulates the adrenal glands, upset my blood sugar levels even further.

Sometimes my hypoglycemia would show up on blood tests, and sometimes it wouldn't. I would come up low in blood sugar ranges even after eating candy, for example, but at other times, the clinical tests indicated I had no problem. I hated having my sugar levels drawn because I had to forgo breakfast before the tests. On one occasion, I remember being so disoriented without breakfast that I got lost on the way to the lab and missed my appointment, even though I had been there on several other occasions.

Why all the concern about blood sugar when it comes to depression?

Because sugar is the brain's primary source of fuel. Unlike our muscles, which can store sugar, the brain has low levels of reserves. Roughly 90 percent of the energy needed for the brain must come from glucose.[1] And the brain uses about half of all the blood sugar in the body.[2] In fact, while most of us eat to maintain our physical health, few realize just how demanding our brains are when it comes to proper feeding. In a recent lecture to the National Alliance for the Mentally Ill, nutritional consultant Janet Aiken pointed out that the central nervous system needs more than fifty different vitamins, minerals, amino acids, and fatty acids in order to maintain itself and synthesize neurotransmitters. Over time, poor diet can combine with stress to create all the conditions necessary for mental illness.

Low levels of blood sugar in the brain lead to low levels of neurotransmitters, including low levels of serotonin, a deficiency of which can cause depression. Recent research has found that if blood sugar levels fluctuate widely enough we can manifest the symptoms of manic depression, swinging high and low without much of a rest in between.[3]

Low blood sugar levels can trigger an attack of asthma or allergy symptoms,[4] which can also aggravate depression. Also, individual responses to various allergies can alter blood sugar levels[5] because histamine, a substance emitted during allergy attacks, tends to rise as blood sugar levels fall.

The yeast *Candida albicans* can cause low blood sugar,[6] as can high levels of cortisol, which make the body less sensitive to insulin. At the same time, low blood sugar levels can place stress on the body, further pulling other hormones out of balance.

The mechanisms that maintain the proper balance of glucose in the brain are amongst the most important survival mechanisms in the body. In brief, the hypothalamus and pituitary glands in the brain control two organs in the endocrine system: the adrenals and the pancreas. The adrenals secrete cortisol, a hormone which raises the blood sugar. The pancreas secretes insulin, a hormone which lowers the blood sugar level and orders the liver to store it in the form of glycogen. A rapid rise in blood sugar levels stimulates the production of insulin, which in turn causes a drop in blood sugar levels.

Clinically, hypoglycemia is defined by blood glucose levels of 50 mg/dl or less.[7] However, the hypothalamic-pituitary-adrenal axis is so sensitive that it can detect changes in blood sugar levels of as little as 2 mg. either up or down. This sensitivity is one reason that nutrition is so important—your mood can change with every meal.

There are both physical and mental symptoms associated with hypoglycemia, but it is important to note that blood sugar can drop without causing symptoms and symptoms can be felt without reaching a clinical level of hypoglycemia.

SYMPTOMS OF HYPOGLYCEMIA

Physical Symptoms	Mental Symptoms
Headaches	Depression
Heart palpitations	Fatigue
Muscular aches and twitches	Dizziness
Excessive sweating	Confusion
Trembling	Forgetfulness
Fainting	Irritability
Double or blurred vision	Paranoia
Cold hands and feet	Anxiety
Craving for food, especially sweets	Light-headedness
Tingling of the skin	Insomnia

Source: Carl C. Pfeiffer, *Mental and Elemental Nutrients*, pp. 384-85.

Some doctors divide hypoglycemia into two basic types—hypoglycemia that occurs after fasting, which is relatively rare, and functional or reactive hypoglycemia, which can occur after eating. Food allergies or food sensitivities can also upset the balance of blood sugar in the body.

Although the mechanism by which food sensitivity can cause the blood sugar to drop is not well understood, it is believed that food sensitivity can make the insulin-producing cells in the pancreas overactive.[8]

It is this latter kind of hypoglycemia, functional or reactive hypoglycemia, that is found to be common amongst those with manic depression and other psychiatric maladjustments.[9] Drops of 10 to 20 mg/dl in blood sugar after meals—without necessarily reaching the clinical level of hypoglycemia—have been found to mimic a wide range of psychiatric disorders.[10]

Another possible factor in chronic hypoglycemia may be mercury amalgam tooth fillings, which have been suspected in playing a part of the vicious cycle of yeast infections, allergies, and hypoglycemia. Mercury itself is a neurotoxin, which poisons the nervous system and the brain.[11] It has been shown to depress the immune system. High sugar diets cause tooth decay, which in turn requires tooth fillings, which may lead to toxic levels of mercury in the body. Mercury toxicity may trigger yeast infections as well as the symptoms of hypoglycemia.[12]

Action Plan

Question 17. Are you hypoglycemic?

1. List here any symptoms you have that may indicate hypoglycemia:

2. In your food, mood, and weather diary, take note of how your emotions change before and after meals. Do you feel depressed, anxious, or irritable between meals? How often do you have to eat to maintain balanced emotions?

3. If your symptoms of hypoglycemia are obvious to you, there may be no need to undergo the expense and discomfort of a blood sugar test. If so, you may simply want to adopt dietary and lifestyle changes to balance your blood sugar (see Question 23).

4. If your doctor recommends a blood sugar test, ask him or her about whether a carbohydrate challenge test, which simulates what happens in real life, would be more appropriate for you than a glucose challenge test, which requires you to drink a sugar solution.

Question 18. Do you need to detoxify your body?

> *"Your body is like a house. It needs regular cleaning and, occasionally, a thorough 'spring cleansing' to operate at peak performance. Signs of toxic buildup include headache, fatigue, depression, belching, flatulence, irritability, insomnia, nausea, abdominal discomfort, tender abdomen, loss of memory or concentration, lack of sexual desire, skin blemishes, sallow complexion, bad breath, coated tongue, body odor, lower back pain, menstrual problems, and aches and pains."* — Cherie Calbom and Maureen Keane, *Juicing for Life*.

If you suspect your depression may be caused by chronic exposure to toxic substances, you may feel overwhelmed, not knowing where to begin figuring out how to begin cleaning up your diet and environment.

Until you find doctors skilled in identifying your sensitivities, there is one program you can begin yourself: detoxification. Nutritionally-oriented doctors have known for a long time that detoxification programs may be a short cut for many patients to eliminate the underlying causes of many mental and physical diseases.[1] Appropriate detoxification may eliminate your allergy symptoms, food sensitivities, hypoglycemia, heavy metals, chemicals, and many other important causes of depression. However, before undertaking any such program, you should understand that the process may take time and require you to make other changes in your lifestyle. Plan to be both patient and prudent.

Many people think of detoxification as a process involving a complete fast, the very thought of which makes hypoglycemics like me head for the nearest available pantry. The process of fasting, abstaining from food for a period of one to several days, is one alternative to clear out digestive problems that may be aggravating your moods, but it may also put additional stress on your blood sugar levels, thereby driving you further into depression.

Doctors today are finding that the body is often better able to detoxify itself when supported with proper nutrition,[2] including:

rotein, low-carbohydrate diet to support the liver;
ant supplements such as flavonoids, vitamin C, vitamin
E, and selenium;
Essential fatty acids;
Supplements that support the so-called friendly bacteria in the
  gut, such as fructooligosaccharides.[3]

You should seek the advice of your doctor before attempting any fast, particularly if you have any preexisting medical condition. These are some of the alternatives you may consider to detoxify your body.

A juice fast. You may want to consider drinking only fruit and vegetable juices, which contain high amounts of vitamins and minerals, along with bulking agents such as psyllium seed husks as bulk laxatives. There are numerous excellent recipe books to tell you how to make your own fresh juices. Keep in mind that initially you may feel worse on any kind of fast, as your body releases toxins.

Special nutritional supplements. Various companies manufacture products to provide high-quality protein; complex carbohydrates; and essential fats, vitamins, and minerals to prevent muscle and organ breakdown while clearing the liver, intestinal tract, and kidneys. Ask your doctor which would be most appropriate for you.

Chelation therapy. Particular compounds of vitamins and minerals may be fed intravenously under a doctor's supervision. These bind to heavy metals and carry them out of the body.

A weight-loss diet and exercise program. Because chemicals and toxins are often stored in our fat cells, many environmentally-oriented physicians encourage diets to lose weight as a means of reducing the total load on the liver.

Salt water and baking soda baths. Many of us forget that the skin is also part of our elimination system. In addition, our skin is the largest organ in the body. I like to take one pound of baking soda and one pound of sea salt, pour it into a hot bath and sit at least twenty minutes or until I feel better. Modern mystics claim that, in addition to providing a deserved rest from the stresses of everyday life and opening the pores for cleansing, these baths cleanse the aura of negative emotions. However these baths actually work, you may be surprised how much better you feel afterwards. Even if you choose not to fast, you can take mineral baths regularly.

Aerobic exercise and saunas. Sweating will help to mobilize only about 10 percent of the toxins in the body,[4] but the process of exercise and saunas also helps to mobilize stored fats.

Body brushing or massage. After you take a mineral bath, sauna, or exercise, consider brushing your skin with a dry brush or towel to detoxify the skin. Massage may also stimulate the lymph glands, also known as the body's sewer system, to carry toxins away from your organs.

A trip to the seashore or mountains to breathe fresh air. In addition to our digestive tract, our skin, and our kidneys, another important organ of elimination is our lungs. Numerous books have been written about the importance of deep breathing to improving state of mind, but many of us never consider the quality of air we're breathing in. Constant exposure to hydrocarbons, both on the highways and in our homes from gas appliances, has been found to cause serious depressions and a wide range of psychotic states.[5]

Action Plan

Question 18. Do you need to detoxify your body?

1. Consult with your doctor to determine if you are a good candidate for a detoxification program, or whether you need to wait until you are physically stronger or more mentally balanced. If you are ready to detoxify, ask him or her what the best method would be.

2. Even if you are not a good candidate for a medically-supervised fast:
   Supplement your diet with vegetable juices.
   Schedule a time to take a salt water and baking soda bath.
   Get a soft-bristle brush or towel and massage yourself afterwards. If you learn Touch for Health or consult with a Touch for Health practitioner (see Question 36), you can get a chart of neurolymphatic reflex points to refer to when you want to stimulate your lymph system.
   Plan a vacation to the seashore or mountains to relax and breathe fresh air.
   Plan to get 30 minutes of aerobic exercise every day.
   Take a sauna.

PART III

THE STRESS CONNECTION

19. Do you have high levels of cortisol in your body?

20. Do you need to lower your stress level?

21. Do you have an adequate stress management program and support system?

Question 19. Do you have high levels of cortisol in your body?

"Disease states in which alterations of the cortisol rhythm have been observed include...severe depression." — Kenneth L. Becker, *Principles and Practice of Endocrinology and Metabolism.*

Anyone who wants to understand depression needs to understand one simple equation:

High levels of cortisol = Depression.[1]

Forgive me here for becoming technical, but I would like to try to explain this biochemical fact in a way that will make you reconsider your entire lifestyle, whether your depression is of the long-term or the short-term variety.

Cortisol is a hormone secreted by the body in response to stress. It is also secreted by the adrenal glands, two tiny organs on top of our kidneys, whenever blood sugar levels drop. Its function is to raise the blood sugar level. You're in a life-or-death situation, so you need quick access to energy, right? Cortisol comes to the rescue. You're hungry, so you need to raise your blood sugar? Cortisol comes to the rescue. To make this point simply, think of two other equations.

High stress = high cortisol.[2]
Dropping blood sugar levels = high cortisol.

The trouble is that a high-stress life aggravated by a lousy diet and erratic blood sugar levels will prolong mild depression and make chronic depression much worse. And that means that when we feel depressed, whatever the cause, we need to lower our stress level and do our best to eat better so as to reduce the total biochemical stress on our bodies.

Why? Cortisol has several effects on the body that in turn affect our emotions. First, cortisol suppresses the function of insulin and raises blood sugar levels,[3] theoretically so we can respond well to a fight-orflight situation. In states of chronic stress, however, it's as if our minds have cried wolf. The adrenal glands have been so overstimulated that they may not be able to produce enough hormones to raise blood sugar when necessary and hypocortisolism, or Addison's disease, may result. On the other hand, excessive production of cortisol may result in a physical disease called Cushing's syndrome,[4] which is accompanied 50 to 90 percent of the time by psychiatric symptoms, including mania or depression.[5]

Second, cortisol speeds the uptake of serotonin, an important neurotransmitter. Low levels of serotonin have been associated with depression, fatigue, eating disorders, suicidal thoughts, and insomnia. Cortisol speeds serotonin through the synapses of the brain's nerve cells so whatever serotonin is around isn't there long enough to produce the usual calming, soothing effects. Result: The same as taking a downer. Animal studies suggest that cortisol acts like a barbiturate and depresses nerve cell activity in the brain.[6]

Even under highly stressful conditions, so-called "normal" individuals may secrete high levels of cortisol, but the feedback mechanisms of the hypothalamic-pituitary-adrenal axis suppress it, ultimately lowering the level of cortisol in the body within a matter of time.

Studies have found that those who tend to be depressive maintain higher levels of cortisol after stressful events and even at night, when the body is resting and supposedly not under any emotional stress. Although doctors have long known that high cortisol levels are a common symptom in depression, they frequently don't test a patient's cortisol levels, arguing that there is no objective measure to determine "normal" cortisol levels for any one individual.[7]

At least one laboratory company, however, Diagnos-Techs Inc. of Seattle, offers an adrenal stress index to help doctors assess how the physiological effects of stress may be contributing to a patient's depression. Their research shows that in most patients suffering from depression, cortisol levels run 43 mg/day or more compared with about 23-42 mg/day for normal control subjects.[8]

In addition, altered cortisol levels may lead to functional hypoglycemia, which deprives the brain of the energy needed for normal function.[9] High levels of cortisol reduce the uptake of glucose, the usable form of blood sugar in the body, by 20 to 35 percent. That's also partly because high cortisol levels have two unhealthy effects on the protein we take into our bodies. For one, high cortisol levels decrease protein synthesis by about 35 percent and increase protein degradation by about the same amount, resulting in a total reduction in protein turnover by about 70 percent. Adequate levels of protein are necessary to ward off hypoglycemia (See Question 17), with its unpleasant highs and lows in mood resulting from fluctuating blood sugar.[10]

High levels of cortisol have also been found to physically dismantle the hardware of the brain, reducing the conductivity of brain cells and leading to problems with memory, spatial distortions, learning problems, and so-called brain fog, where thinking itself feels difficult.[11] They can also affect the balance of electrolytes, or minerals, in the body, and change blood pressure.[12]

There is nothing new about these findings. In fact, medical students learn about high cortisol levels in basic neurochemistry textbooks.[13] Nevertheless, we as a society continue to ignore the fact that chronic stress, whether the source be psychological or physiological, can lead to high cortisol levels and depression.

Taken together, studies of thyroid function and cortisol levels have been found to identify biological malfunction in approximately 85 percent of what's called unipolar depressives, or people who tend to get depressed without alternating to manic episodes.[14]

We now know that chronic stress can alter brain chemistry permanently, and what goes on with our adrenal glands plays a huge role in the changes that take place.

SYMPTOMS OF ADRENAL DYSFUNCTION

Inability to concentrate
Excessive fatigue
Nervousness and irritability
Depression
Apprehensions

Excessive weakness
Lightheadedness
Faintness and fainting
Insomnia

Source: John W. Tintera, "Adrenal Dysfunction," *Hypoglycemia Association Bulletin* 96.

Many researchers now believe that depression is really a malfunction of the hypothalamic-pituitary-adrenal axis, basically a feedback loop between the hypothalamus and the pituitary gland in the brain, and the adrenal glands.[15]

If you have suffered from prolonged stress and feel depressed, you may want to ask your doctor about tests to see if your adrenal glands are functioning normally. If they aren't, adrenal supplements are available to help you deal with the biochemical effects of your current stress while you make the changes necessary to return to mental health.

Action Plan

Question 19. Do you have high levels of cortisol in your body?

1. List here any symptoms you have that may indicate adrenal dysfunction:

2. Ask your health care practitioner about medical tests of your adrenal function. Even if your cortisol level is not high, you may have alterations in the normal daily rhythms of your stress hormones that may need to be addressed.

3. If your cortisol level is high, plan to make a serious reassessment of your stress management program (see Questions 20 and 21). Ask your doctor what other measures you might take to restore the balance of your adrenal hormones.

Question 20. Do you need to lower your stress level?

"By learning to gauge our own innate energy, potential weaknesses and strengths, we can all benefit from it. True, this requires a great deal of self discipline and will power, but we must not lose sight of the fact that in the last analysis, each of us is responsible for his or her own well being. Otherwise we will continue to be plagued by stress-induced diseases, no matter what treatments we devise." — Hans Selye, as quoted in *Physical Illness in the Psychiatric Patient*, Erwin K. Koranyi, ed.

Stressed out? Wonder why you're depressed?

Sixty percent of patients with major depression meet the criteria for generalized anxiety disorder, and 30 to 90 percent of anxiety disorder patients have a history of major depression.[1]

Throughout my life, even times of high achievement were not necessarily enjoyable if they were accompanied by a lot of stress. Thus, I found myself bummed out as a successful newspaper reporter even when beating major dailies on big business news stories. As a playwright, I endured years of anonymity, only to feel even more misery when my plays came to light because the emotional cost of play productions would wipe me out for months afterwards. I was caught in a trap: I was not able to handle stress particularly well, yet I was always drawn to high achievement. I couldn't enjoy the peaks of my professional or personal life, and I suffered equally hard times in depression. Life didn't seem exactly fair.

More than forty definitions of stress can be found in psychiatric literature,[2] but in the final analysis, what is stressful to one man is a thrill to another. Life comes down to a question of perspective and how we view what happens to us. As I pondered this point, I wondered what the evolutionary reason was for depression. In a perfect world, nobody would be depressed, right?

Not necessarily.

Hans Selye, a leading researcher on the human stress response, has theorized that depression may have been designed to get us to stop stressful activity before we exceed our personal emotional and/or physical breaking points.[3] Other researchers have added that because depression is essentially a reaction to stress, in many real-life situations it is the only psychologically healthy way to react. As Selye noted, "It automatically prevents people from persisting in activities that exceed their powers of resistance."[4] So, from an evolutionary perspective, depression may be thought of as a logical response to prevent individuals from driving themselves over the brink—a fact worth considering in a society that encourages us to have it all and do it all or face feeling unfulfilled.

According to yogic philosophy, anxiety stems from attachment. Whether the attachment is to persons, places, or things, inability to let go in proper time crowds the unconscious mind and clouds our ability to interpret the overarching truth of every present moment.

If you have practiced the postures of hatha yoga, you are familiar with the concept that thoughts carry actual weight—thinking too much not only can throw your body off balance but also may cause you to lose total focus and control, no matter what your level of strength or physical coordination. Hatha yoga has much to teach about the process of stress management, but you need not practice actual physical yoga to benefit from the philosophy behind it.

Part of lowering our stress level obviously has to do with lightening the load in our schedules, but it also has to do with unburdening ourselves of tiresome thoughts. Attachments to thoughts of the past or fears of the future literally reduce the amount of energy available to us—psychic energy as well as actual physical energy. When our energy is bound up in memories of past wrongs or fears of the future, we are unable to fully invest ourselves in the present moment, which is where our hearts are most able to find peace. Thus, you may try your best to relax—you may charter a jet to the most exotic, remote corner of the globe—but if you are unable to let go of the thoughts that are literally weighing you down, you will have difficulty lowering your stress level, no matter where you are.

Stress management is important for everyone, but it is an even higher priority for those with chronic depression and high levels of cortisol, the hormone secreted in response to stress. In most individuals, cortisol levels can rise in response to a stressful event and then return to normal. That's not always the case, however, among those with chronic depression. In some cases, cortisol levels may go up and stay up, leading to further depression.

Cortisol has a biological half life of thirteen hours, which means that we will continue to feel the physical and emotional effects for up to thirteen hours after a stressful event.[5] One study by the Institute of HeartMath, a biomedical research center in Boulder Creek, California, showed that when an event triggers an angry response for as short a period as five minutes, the immune system is depressed for more than six hours.

The same study asked subjects to think about someone or something they cared about. Results: positive, caring thoughts actually lowered cortisol levels and increased the number of immune cells.[6] Such scientific data should encourage even the most skeptical to consider the physiological effects of positive thinking. What this means in practical terms is that those of us who tend to be easily depressed need to focus greater attention on our personal need for relaxation. Stress—even "good" stress from outstanding personal achievement—is likely to send us into depression. And when we feel bad to begin with, more stress will make us feel worse. Either we face this fact and take greater care of our minds and bodies, or we continue to drive ourselves from one breakdown to another.

A key factor in my recovery from chronic fatigue and depression was learning that, first, I could actually be more productive if I spent more time taking care of myself. I simply had more to give if I took better care of myself. And, second, I had to change the way I viewed stress.

Researchers at the University of Washington School of Medicine developed a scale for ranking stressful events, with the underlying theme that the more changes there are in your life, good or bad, the higher your stress level and the greater your chances of becoming ill.

However, in my own research, I found that a key factor in stress resistance was the element of control. The famous stress scale does not take into account how each of us reacts to sitting in rush hour traffic or waiting on hold for a customer service representative to pick up the telephone.

We can choose to reduce the amount of stress in our lives to some extent by the way we organize our lives and by the amount of time we invest in relaxing, but perhaps even more importantly, by the way we interpret what happens to us. Once we truly understand that the biochemical effects of stress lead to depression, we have to face the question of how we choose to react to what goes on in our lives.

Action Plan

Question 20. Do you need to lower your stress level?

Choose a day to monitor the thoughts behind your thoughts. Spend the day listening to your inner voice and make a list of the top five issues that dominate your mind. It doesn't matter whether the thought is a memory of an actual past event or a worry about what may have happened or what may happen in the future.

As you list them, notice how long each particular issue has been troubling you.

After you have brought this list of worries to light, write beside each one what it would take for you to let go. If you can't imagine letting go, forgetting, or forgiving, that's O.K. Don't judge. Just ask yourself the question and allow your mind to come up with the answer in its own perfect time.

After you have made your list and noted what it would take for you to let go, place each worry on a separate piece of paper. Then fold the papers and set them aside. Spend the next hour totally relaxing your body in whatever way seems most nurturing to you. Take a bath. Meditate. Listen to your favorite music. Dance. Stretch. Do yoga. Go for a walk. Watch the sunset. Pray or read the scriptures. You will know you are fully relaxed when the tension has disappeared from your body. Your shoulders and back will feel supple. When you feel soft and at peace, return to the pieces of paper and unfold each one, discovering your previous thoughts as if for the first time. See if perhaps some of the worries no longer concern you.

If you are ready to release a major worry, create a special ceremony for it. Burn the paper in a candle. Tear the words into a thousand bits and cast them off the top of a bridge. Blow the tatters from your hand like feathers. Say a prayer and give thanks for lightening your burden.

If, when you are completely relaxed, you feel unable to let go of any worry, just take note. Don't increase the weight of that thought by blaming or judging or intensifying the memory. Say to yourself, "One day I will be ready to let go of this, but there is something here still to benefit me. I accept myself for where I am now. I am in the perfect place in perfect time."

Then return to the rest of your day, and go on.

Question 21. Do you have an adequate stress management program?

"The World is too much with us; late and soon,
Getting and spending, we lay waste our powers;
Little we see in Nature that is ours;
We have given our hearts away, a sordid boon!"
— William Wordsworth, "The World Is Too Much With Us."

If you remember nothing else that you read in this book, remember this one simple equation:

$$\text{High cortisol} = \text{Depression.}[1]$$

Again: cortisol is a hormone secreted by the adrenal glands in response to stress. It's also secreted when our blood sugar levels drop to signal our bodies to release more energy into the bloodstream.

Because high cortisol levels are a consistent finding in depressed patients, we may conclude that the fastest way to alleviate depression is to lower the stress we are placing on ourselves—both emotional stress and physiological stress. Each of us must identify our own stressors. The key element is the feeling of control, and that perception of control can only come from the realization that we have the power to make choices every day of our lives.

Many of us instinctively know that when we get stressed at home or at work, we are more likely to become depressed. The connection should no longer be ignored. We know that long-term stress can change the biochemistry of the brain, and that the body does not differentiate whether the source of our stress is mental or physical. That's why it's important to do everything we can to boost our immune system, develop positive habits of thinking, and manage whatever stress comes along in our lives.

For years, I chose to deal with stress by ignoring it. Feeling unable to cope with the sadness at my very core, I chose to cover it up with decades of nonstop achievement. If I chose to be a reporter, I had to be the very best reporter. If I chose to write plays, I had to be writing all the time or I would feel terribly guilty. I allowed myself little time for relaxation because I felt I might miss something in the time I thought I was wasting. Ultimately, when I got so sick that I was forced to sit back and reevaluate how I had been managing my life, a healer commented to me, "You cannot drive your body like it was a car."

Like a reformed smoker who is ever more acutely aware of the perils of nicotine, I now counsel my personal training clients to focus more on relaxation and can only hope one day they will be ready to listen. Some of the people I train get up at 4:30 A.M., never eat breakfast or lunch, never stop to take a breath, and wonder at the end of the day why they feel so unfulfilled. "If you don't take care of yourself, you can't take care of anybody else," I advise them.

I had to reach the grand old age of thirty-seven before I could convince myself that I could be more productive if I spent more time taking care of myself. At first, I thought I was being quite selfish, and then I began to comprehend the fact that if I do not take care of myself, I have nothing to give—no enthusiasm to share, no inspiration to write down—and everybody loses, including me.

Just as stress will look different to each of you who reads this book, so should your stress management program. However, I believe you must consider:

❖ What amount of time you need alone every day to nourish your mind, body, and spirit.

❖ How to make time to be around those who support you and love you unconditionally.

❖ Activities you need to include every week to gain a different perspective of your routine.

❖ Physical exercise and rest, such as a daily walk and assured number of hours of sleep.

❖ Mental exercise and rest, such as yoga or meditation.

❖ Spiritual exercise and rest, such as time pondering scriptures or contemplating the beauty of nature.

It may seem at first that you should not take the time to do these things for yourself. Better to assume that you could go on living your life to the fullest if you did not eat or sleep! If you are driven to succeed, rest assured that the more you can successfully integrate these kinds of activities into your routine, the faster you will be able to overcome your depression.

Action Plan

Question 21. Do you have an adequate stress management program?

1. Create an Emotional Survival Kit. Get a box or clear out a drawer. Perhaps you could even treat yourself to a special, pretty box. Place inside:

A list of names and phone numbers of your dearest loved ones
Favorite photographs
A copy of sacred scriptures
Clippings of funny jokes
Faded flowers from your garden
Inspirational quotations
Anything near and dear to you that makes you laugh or smile
Anything that reminds you of how much you are loved and valued
Any object that represents your security

Long ago, I took a train to my first day of a new school. I didn't know any of the other girls, and felt odd and uncomfortable in my ugly school uniform. No one seemed to take any notice of me, except a funny old man. We didn't speak, but as he departed he turned to me and gave me a tiny pamphlet that he had been reading. It was called "The Reason Why." For many years, during my darkest depressions, I told myself, "When I get very desperate, I will always be able to read, 'The Reason Why.'" I don't remember ever reading it, but I carried it with me through numerous moves, in a special box with favorite pictures and crumbling roses. When you are tired and down, with no one available to comfort you, you should always be able to turn to your Emotional Survival Kit.

2. In your food, mood, and weather diary, schedule one week to monitor the amount of time you spend in any activity that nourishes your mind, body, or spirit. Do you feel guilty when you take care of yourself? Try to look at your record as if it belonged to your dearest friend— would you want your dear one to give more to himself or herself? In what ways can you make the space to nurture?

❖ List the ways you manage your physical stress.

❖ Describe how you relax your mind in any activity other than sleeping.

❖ Listen to your spirit and ask what ways it wants to be exercised or rested. When was the last time you worshiped—at a church, synagogue, or mosque, in quiet ceremonies, or by reveling in the creation all around us?

As you become aware of how much time you need in activities that nourish your body, mind, and spirit, schedule time for each one on a daily basis. Make an appointment and develop your will by honoring your commitment to yourself. Notice what kinds of outside influences convince you to break your personal appointments. Are you valuing yourself as much as you value the needs and demands of others?

3. Make a pie chart of your life's activities for an average week. Include the amount of time you spend working, taking care of family, commuting, eating, resting, exercising, worshiping, taking care of errands, managing finances, enjoying hobbies, as well as any other major activities. Now draw the chart again, this time dividing up the pie how you would like it to be.

4. List the favorite people in your life and why you feel good when you're around them. Now list those who seem to drag your energy level down. Develop an awareness of how other people affect you. Notice whether they celebrate your accomplishments, support you in your dreams. Are you bringing joy and light to their lives? Is there a mutual benefit, or a divine purpose that is being served?

PART IV

THE NUTRITION CONNECTION

22. Are you willing to adopt a healthier diet?

23. Do you need to adopt dietary and lifestyle changes to stabilize your blood sugar?

24. Do you need to psyche yourself to change your eating habits?

25. Are you willing to give up the ten kinds of foods most likely to aggravate depression?

26. Are you willing to eat more of the ten kinds of foods most likely to improve depression?

27. Should you learn to appreciate vegetables?

28. Are you willing to give up antibiotics and other additives in your food?

29. Do you need to rotate your diet?

30. Do you drink enough water and ingest enough salt?

Question 22. Are you willing to adopt a healthier diet?

"If someone had told me a year ago that I would give up bread and cheese, I would have replied, 'I'll die first,' and I felt as though I almost did. No food is worth that. There are many other pleasures, the best one being the joy of optimum health."
— Charlene Grimmett, *Beat The Yeast Cookbook*.

I would be the first to admit I was less than thrilled the first time I heard about a yeast-free, sugar-free diet. It was as if the bony finger of fate had pointed at me directly, and all I could do was look around as if to say, "Who, me? There must be some terrible mistake!"

For me, among food's many purposes, the first and most important has always been a kind of entertainment value. I love to eat. I love to cook. Even the most mundane meal is an event to be enjoyed, a break from the pressures of the day, a time to reward myself. When I have the time, I love to entertain large numbers of friends and family members, as many as will fit around our dining room table, with memorable feasts that linger on for hours. And even on the most unmemorable occasions, I used to like to treat myself. Chocolate chip cookies? Fresh bagels with homemade jam? Frozen yogurt? This is what heaven on earth is all about, I used to think.

The good news is this: Changing your diet to go yeast-free and sugar-free is not about deprivation at all. In fact, if you like to eat, this is the diet for you!

When you switch to eating a balanced diet of fresh vegetables and some fresh fruits, whole grains, and what I call clean meats without antibiotics and steroids, you can eat a lot more than you ever thought possible and most of the time either lose or maintain your weight while attaining new levels of mental well-being.

After much trial and error, I have come up with this recommendation for the optimum depression-fighting diet:

The worst 10 kinds of foods to put in your body:

1. Anything moldy, malted, or fermented.
2. Anything processed.

3. Anything dried or aged.
4. Anything made with sugar or honey.
5. Anything made with yeast.
6. Any meat raised with antibiotics or steroids.
7. Leftovers unless frozen.
8. Alcoholic beverages, coffee, tea, chocolate, and colas.
9. Food colorings, chemicals, preservatives, and additives.
10. Tap water.

The best 10 kinds of foods to put in your body:
1. Fresh vegetables.
2. Fresh, unsweet fruits in moderation.
3. Protein, keeping a 2-to-1 ratio of carbohydrates to protein.
4. Range-fed meats.
5. Cold-pressed vegetable oils.
6. Whole grains.
7. Fiber.
8. Nuts, but not peanuts or pistachios.
9. Organic foods.
10. Anything homemade and fresh, as opposed to packaged or processed.

Action Plan

Question 22. Are you willing to adopt a healthier diet?

In my work as a personal trainer, I have learned that most people are capable of making profound changes in their health when they are motivated to do so, especially when they begin to see results. However, in order to make not only profound but also permanent changes, we need to take our steps one at a time.

I can remember in my twenties reading a book about PMS that recommended giving up diet sodas, chocolate, and pastries—all the basic food groups for a single woman my age—and deciding to give up, even before I started. Don't do that! Be realistic with yourself.

1. Look over the list of the top 10 worst and top 10 best kinds of foods and make two more lists:

FOODS I AM WILLING TO GIVE UP NOW

FOODS I AM WILLING TO EAT MORE OF NOW

Begin where you are ready to start—even if you can give up just one thing, and start adding in one other healthy kind of food. Don't worry about being perfect—for most of us, perfection in any realm is never going to be a realistic option. Decide ahead of time the changes you are ready to make at this particular point in your life, and write these two lists in your mood, food, and weather diary, so you can remind yourself whenever necessary.

2. Make a commitment to yourself to stick to your self-prescribed lists for at least two weeks. After two weeks, make a note:

IMPROVEMENTS I HAVE SEEN:
IN MY MOODS

IN MY SKIN

IN MY ENERGY LEVEL

IN MY BODY

IN MY WILL POWER

OTHER

3. When you are ready, on your own, go back and re-examine your lists. As you notice improvements, you may want to add more items to each list, or what you have already done may be enough. On the other hand, you may find a more dramatic improvement in your moods when you are willing to make more changes.

Question 23. Do you need to adopt dietary and lifestyle changes to stabilize your blood sugar?

> "For many diseases of lifestyle the outlook is grim, but not so for hypoglycemia. All that is needed for the disease to go away is a change in lifestyle." — Carl C. Pfeiffer, Nutrition and Mental Illness.

You don't have to be clinically hypoglycemic to suffer the psychological effects of low blood sugar. Everyone knows children who become cranky, exhausted, and tearful when they're hungry. Why should we expect to be immune to these symptoms when we grow up to be adults?

Predisposing Factors To Hypoglycemia
Overconsumption of starchy or sugary food
Smoking
Alcohol, tea, and coffee
Too little or too much thyroid hormone
Vitamin and mineral deficiencies
Stress
Overgrowth of *Candida albicans*
Food sensitivities
Overproduction of insulin by the pancreas
Excessively slow or fast metabolism

Sources: Jonathan Brostoff and Linda Gamlin, *The Complete Guide To Food Allergy and Intolerance*; William Duffy, *Sugar Blues*; Martha Sanbower, "Recognition and Treatment of Physical Factors in Psychotherapy Clients," *The Journal of Orthomolecular Medicine*.

The average person consumes 20 percent of his or her calories in some form of refined sugar. Sometimes we think of the sugar in our diet as simply empty calories—perhaps a better way to think of it is as a drain on our nutritional resources. That's because the body requires vitamins and minerals to metabolize sugar, and sugar leaves little to nourish the mind or body in return.[1]

Eliminating sugar not only can be of great assistance in getting off the roller coaster of blood sugar swings, but also can force you to eat more nutritious foods to support your immune system.

A word here on smoking: because cigarettes are not a food, you may not be aware of how they affect your blood sugar levels. However, as you inhale, the addictive ingredient in cigarettes, nicotine, stimulates the adrenal glands to constantly order the release of glucose into the blood.[2] In addition, smoking destroys vitamin C, which is a depression-fighting vitamin and an important factor in sugar metabolism.[3] According to the Hypoglycemia Association, every cigarette destroys about 50 mg. of vitamin C, and the cadmium that coats the cigarette papers goes directly to the kidneys where it further deactivates zinc.[4] William H. Philpott, an expert in the way that common substances affect our moods, has observed that the most common psychological reaction to smoking is paranoia.[5]

In some cases, smoking may lead to an allergy to tobacco that can cause severe depression. Dr. Abram Hoffer, a leading researcher in orthomolecular medicine, cured one patient who had been hospitalized for depression merely by taking him off tobacco.[6]

Bottom line: If you want a more even disposition and higher energy levels, give up tobacco products and other stimulants.

The Hypoglycemia Association recommends beginning dietary treatment by gradually giving up caffeine, sugar, alcohol, nicotine, grains, flours, and any foods with molasses, fructose, or corn sweeteners.[7] Listen to your body to determine when you need to eat, and be sure to eat breakfast—don't put it off.

According to James Hill, a doctor who spoke to the Houston branch of the Hypoglycemia Society, "Within one hour after you get up in the morning, after your longest period of sleep, certain hormones are at their lowest ebb for any 24-hour period. If you do not eat an adequate breakfast within that first hour after you get up, you will not build those hormones for that day. Certain other hormones are at their highest. If you do not eat an adequate breakfast, they begin to fall off, and within three hours of arising, they will have fallen off to practically nothing and then you have a worthless, washed-out day."[8]

It is also important to eat protein at every meal and keep it in a healthy balance with the amount of carbohydrates you take into your body. Studies show that many people with depression try to compensate for their low moods by eating large amounts of carbohydrates as a means of unconscious self-medication. That's because carbohydrates stimulate the brain's production of serotonin, a depression-fighting neurochemical.[9] But that strategy is shortsighted and ultimately self-defeating because a high-carbohydrate diet may crank up the roller coaster again.

I believe the ideal diet to maintain blood sugar levels is about 1.7 to 2.3 parts of carbohydrate for every 1 part of protein.[10] Since protein and carbohydrate foods have the same number of calories (4 calories per gram), if you are trying to measure this out in your diet you can use either calories or grams for your guide. Taking into account the different densities of carbohydrates and proteins, try to make sure about 25 percent of your plate is filled with protein, with the rest complex carbohydrates such as fruits and vegetables. These complex carbohydrates are far superior to simple ones such as table sugar, honey, and molasses because they are metabolized much more slowly.

Dietitians refer to something called the "glycemic index," which is a measure of how quickly a food is metabolized. For example, white sugar is rated at 59 on the glycemic index, which is actually lower than honey at 87.[11] The more slowly a food is metabolized, the more desirable it is for hypoglycemics. Compare the glycemic index for sugar with that for soybeans, 15, or skim milk, 32. The amount of simple sugar in a food is just part of the reason it may rate high on a glycemic index. Also factors are the amounts of processing, cooking, and fiber. Fresh, unprocessed foods high in fiber are generally preferable to those highly refined.

When the ratio of carbohydrates to protein goes above this 2-to-1 ratio, as it does so frequently in the standard American diet, with an average of about 4 parts carbohydrates to 1 part protein,[12] you can stimulate a hypoglycemic response. That's why you may have roller-coaster moods even if you're eating high volumes of food at frequent intervals throughout the day.

Another reason: when the ratio of carbohydrates to protein is too high, your pancreas is not stimulated to produce the hormone glucagon, which mobilizes fats and protects against the shaky, nervous feeling you get with hypoglycemia. Added bonus: when you eat carbohydrates and protein in this proper 2-to-1 ratio, your body mobilizes your fat stores and it's much easier to lose weight and avoid overeating.

Although many experts recommend a vegetarian diet to combat *Candida*, others point out that it's often difficult to maintain the ideal 2-to-1 ratio to combat hypoglycemia on a meat-free diet.[13] If you are a vegetarian who has trouble with hypoglycemia, you may want to consider adding egg whites and dairy products in addition to meat-free protein sources like soy, providing you aren't sensitive to them.

If you are uncertain what your average ratio of carbohydrates to proteins is, you may want to consult a local laboratory for a dietary analysis, complete with a measure of the amounts of nutrients you are taking in.

Action Plan

Question 23. Do you need to adopt dietary and lifestyle changes to stabilize your blood sugar?

1. Go back and re-examine your Action Plan for Question 17, "Are you hypoglycemic?" If your moods tend to roller coaster in tandem with your blood sugar, look over the list of predisposing factors to hypoglycemia. Some of these factors, such as smoking or drinking alcoholic beverages, you will recognize right away. Some of the other factors you may need to ask your doctor about, such as whether your body is over-producing insulin or whether you have an excessively fast or slow metabolism. Make a list.

THINGS I DO TO MYSELF TO AGGRAVATE MY MOOD SWINGS:

2. Now look over this list and decide which factors you are ready to change. If you have life-long habits that are difficult to change on your own, such as smoking or drinking, you may want to consult your doctor or a local support group, such as Alcoholics Anonymous. Make a list.

HABITS I AM READY TO CHANGE:

3. Adopt a high-protein, low carbohydrate diet (see also Question 26).

4. Begin substituting fresh fruit for sugary desserts.

Question 24. Do you need to psyche yourself to change your eating habits?

> *"It is surprising how often diet and nutrition are factors in depression, and how effective enhanced or improved nutrition can be in helping someone suffering from depression to improve their mood."* — Gary Null, *Nutrition and the Mind.*

"O.K.," you may say, "maybe this is beginning to make sense. Maybe I already know she's right. But I have to be pretty depressed to make any changes, and then I just may be so depressed that I need to eat a lot of chocolate fudge pies because everything else in my life will be going to hell and I have to have something good to fall back on!"

So let me have a little chat with your unconscious mind. Take a deep breath and just listen—remember, you don't have to make any changes until you are ready.

You have too much pain and suffering in your life already and you don't want to add any more? That's good. In fact, you should develop that attitude further. That's the point of all these changes! Hey, I don't like to do anything that doesn't feel good, either. I'm not going to ask you to do anything that makes you feel like you're starving. Deprivation is not a fun feeling, and in the case of us hypoglycemics, it can be downright terrifying. Who wants to faint from lack of food? Realize that the kind of eating program we're aiming for is not a "die-it," but one of true health and abundance.

You may want to tell me you have no will power. Every other time you have tried to change your eating habits—say when you went on a diet to lose weight—you failed miserably and ended up fatter than before? As a personal trainer, I have seen this syndrome frequently. The whole experience left you frustrated with yourself, bitter about anybody who doesn't have a pot belly, and more determined than ever to give up this health-nut business and eat whatever you want, regardless of the consequences.

I'll say it again: It doesn't take will power to go on a yeast-free, sugar-free diet. All it takes is a sincere desire to be as healthy as you can possibly be. Don't concentrate on being deprived. Think of all the good things you are bringing into your life.

As you begin this new lifestyle, go to the library or your local bookstore and find yeast-free, sugar-free cookbooks and spend plenty of time imagining yourself feasting on a wide variety of new and delicious dishes. Some of my favorites: Ratatouille. Pot roast with parsnips, carrots, onions, green peppers, and potatoes. Butternut squash pudding. Millet salad with peas, carrots, and tahini. Tofu quiche. Fresh pesto made without cheese over rice pasta. Kiwi sorbet. Spinach salad with homemade dressing made of exotic flavored oils such as olive oil with basil, olive oil with oregano. Plantain bread. Grilled lamb chops. Sweet potatoes with brazil nuts. Fresh peaches. Yucca French fries not fried but baked in the oven. Mmmmm! Any kind of growth is easier if you reach for the new and let go of the old, and that means focusing on all the delicious foods that maybe you've never tasted before. Clean out your pantry, give away the old cans of cherry pie filling and fried onions to the local food bank, and have fun exploring.

When I first started this eating program, I'd buy one or two new vegetables every week and figure out how to cook them. Sometimes, of course, I decided that I didn't really like jicama, or that I prefer summer squash over chayote squash, but other times I'd discover some new exotic vegetable such as celery root that I enjoyed, or even something I wasn't wild about, like fennel, but took in anyway, just to add variety.

The first breads I made without yeast could have been better used as playdough, but I kept trying and my batter-ing average (to make a pun) improved. I traded in my bread machine for a tortilla maker, and I made a lot of flat breads that could be stored in the freezer. I bought a waffle iron at a yard sale and made a big hit with carob-buckwheat waffles, and when my husband and I have weekend guests sometimes I make pancakes, which can also be frozen and eaten at a later date.

Now I can honestly say I don't need will power to hold me back from anything. I like what I eat now so much better than what I ate before I wouldn't want to go back to my old habits.

For all the mechanics of it, changing your diet in this way is indeed a kind of spiritual growth because you reach for all the things that take care of your body and calm your soul.

O.K., so you're trying to concentrate on what will make you feel better—but you're human and you still slip up. What if you can't help yourself and you give in to that hot fudge brownie with a cherry on top? Then what? As the cliché goes, Rome wasn't built in a day. This is not a weight control program where a group leader will embarrass you publicly if you eat the wrong thing. Only you will be able to tell right from wrong—and right only means right for you, right for your body, and right for your individual, overall health. Be kind to yourself. It may take longer to give up certain foods than others—especially if you are also in the process of giving up alcohol. But as you progress, your desire to get better will increase and it will be easier for you to identify the foods that you need to avoid.

Will the diet really get easier? It will. The reason: your body will let you know. If you pay attention, you will develop internal mechanisms to tell you what feels right. That's where your food, mood, and weather diary will come in so handy (see Question 2). Figure out which foods make you feel calm and happy, and I promise you will develop a liking for them.

Another strategy: if temptations prove strong initially, develop a cross visualization strategy. For example, say you crave a hot fudge sundae. To get to your job, you have to pass an ice cream parlor every day and you can't avoid looking in the window where you can see other people slurping down bananas, creamy chocolate, whipped cream, and cherries. Have you got that picture in your mind? Now, visualize the most revolting thing you can imagine, something that really turns your stomach. I leave it up to you what that will be! I think of compost that I put out in my garden, a revolting, sticky black sludge. Now weld the two images together in your mind. Every time you think of ice cream sundaes, think of covering it with stewed, stinky compost. Could you eat the sundae now? No way! Your craving will definitely go away.

Once you make these kinds of connections, your desire to have a free and easy spirit will far outweigh your desire for your old favorite foods. Although I have my moments when I walk past the bakery aisle in the local grocery store, I no longer think I could really relax with a chocolate chip cookie because of the associations I now have with my sensitivity to wheat, eggs, and sugar. Over time, I can only hope that these sensitivities will diminish. I know the cookies will be there waiting for me when and if that happens, but, in the meanwhile, there are plenty other delicacies to keep me satisfied.

You say you don't like vegetables? You never have and never will? Or you don't like fish. Or you're a vegetarian, and you're afraid that if you give up any more foods there won't be anything left for you to eat. Remember, you don't have to eat anything you don't want to eat. It's still a free country. And there really is plenty of delicious food left out there in the universe to keep your taste buds interested.

As you stay on this eating program, your tastes really will change. I used to hate sweet potatoes and now I eat them all the time. In fact, sweet potatoes and carrots and even butternut squash taste very sweet to me now that I don't eat refined sugar. Even if you don't like most vegetables, start with a few that you do—nearly everybody can stomach a fresh carrot or two—and try the others in small quantities. I have always hated fish, a great source of protein and essential fatty acids, but I have plenty to eat without it. Vegetarians can still get their protein by combining yeast-free foods.

You don't like to cook? Great! In fact, even better. Raw foods contain all their original nutrients without any being destroyed in cooking. Learn to make all kinds of salads, or send off for organic food catalogues for pre-baked yeast-free breads of all kinds. You can make sandwiches out of cold meats or various organic nut butters. Carry fresh fruits and nuts for snacks. You can make this diet as easy as you like if you plan to have the right ingredients on hand.

Or maybe you do cook, but you don't have time to cook separate meals for yourself and everyone else in your family. And if you did serve acorn squash, tofu, and Brussels sprouts, your spouse might use that as grounds for divorce, your teenagers would make a mad dash for the nearest fast food restaurant, and what's left of family meal time would be thrown into a chaotic argument about menus. Given time, those attitudes just might change. In my house, if I try to serve my husband the old standard American diet (some doctors call it SAD for short), he would now accuse me of trying to make him fat or give him heart disease. He would think I'm trying to deprive him.

But when I'm cooking for others, what I do is cook a healthy meal and then have plenty of extras for everybody else—fresh bread, the usual desserts. That way the others can get their infusion of vitamins and minerals without having to make too many compromises.

You say you travel and won't be able to find restaurants that serve yeast-free foods? When you eat out, ask the waiter to bring you steamed vegetables and plain, broiled chicken with a side order of baked potato or rice. On long trips, take an electric wok with you. Take advantage of the best restaurants to order seasonal fruits and exotic vegetables cooked to your specifications.

Last, you may wonder how long you have to eat this way. Once you get into it, you'll find that a yeast-free, sugar-free diet ends up being more enjoyable, and the results so worthwhile, that you will want to stick with it for the rest of your life.

The good news is you may be able to add certain foods back to your diet over time as your body gives permission. Some food sensitivities are cyclical, so just because you can't eat corn now, for example, doesn't mean you'll never be able to have it again. Once you've gone on an elimination diet and cut out the real culprits, you should wait and add them back one at a time and see how your body and mind react.

Action Plan

Question 24. Do you need to psyche yourself to change your eating habits?

1. Make two lists:

REASONS I AM READY TO CHANGE MY EATING HABITS

REASONS I WANT TO PROCRASTINATE

Compare the length of your lists. Now argue with yourself. For every reason you have for wanting to procrastinate, think of a logical reason why you may be in error.

2. Go to the library or local bookstore and find cookbooks with healthy recipes. If you think you live in some backwater area and will be unable to marshall the resources necessary, think again. There are numerous companies that specialize in selling healthy cookbooks by mail, including:

Allergy Resources, P.O. Box 444, Guffey, CO 80820 (800-USE-FLAX)
Allergy Resources also sells air and water purifiers, supplements, and organic cleaning products.

Ener-G Foods Inc., P.O. Box 84487, Seattle, WA 98124-5787 (800-331-5222)
Ener-G Foods sells allergy-free foods, and has a computer data base of allergy-free recipes.

Gold Mine Natural Food Co., 3419 Hancock St., San Diego, CA 92110-4307 (800-475-FOOD)
Gold Mine sells a full line of organic foods and products.

Mountain Ark Trader, 799 Old Leicester Highway, Asheville, NC 28806 (800-643-8909)
Mountain Ark also sells organic foods, household cleaners, supplements, and other products.

Natural Lifestyles Supplies, 16 Lookout Drive, Asheville, NC 28804-3330 (800-752-2775)
Natural Life sells a full line of organic foods and products, cookware, and supplements.

N.E.E.D.S. (National Ecological Environmental Delivery System) 527 Charles Ave., 12-A, Syracuse, NY 13209 (800-634-1380)
N.E.E.D.S. represents numerous companies that sell a wide variety of environmentally-safe products.

The Vitamin Shoppe, 4700 Westside Ave., North Bergen, NJ 07047 (800-223-1216)
The Vitamin Shoppe also sells nutritional supplements and organic personal care products.

Starburst Wellness Resources, 8466 Old Poland Rd., Barnveld, NY 13304 (800-852-3821)
Starburst sells a variety of books on various disabilities.

Allergy Alternative, 440 Godfrey Dr., Windsor CA 95492 (800-838-1514)
Allergy Alternative also sells air and water purifiers and other allergy-free products.

Question 25. Are you willing to give up the 10 kinds of foods most likely to aggravate depression?

"At a time when self-indulgence has become commonplace, the development of discipline in one's life is an important steppingstone toward any type of personal or spiritual transformation. Modification of dietary habits, forcing oneself to exercise, and the daily practice of meditation are all crucial facets of self-discipline that one must acquire in order to truly achieve health and wellness of the total mind/body/spirit."
— Richard Gerber, *Vibrational Medicine: New Choices for Healing Ourselves.*

THE 10 WORST KINDS OF FOODS TO PUT IN YOUR BODY:

1. Anything fermented. In his excellent books on the yeast *Candida albicans*, Dr. William Crook has given clear explanations of the unfortunate role yeast has played in the American diet. Fermented foods simply put back into the body the very yeasts that a yeast-free diet is trying to eliminate. What kinds of foods are fermented:

Alcoholic beverages, including wine, beer, and distilled spirits.
Cheese.
Buttermilk, yogurt.
Mushrooms.
Vinegars, and all sauces made with vinegar, including ketchup,
    salad dressings, mayonnaise, soy sauce, and BBQ sauce.
Pickles.

2. Anything processed. The trouble with processed foods is the same trouble as you encounter when eating out. You don't know what you're getting. Even when you read labels, it's not possible to know what's in any given food. My favorite listing on a label: "Natural ingredients." What is processed:

Snack foods.
Cold cuts.
Processed meats such as hot dogs and sausages.

Bottled salad dressings.
Rice mixes.
Commercial pasta.
Packaged cereals.
Canned soups and soup mixes.
Baking mixes.

It's not just that commercial processing typically removes vitamins and minerals from a food, or the fact that many processed foods are also high in saturated fats. It's that processed foods so often contain the kinds of additives and chemicals important to avoid, such as MSG, artificial colorings, chelating agents, emulsifiers, etc. Many of these additives are derived from substances to which you may be sensitive, such as dairy products, gluten, eggs, or corn.

Generally, if I can't tell what's in it, I won't buy it.

3. Anything dried or aged. What is dried:
Raisins, prunes, and other dried fruit.
Sundried tomatoes.

Dried foods often contain molds and/or, in the case of raisins and other dried fruit, may be more concentrated in fructose.

4. Anything made with sugar or honey. Probably the biggest dietary step anyone can make toward improved mental health is the elimination of sugar. I include honey here, but also you should watch out for other forms of sugar, including fructose from fruit, dextrose from corn sugar, maltose from malt sugar, lactose from milk sugar, as well as sucrose made from sugar cane or sugar beets.

For one thing, sugar uses up B vitamins without adding any back. And what do people with depression need to stay calm and relaxed? B vitamins. That's why sugary foods are not just empty calories. Eating sugar is like inviting a thief into your home: it robs you of your most valuable nutritional possessions.

The trouble with kicking the sugar habit, as William Duffy pointed out so well in his best seller, *Sugar Blues,* is that you might as well be addicted to heroin. Sugar is a very hard habit to kick.

How to cope? Develop a taste for fruit that is not too sweet, such as kiwis, or Granny Smith apples. Or try vegetables such as carrots or sweet potatoes when the craving strikes. Another effective strategy: cut down on your consumption of salt, since salt creates a craving for sugar.

Sugar substitutes are rife with their own problems. Some—aspartame, for example, also sold as Equal or NutraSweet—are derived from corn syrup and thus should be avoided by those sensitive to corn. Several scientists are concerned that aspartame might cause altered brain function and behavior changes and many have reported other effects, such as dizziness, headaches, and seizures.[1] If you can't kick your craving, try stevia tea, a herbal sweetener that won't affect your blood sugar. Stevia is outrageously expensive (around $16 for about two ounces), but it's so concentrated you may find yourself using small amounts. When I bought my first vial of stevia, I used less than one ounce in twelve months.

5. Anything made with yeast. If you imagine your stomach as a battleground for a fight, you will be able to understand why eating more yeast would not be a good idea. The yeast team is not on your side. The yeasts in your body are supposed to live in a delicate balance with their antagonists, healthy bacteria. When there's an overgrowth of yeast, the beastly yeasts fight off the intestinal flora that aid the process of digestion. The victorious yeasts then do many unkind things to your intestines. And when that happens, your immune system can't figure out what undigested food is doing in your blood, attacks it, and lo and behold, you have developed antibodies to your favorite snack, say popcorn. So the next time you eat popcorn, a little escapes through your intestinal wall, your immune system attacks it, and you feel terrible. Would a friend of yours do that to you? Of course not. What has yeast:

Bread.
Bagels.
Brewer's yeast.
Many vitamins.

6. Any meat raised with antibiotics or steroids. "Free range" meats are not only generally cleaner, with fewer bacteria, but also more easily digested. When you eat the meat of animals that have been given antibiotics, you diminish the likelihood that antibiotics will work effectively for you if you need them. And that goes back to the idea that you need to keep your immune system as strong as possible to ward off stress and any kind of foreign invaders if you want to stay emotionally balanced. Researchers have been advising doctors not to overuse antibiotics, which can kill off the healthy bacteria in your system and cause an overgrowth of *Candida*. Steroids have likewise been linked to rage and depression. One good way to cut down on the use of antibiotics and steroids is to take them out of the foods in your diet, a place you may not have realized you were getting them.

7. Leftovers, unless frozen. As a general rule, don't eat leftovers unless they have been stored in your refrigerator within the last twenty-four hours or frozen. Don't leave food out at room temperature. However, I would strongly advise against going home to your spouse and making a rash declaration like, "I won't have turkey hash—Carrigan says leftovers will make me crazy." Be sensible. Remember that you're going for two things here: first, to build your immune system with healthy food and, second, to avoid anything moldy or fermented.

Refrigerator temperatures should be 40 to 45 degrees Fahrenheit, and the freezer should be zero. Disease-causing bacteria grow in temperatures between 40 and 140 degrees. Cooked foods that have been in this temperature range for more than two hours should not be eaten. Reheated foods should be brought to a temperature of at least 165 degrees.[2]

8. Alcoholic beverages. Many people with an overgrowth of yeast in their bodies are already unable to tolerate alcoholic beverages because the yeast itself produces too much alcohol. It's like having a chemical factory in your very own stomach. The yeast manufactures toxins the equivalent of formaldehyde, and anyone who has taken high school biology and seen dead animals floating in jars of formaldehyde can imagine what that does to your insides. Lovely, lovely! So adding even more alcohol in the form of an after-work drink will make such a person feel worse, not more relaxed (see Question 6).

In addition, alcohol can induce hypoglycemia, so it's something especially to avoid if your moods tend to swing between meals. It's easy to see how alcohol's effect on blood sugar encourages the addiction cycle. Alcohol lowers the output of glucose by the liver. At first, you may get a lift from drinking, but then your blood sugar will fall and you feel you need another.[3]

Many people who are trying to kick the alcohol habit will find it easier not to eat the grains (such as wheat) or fruit (such as grapes) from which the liquor, beer, or wine they crave is derived. The body may not recognize the difference between ingredient and final product. A hypersensitive person can easily develop a sensitivity/addiction to both.

Aside from its effect on blood sugar, alcohol depresses the central nervous system, and thus should be strictly avoided. On the few occasions when I used to drink, I always seemed to skip the happy phase and become immediately depressed.

In addition, alcohol competes with several other solvents for detoxification enzymes, and can slow down the purification process of the body.[4] It also interferes with the normal metabolism of nutrients in the body necessary to maintain a positive emotional balance, including calcium, magnesium, and thiamine. A single dose of alcohol, for example, may deplete calcium levels in the brain.[5] Alcohol also depletes other nutrients necessary to prevent depression, including zinc, manganese, potassium, and folic acid. It also interferes with protein metabolism if taken at mealtime.[6]

9. Caffeine in coffee, tea, chocolate, and colas. Various studies have found that measures of depression tend to increase when caffeine and/or coffee consumption goes up.[7] There is also an undeniable association between coffee consumption and higher levels of anxiety, a psychological factor that can increase physiological stress, leading to higher cortisol levels and depression. In larger quantities (eight to twelve cups of coffee per day), caffeine produces a clinical syndrome indistinguishable from anxiety neurosis. High doses of caffeine have also been found to exacerbate psychiatric symptoms in people with depressive and schizophrenic tendencies.[8] In case these facts don't impress you, realize that psychiatrists have thought enough of these effects to include a diagnosis of caffeine intoxication in their standard diagnostic manual.[9]

Caffeine, which is found in coffee, tea, chocolate, and cola drinks, has an effect on body chemistry similar to sugar in that it stimulates the adrenal glands to increase blood sugar levels, which in turn stimulates the pancreas to secrete insulin, leading to a drop in blood sugar levels. Anxiety and other emotional symptoms have been recorded in people consuming as little as two to three cups of coffee per day.[10]

Like alcohol, caffeine interferes with protein metabolism and depletes important depression-fighting nutrients, including magnesium, zinc, and chromium.[11] It is also a common food allergen.[12]

The highest concentration of caffeine is found in chocolate—about 160 mg. per 8 ounces—followed by aspirin, which has about 15 to 30 mg. in each tablet. Coffee contains about 100 to 150 mg. per cup, followed by tea, with about 60 to 75 mg. per cup, and cola drinks, which contain about 40 to 60 mg. per cup.[13]

10. Food colorings, chemicals, preservatives, and other additives. For more detailed information on this subject, see Question 28. Perhaps the worst additives to avoid are monosodium glutamate (MSG) and aspartame, an artificial sweetener. Again, the guiding principles are (1) eat to strengthen your immune system, (2) avoid unnecessary chemicals, and (3) avoid additives that may be derived from foods to which you may be sensitive.

Action Plan

Question 25. Are you willing to give up the 10 kinds of foods most likely to aggravate depression?

For every food you want to give up, find an alternative and stock your pantry accordingly. That way you will be prepared. Also, by recognizing that you still have plenty of choices, you won't feel deprived.

Instead of:	Try:
Alcoholic beverages	Fruit or vegetable juices, sparkling water
Chocolate	Carob powder
Coffee, caffeinated tea	Herbal teas, Dacopa, Caffix
Cola drinks	Bottled water
Conventional meat	Organic meat
Dried fruit and vegetables	Fresh fruit
Junk food	Cut-up vegetables, nuts, fruit
Leftovers	Fresh or frozen foods
Packaged cereals	Whole grains
Processed foods with additives	Organic or homemade foods
Salad dressings with vinegar	Herb-flavored oils
Sugar, honey, or sugar substitutes	Stevia tea
Sugary desserts	Fresh fruit
Yeast	Baking soda and vitamin C crystals
Yeast breads	Homemade quick breads, yeast-free breads

Question 26. Are you willing to eat more of the 10 kinds of foods most likely to improve depression?

"Once you have experienced a more healthful diet, you are forever changed." — Sherry A. Rogers, *You Are What You Ate: An Rx for the Resistant Diseases of the 21st Century.*

The best 10 kinds of foods to put in your body:

1. Fresh vegetables. Very few Americans come close to consuming the three to five servings or more a day of vegetables recommended by the U.S. Department of Agriculture. A serving is ½ cup of cooked vegetables, ¾ cup of juice, 1 cup of leafy greens, or ½ cup of dried peas or beans. These are some of the reasons why people who tend to be depressed need to eat at least this much or more:

❖ **To build the immune system.** Fresh vegetables are an excellent source of vitamins and minerals necessary to ward off all sorts of mind-body diseases.

❖ **To ward off flus and colds.** Fresh vegetables contain loads of vitamins and minerals to fight off minor illnesses that can sap your spirit.

❖ **To prevent fatigue.** In order for your body to use the food you take into your body, you must have adequate amounts of vitamins and minerals, many of which can be found in vegetables.

❖ **To provide the body with nutrients to support mental health.** These include especially vitamin C, which is found in fruits and vegetables, as well as other vitamins and minerals.

❖ **To improve digestive function.** As you consume more vegetables, you will move your bowels more regularly, a recommended two to three times daily, and feel less sluggish. As the bowels move more regularly, you will be able to remove toxins from your body and will be less susceptible to fungi and yeasts, and thereby increase your resistance to all diseases. Improved diet, including more vegetables, has also been shown to reduce the permeability of the intestines, and thus you will be less likely to develop food sensitivities, a cause of mood swings.

❖ **To maintain proper acid-alkaline balance.** Japanese nutritionists have long noted that the foods we take into our body increase either the acidity or the alkalinity of our fluids. The major components of the standard American diet—sugar, beer, beef, eggs, cheese, and grains—tend to raise the acidity of body chemistry. The major effect of acidosis is depression of the central nervous system.[1] Vegetables and fruit, on the other hand, tend to raise the alkalinity of the body. For that reason, Japanese nutritionists recommend a diet high in vegetables as the basis for a more clear-headed and spiritual approach to life.

2. Fresh, unsweet fruits in moderation. Some *Candida* experts recommend giving up fruit, especially in the early stages of a yeast-free diet, because fructose, a naturally occurring sugar, will feed the yeasts in your intestines. Those who are knowledgeable about food combining advise against eating fruits at any meals when vegetables are also eaten, so as not to slow down the digestive process and thus promote the growth of *Candida* in yet another way. In addition, many fruits, such as grapes, have yeasts growing on their skins.[2]

If you don't want to eat fruit but would like to have a sweet taste, try sweet potatoes, carrots, or desserts made from butternut squash. If you do want to continue eating fruit, at first try those that aren't too sweet, such as fresh berries, Granny Smith apples, kiwis, melons. Citrus is a common food allergy, and if you are sensitive to oranges you may also be sensitive to grapefruits, limes, and lemons.[3] Try eliminating these from your diet at first and then adding them back one at a time to see how you react.

In addition, check out your grocery or local farmers' market for unusual fruits to which you may not have a sensitivity, such as cherimoya, cactus pears, mangos, kumquats, plantains, papaya, and coconut.

A hint here on using fruits as natural sweeteners: use a juicer to create fresh fruit juice and freeze the juice in ice cube trays. That way you can thaw out one or two cubes for sweetener when you make yeast-free breads.

3. Protein. Protein is a basic nutrient required by the human body and is made up of various amino acids. It is found in animal products and in fruits and vegetables. Vegetarians can get adequate amounts of proteins in their diets by combining certain plant foods, such as beans and peas with grains and nuts. Although the Recommended Dietary Allowance set by the U.S. government is somewhat lower, you should consume about 1 gram of protein daily for every 1 kilogram of your body weight. That means, for a person who weighs 150 pounds, or about 68 kilograms, you should be getting about 68 grams of protein per day. You will need less if you weigh less, and more if you weigh more. Many of us get far more protein than we actually need, so in recommending protein I am not necessarily recommending more, but a balance. The best way to determine if you are getting enough protein in your diet is to look at what you're eating in terms of grams or calories. Protein and carbohydrates are equal in grams and calories, about 4 calories for each gram, so you can either measure by gram weight or by calories.

Protein is important in an antidepression diet as a means of stabilizing the blood sugar. Eating only carbohydrates at a meal tends to promote hypoglycemia, which, in turn, promotes the release of stress chemicals from the adrenal glands, which then leads to depression. Some form of protein should be consumed at every meal.

I believe the ideal ratio is 2 parts carbohydrates to 1 part protein. Most Americans also consume too many carbohydrates—about 1 part protein to 4 parts carbohydrates. Measurable changes in brain chemistry can occur at every meal.[4] That's why it's far better to stabilize blood sugar by aiming for a balance between protein and carbohydrates in every meal.

Some anti-*Candida* programs recommend low carbohydrate diets or all-vegetarian diets. I believe the best approach, to combat both *Candida* and hypoglycemia, is a more balanced diet. Although you can get adequate levels of amino acids in a vegetarian diet, keeping some meat in your meals will insure you get enough amino protein on a regular basis, as well as B12, an important depression-fighting vitamin, although you can also get B12 in dairy products and eggs.[5]

4. Range-fed meats. If you decide to continue to eat meat—and I recommend that you do—the best kind to get is organic or so-called range fed. Organic meat will have been raised without antibiotics, steroids, or other pollutants. This is important for fighting depression in several respects. First, antibiotics and steroids promote the growth of *Candida.* Second, your goal is to strengthen your immune system. If you continually take into your body meats from animals raised with antibiotics, you will reduce you own chances of being able to use antibiotics effectively if you get sick. Third, lead, cadmium, arsenic, and other heavy metals associated with mood problems and decreased memory are put into many animal feeds.[6]

Do not eat processed meats, such as hot dogs, bacon, or cold cuts, as these not only may have been produced from non-organic meat sources, but also may contain additives such as MSG.

Range-fed meats are also usually leaner, which is another plus. The typical American diet contains too much fat—far more than the 30 percent recommended by the U.S. Department of Agriculture—and high-fat diets have been linked to increased risk of suicide. Toxic chemicals are often stored in fatty tissues.

5. Cold-pressed vegetable oils. Cold pressed vegetable oils provide the essential fatty acids for the development of the brain, nervous system, and cell membranes.[7] Although we most often think of fat as residing in undesirable places in our bodies, fat is essential to the proper function of the central nervous system. Highly unsaturated fatty acids attract oxygen and help generate electrical currents.[8] Again, as in the case of protein, it's not that we need more fat, but we need better fats and in the proper proportions.

Despite all the information circulating about the role of fats and diet, few Americans are aware of the role that fats play in chronic pain and stress. Simply put, a kind of fat commonly found in animal foods, including meat, eggs, and dairy products, arachidonic acid, is the parent compound from which substances that cause chronic inflammation in the body are made.[9] Chronic inflammations, in turn, place greater physiological stress on the body, leading to higher cortisol levels (see Question 19), which can predispose a person to depression.

A study of Eskimos who ate diets high in fish and marine animals showed they were less susceptible to SAD, or seasonal affective disorder, even when the sun never shone. Researchers have theorized that the natives' diets contained high amounts of EPA, or eicosapentaenoic acid, and DHA, or docosahexaenoic acid, both of which help to store the chemical energy of sunlight in the human body.[10] Saturated fats and monounsaturated fatty acids may interfere with this important function.

6. Whole grains. Whole grains are excellent sources of B vitamins, which are necessary to maintain emotional calm, as well as protein, which is necessary to consume in balance with carbohydrates. One-third cup of whole grain wheat contains between 12 and 15 percent of an adult's daily requirement for protein, including adequate amounts of four essential amino acids. Many people who are sensitive to wheat or gluten (a protein found also in oatmeal, rye, and barley that has been implicated in many kinds of mental illness) should consider high-protein wheat alternatives such as quinoa or amaranth.

7. Fiber. Fiber is the part of food that is not digested by the human body. It can be found in fruits, vegetables, whole grains, beans, and peas, and consists of cellulose, hemicellulose, lignin, pectin, and gums. Its role in nutrition is to clean out the intestinal tract. The health of our gastrointestinal tract relates to our mental health in several important ways.

First, *Candida albicans* thrives in an underactive colon, and various GI diseases, including colitis, Crohn's disease, and leaky gut syndrome, are often symptoms of a yeast overgrowth. Leaky gut syndrome is of key importance to mental health because it often leads to the development of food sensitivities. As the intestinal walls become permeable, undigested food particles can escape into the blood. In turn, the immune system recognizes these substances—say, the molecules of a piece of bread—and develops antibodies to that particular food so that the next time you eat bread or anything else containing wheat, yeast, sugar, eggs, or other ingredients, you feel lousy.

Second, toxins that build up in the intestines can affect all parts of the body. As digestion is delayed in the intestines, *Candida* grows more easily and the 100-odd toxins it alone produces wreak a wide range of nasty effects on our central nervous system. One study of children with brain injuries found that they had an impaired gut/liver detoxification system. Simply put, they were exposed to more toxins originating in their gastrointestinal system, which in turn overloaded their livers and resulted in adverse impact on brain chemistry.[11]

Maintaining a healthy gut is also important because this is where our body manufactures many important vitamins, including B vitamins, vitamin K, and biotin. The presence of fiber clearly favors the growth of aerobic bacteria, such as acidophilus, as opposed to anaerobic types that produce toxic waste products.[12] Certain kinds of fiber, especially fiber from okra, psyllium, and flax, provide food for these beneficial bacteria.[13]

Many anti-*Candida* programs recommend colon-cleansing routines such as enemas, but a gentler way is to include more fiber in the diet on a regular basis. Nutritionists generally recommend that we include between 20 and 35 grams of fiber a day in our diet.[14] One gram of fiber can be found in 1 cup of popcorn, half a cup of asparagus or cauliflower, or about one quarter of a cantaloupe. You may also want to include at each meal 1 teaspoon of flax or psyllium seeds, which scrub accumulated deposits from the intestines.[15]

In addition to promoting a healthy gut, fiber also slows down the absorption of food and thus works in favor of anyone combating hypoglycemia.

8. Nuts, but not peanuts or pistachios. Brazil nuts are excellent sources of selenium, a depression-fighting mineral,[16] and, although high in fat, many nuts—including pignola nuts, pumpkin and squash seeds, sunflower seeds, cashews, sesame seeds, and walnuts—are also high in protein. Avoid peanuts and pistachios, which are often processed with other ingredients and/or covered with mold. Because they are concentrated and don't need to be cooked, nuts make excellent snacks for those on an anti-hypoglycemia, yeast-free diet.

9. Organic foods. One of the ironies about including more fruits and vegetables in your diet is that these nutrition-packed foods are often higher in pesticides, fertilizers, herbicides, fungicides, chemical additives, and other neurotoxins. In a perfect world, we would all have access to unlimited amounts of affordable organic food. Although there is some mislabeling, organic foods are those usually grown without pesticides and other additives.

Most of us can imagine cancer patients and others with sensitive immune systems wanting to eat only organic food, but why should those with depression bother? Because pesticides, herbicides, and fungicides are known to affect the nervous system and therefore, by definition, our brains.[17] Pesticides and herbicides have both been found to reduce the nutritive value of foods,[18] in ways that include reducing the carbohydrate, free amino acid, vitamin, and mineral compositions. Canning, drying, freezing, smoking, pasteurizing, and other methods of processing foods also often rob them of many of their vitamins and minerals. Organic foods are not only safer, but also often more nutritious.

Eating organic foods also lightens the load on the liver, which filters the blood to remove contaminants from the body. Although modern medicine has overlooked the role of nutrition in mental health, Ayurvedic medicine, long practiced in India, links an overburdened liver with depression because circulating wastes are able to enter the nervous system and may directly interfere with the functioning of the brain.[19]

In some cases of food sensitivity, such as, for example, a sensitivity to apples, you may not be sensitive to the food itself but to the chemicals and pesticides with which the food has been treated.

10. Anything homemade and fresh, as opposed to packaged or processed. Homemade and fresh is always going to be better than anything packaged or frozen for two primary reasons: You know the ingredients, and you can control the freshness of the food.

At first, when you begin this eating program, you may find yourself unleashing your creativity in the kitchen, doing your best to make something you might consider edible from the long list of healthy foods allowed. As you progress, however, you may find yourself eating at home but cooking less. Raw or simply cooked vegetables will appeal to you, and, when you do cook, you can use your freezer to good advantage to store homemade soup, yeast-free breads, cheese-free pesto, curried dishes, sugar-free desserts, etc.

Action Plan

Question 26. Are you willing to eat more of the 10 kinds of foods most likely to improve depression?

1. Plan an adventure. Make a trip to the local health food store or farmers' market, and purchase three new foods that will help you feel healthier.

2. Invest in cookbooks. You may want to try:
   Allergy Cooking with Ease by Nicolette Dumke
   The Food/Depression Connection by June Roth
   If This Is Tuesday, It Must be Chicken by Natalie Golos and
       Frances Golos Golbitz
   Who Killed Candida? by Vicki Glassburn
   The McDougall Plan by John A. McDougall and Mary A.
       McDougall
   The Yeast Connection Cookbook by Marjorie Hurt Jones and
       William Crook

3. Make a recipe book of your own. Collect recipes that will build your health.

4. Ask your health food store or local grocery where you can find classes in healthy cooking.

5. Instead of counting fat grams, find out if you are getting enough fiber by counting fiber grams for a day or two.

6. At every meal, make sure you are getting the proper balance of protein. If you look at your plate as a pie chart, about 25 percent of the plate should have a protein dish.

7. Experiment with wheat alternatives such as quinoa, amaranth, spelt, and millet.

8. Purchase an electric slow cooker and make homemade soups.

9. Invest in a juicer and make your own vegetable juices.

10. For an alternative to yeast breads, make tortillas or waffles and freeze them.

11. Reward yourself with exotic fruits such as Asian pears, kumquats, or mango.

12. Try a taste test. Invite your whole family to experiment with small portions of organic versus conventional products. Compare labels. See if you can taste the difference.

13. Rethink your concept of conventional meals. Instead of cereal and toast for breakfast, grill a lamb chop and prepare a salad. Instead of a sandwich for lunch, take a cold chicken breast, nuts, and fresh fruit. If you are pressed for time, try a protein shake made without sugar or sugar substitutes.

14. Instead of frying, try using small portions of cold-pressed vegetable oils in a wok.

15. If you don't like to cook, try raw foods and cold meats.

Question 27. Should you learn to appreciate vegetables?

"Only a third of Americans meet the U.S. government's Healthy People 2000 goal of consuming five or more servings of fruits and vegetables a day.... Broken down, people's average intake was only 1.2 servings of fruits and 3.1 servings of vegetables a day.... A staple of the American diet—French fries—made up 11 percent of people's vegetable intake."
— "Americans Doing Better at Eating Their Veggies," Medical Tribune News Service.

If we decide to take a nutritional approach to treating depression, it's time to grow up and learn to like what's good for us. According to the U.S. Agriculture Department, we eat more snacks such as crackers, popcorn, and chips than we do dark green vegetables—the stuff that has all the depression-fighting vitamins and minerals.

Most vegetables are sugar-free, yeast-free, and full of fiber. According to even the most conservative government recommendations, we should be eating three to five servings a day, along with two to three servings of fruit. Aside from protein (and besides, many vegetables contain small or adequate amounts of protein), vegetables may be the most important kind of food to include in a depression-fighting diet. Here are the top vegetables to eat and a breakdown of the key nutrients contained in 3.5 ounces:

Alfalfa Sprouts, 3 cups
Vitamin C 8 mg.
Folacin 36 mcg.
Magnesium 27 mg.

Artichoke, about ⅔ of one lg.
Vitamin C 12 mg.
Folacin 68 mcg.
Magnesium 60 mg.

Asparagus, 8 spears
Vitamin B6 0.2 mg.
Vitamin C 33 mg.
Folacin 119 mcg.

Beets, ¾ c. sliced
Vitamin C 11 mg.
Folacin 93 mcg.

Butternut Squash, 1 c. cubed
Vitamin B6 0.2 mg.
Vitamin C 21 mg.
Folacin 27 mcg.
Magnesium 34 mg.

Broccoli, 1 c. chopped
Vitamin B6 0.2 mg.
Vitamin C 93 mg.
Folacin 71 mcg.

Brussels Sprouts, 1 c.
Vitamin B6 0.2 mg.
Vitamin C 85 mg.
Folacin 61 mcg.

Cabbage, 1½ c. shredded
Vitamin C 47 mg.
Folacin 57 mcg.

Carrots, 1⅓ carrots
Vitamin C 9 mg.

Cauliflower, 1 c. florets
Vitamin B6 0.2 mg.
Vitamin C 72 mg.
Folacin 66 mcg.

Celery, 2½ stalks
Vitamin C 7 mg.
Folacin 28 mcg.

Corn, ⅓ c. kernels
Vitamin C 7 mg.
Folacin 46 mcg.
Thiamine 0.2 mg.

Eggplant, 1¼ c. sliced
Folacin 18 mcg.

Fennel, 1 c. chopped
Vitamin C 93 mg.
Calcium 109 mg.
Magnesium 49 mg.

Kale, 1½ c. chopped
Vitamin B6 0.3 mg.
Vitamin C 120 mg.
Calcium 135 mg.
Folacin 29 mcg.
Magnesium 0.8 mg

Leeks, 1 c. chopped
Vitamin B6 0.2 mg.
Vitamin C 12 mg.
Folacin 64 mcg.
Magnesium 28 mg.

Lima Beans, ¾ c.
Vitamin B6 0.2 mg.
Vitamin C 23 mg.
Folacin 34 mcg.
Magnesium 58 mg.
Thiamine 0.2 mg.

Mung Bean Sprouts, 1 c.
Vitamin C 13 mg.
Folacin 61 mcg.

Mushrooms, 5 mushrooms
Folacin 21 mcg.
Niacin 4 mg.
Riboflavin 0.4 mg.

Okra, 1 c. sliced
Vitamin B6 0.2 mg.
Vitamin C 21 mg.
Calcium 81 mg.
Folacin 88 mcg.
Magnesium 57 mg.
Thiamine 0.2 mg

Onions, ½ c. chopped
Vitamin C 6 mg.
Folacin 19 mcg.

Parsnips, ¾ c. sliced
Vitamin C 17 mg.
Folacin 67 mcg.
Magnesium 29 mg.

Peas, ⅔ c.
Vitamin B6 0.2 mg.
Vitamin C 40 mg.
Folacin 65 mcg.
Magnesium 33 mg.
Niacin 2 mg.
Thiamine 0.3 mg.

Peppers, Hot Red, 2 peppers
Vitamin B6 0.3 mg
Vitamin C 243 mg.
Folacin 23 mcg.

Potato, ½ potato
Vitamin B6 0.3 mg.
Vitamin C 13 mg.
Magnesium 27 mg.
Niacin 2 mg.

Radishes, 1 c. sliced
Vitamin C 23 mg.
Folacin 27 mcg.

Romaine Lettuce, 2 c. shredded
Vitamin C 24 mg.
Folacin 136 mcg.

Rutabaga, ¾ c. cubed
Vitamin C 25 mg.
Folacin 21 mcg.

Scallions, 1 c. chopped
Vitamin C 19 mg.
Folacin 64 mcg.

Snap Beans, 1 c.
Vitamin C 16 mg.
Folacin 37 mcg.

Spinach, 2 c. chopped
Vitamin B6 0.2 mg.
Vitamin C 28 mg.
Calcium 99 mg.
Magnesium 79 mg.
Riboflavin 0.2 mg.

Sweet Potato, ¾ sweet potato
Vitamin B6 0.3 mg.
Vitamin C 23 mg.

Tomato, ¾ tomato
Vitamin C 19 mg.

Turnip, ¾ c. cubed
Vitamin C 21 mg.

Water Chestnut, ¾ c. sliced
Vitamin B6 0.3 mg.
Riboflavin 0.2 mg.

Zucchini, ¾ c. sliced
Vitamin C 9 mg.
Folacin 22 mcg.

Source: Thomas Dickey, ed., *The Wellness Encyclopedia of Food and Nutrition.*

Action Plan

Question 27. Should you learn to appreciate vegetables?

1. Make three lists:
VEGETABLES I CAN'T STAND

VEGETABLES I LOVE

VEGETABLES I HAVE NEVER TRIED

Note the length of the lists. If you can't stand more vegetables than you like, begin to notice recipes that sound palatable. At restaurants, observe how different vegetables are cooked and think of how you may be able to duplicate each gastronomic achievement in your own home. Note: If you are like George Bush and can't stand broccoli, don't force yourself to do something you don't want to do—eating vegetables shouldn't be a form of punishment. I'm confident that you'll find plenty of veggies that you do like.

2. Make a Week for Vegetables. For one week, note in your food, mood, and weather diary how many servings of vegetables you consume on a daily basis. You may be surprised. Note which ones taste the best, and make conscious plans to repeat the pleasure. As you consume more, notice any improvements in your health, particularly your gastrointestinal functions. Are you less hungry all the time? Has your hypoglycemia improved?

3. Designate a folder, notebook, or box as a keeper of vegetable recipes. Watch for new recipes to collect and make an effort to try them.

4. Explore the Great Unknown: Once a week, when you visit the grocery, purchase a vegetable you have never eaten before. There is more to the life of vegetables than iceberg lettuce and hothouse tomatoes. If you don't like it, that's fine. Buy small amounts so you don't feel guilty relegating what you don't want to the compost heap. If you keep trying, you may run across one or two that you actually adore and, in the process, broaden your appreciation of just how delicious a health-conscious diet can actually be. As you appreciate the joys of, say, alfalfa sprouts, butternut squash, and mini zucchinis, add these to the list of vegetables that meet your approval and be on the lookout for recipes that use them and add to your collection of vegetable recipes.

Question 28. Are you willing to give up antibiotics and other additives in your food?

"One of the most common negative claims about food additives is that they can provoke or exacerbate a variety of behavioral problems, including depression, dizziness, blurred vision, insomnia, nervousness, migraines, and hyperactivity." — Robin B. Kanarek and Robin Marks-Kaufman, *Nutrition and Behavior.*

There are four good reasons why you should do your best to avoid drugs and chemicals in the foods you eat if you want to rise above depression:

1. Many food additives have been proven to depress the central nervous system. A number of food additives have been determined to be neurotoxins, including:

MSG, a common ingredient in Chinese food.[1]

Aspartame, a sugar substitute.[2]

Glutamic acid, an ingredient in amino acid mixtures, flavor enhancers, and salt substitutes.[3]

Aspartic acid, an amino acid found in proteins and in aspartame.[4]

Whether or not these additives cause toxic symptoms depends not only on the amount ingested but also on the sensitivity of the person consuming them.[5]

2. To fight off depression, you need to strengthen your immune system. When you take antibiotics into your body, you increase your risk of developing *Candida albicans*.[6] Many consumers are unaware that the meats and often the dairy products they take into their bodies are laced with antibiotics. Today, about half the antibiotics produced annually in the United States are used in animal feed.[7]

You also decrease your chances of being able to use antibiotics effectively should you happen to get really sick. Researchers are advising doctors to use antibiotics less frequently with their patients because of the increasing incidence of antibiotic-resistant strains of infectious agents. Shouldn't they also be advising you to stop using these drugs unwittingly in your diet?

Antibiotic residues in meat alter the intestinal flora, lowering your ability to synthesize vitamins.[8]

3. Many food additives are derived from common food allergens. If you find that food sensitivities play a large factor in your depression, then you need to educate yourself about which additives are made from foods to which you are sensitive. See Question 14 for a list of additives and ingredients made from common allergens.

4. You may be allergic to the additives in your food rather than intolerant to the food itself. Artificial food colorings and preservatives are the most common additives associated with food intolerance.[9]

Many health-conscious individuals are instinctively aware of the chemicals in fast food and stay home to eat. But without a deliberate effort to avoid foods that are processed, canned, frozen, or freeze-dried, it's a challenge to elude the 2,500 to 3,000 substances currently estimated to be used as food additives.[10]

Dr. Ben Feingold, a California allergist, drew attention to food additives about twenty years ago when he postulated that additives caused hyperactivity in children[11] and migraine headaches in adults.[12] Since that time, his studies have been repeated and many doctors now agree that at least a certain percentage of children can improve their behavior by following an additive-free diet.

Even an additive that the U.S. Food and Drug Administration has decided is safe for 98 percent of the population—such as monosodium glutamate (MSG)—may pose significant risks for 2 percent of the population (roughly 5 million people, well over the population of metropolitan Atlanta).[13] High doses of MSG have been found to cause lesions in the nerve cells of the hypothalamus. Even low doses were found to affect the level of serotonin, an important neurotransmitter needed to combat depression.[14] One expert on the adverse side effects of MSG, George R. Schwartz, has documented numerous case studies in which he found a link between the additive and subsequent depression. He speculates that MSG may release acetylcholine in the body, a substance that may induce depressive reactions.[15]

Although there are hundreds of additives that may cause adverse health effects, the most important ones to be avoided by anyone prone to depression include:

ASPARTAME

Often Found In:
Diet drinks
Children's multivitamins
Sugar-free products

May Cause:
Panic attacks
Visual hallucinations
Mood swings
Mania
Headaches, seizures
Insomnia

BUTYLATED HYDROXYANISOLE AND BUTYLATED HYDROXYTOLUENE (BHA AND BHT)—Antioxidants and preservatives

Often Found In:
Chewing gum, candy
Active dry yeast
Cake mixes
Enriched rice
Potato chips
Margarine, vegetable oils
Breakfast cereals

May Cause:
Asthma, rhinitis
Dizziness, confusion
Cancer

CARAMEL COLORS

Often Found In:
98 percent of all colors in foods

May Cause:
Reduced dietary levels
    of Vitamin B6

MSG

Often Found In:
Meat tenderizer,
    Natural flavorings,
    Natural seasonings,
    Seasonings and spices,
    Natural chicken and
    pork flavorings,
    Autolyzed yeast
Bouillon cubes
Soy sauce

May Cause:
Chinese restaurant syndrome—
    numbness and palpitations
Headaches
Asthma
Depression, mood swings,
    paranoia
Visual disturbances
Brain damage, especially in infants

Canned soups and gravies
Chinese restaurant food
Lunch meats, sausages,
   pot pies, beef burgers
Cheese
Mushrooms
Tomatoes

SACCHARIN

Often Found In:
Over-the-counter and
   prescription drugs
Sugar-free products

May Cause:
Depression, hallucinations
   in children
Cancer

SULFITES

Often Found In:
Baked goods
Beer, wine, and colas
Canned foods
Seafood
Gelatin, jams, jellies
Salad dressings
Potato chips, frozen potatoes
Maple syrup, corn syrup,
   pancake syrup

May Cause:
Asthma
Fainting
Low blood pressure

Sources: Susan C. Smolinske, *Handbook of Food, Drug, and Cosmetic Excipients*; and George R. Schwartz, *In Bad Taste: The MSG Syndrome.*

A special word on aspartame: This artificial sweetener can change the ratio of amino acids, the building blocks of protein, in the blood stream. That aspect has relevance to people with depression because many depressives have low levels of amino acids already. In addition, aspartame may cause a blockage in the formation of serotonin, a neurotransmitter in the brain necessary to prevent depression. As it breaks down in the body, one of the byproducts of aspartame is methanol, or wood alcohol, which turns into formaldehyde, a neurotoxin used for embalming bodies.[16]

In addition to the additives listed above, you may want to avoid certain spices, at least at the beginning of your diet and depending on your overall state of health, as a means of battling yeast infection, a possible contributing factor toward your depression. These spices may irritate the stomach and destroy the mucous layer of the intestinal tract, allowing toxins to enter other areas of the body:[17]

Pepper   Mustard
Cinnamon   Curry
Ginger   Chili powder
Cloves   Cayenne
Mace

When you use spices, choose only the freshest ingredients because yeast-encouraging molds often grow in seldom-used spices. In addition, many spices may contain other ingredients to which you may be allergic, such as cornstarch or gluten, a protein found in wheat.

Some spices have been documented as having psychoactive properties. Ingesting 5-15 grams of nutmeg, about the amount in several teaspoons, for example, has produced visual hallucinations, distortions of time and space, and, in some cases, depression and stupor.[18]

The additive most commonly implicated in food intolerance reports is tartrazine, also known as FD&C yellow No. 5 or E102, an artificial color.[19] You may also want to monitor how you react to foods containing these additives:

Annatto, a natural orange-yellow coloring found in cereals, cheese, margarine, oil, and ice cream

Ponceau4R, Amaranth, Sunset Yellow FCF, synthetic colors

Balsam of Peru, a flavoring in candies, gum, cola drinks, and ice cream

Benzoate derivatives (including sulphur dioxide, a preservative) that occur in cranberries and certain types of honey

Salicylates, a natural ingredient in curry powder, paprika, many other spices, tea, oranges, and honey.[20]

Action Plan

Question 28. Are you willing to give up antibiotics and other additives in your food?

1. When you go out to eat, especially at Chinese restaurants, ask if the food has been prepared with MSG, aspartame, or other additives.

2. Avoid additives made from foods to which you know you are sensitive (see Question 14).

3. If you are unable to find organic or range-fed meats such as Coleman, Maverick Light, Homestead beef, or Welsh Family Organic Farm meats at your grocer or health food store, you may want to try mail order houses. Walnut Acres Organic Farms, Penns Creek, PA 17862 (800-433-3998) sells a variety of organic meats and other products.

4. Before you eat anything processed, read the label.

5. Look through your spice cabinet. How old are your spices? Purchase from a health food store that carries fresh spices in bulk, or contact Frontier Cooperative Herbs, 3021 78th St., Norway, IA 52318-0118 (800-786-1388).

Question 29. Do you need to rotate your diet?

"The whole point of this diet is to let the body recover from the effects of a food before eating it again."— Theron G. Randolph and Ralph W. Moss, *An Alternative Approach To Allergies.*

The reason we tend to eat the same things over and over again seems to me a matter of human nature. We figure out what we like to eat and stick to that. We figure out what's easy and grab the first thing that takes five minutes. Life is short and most of us have higher priorities on our minds. And besides, when it comes to eating, no matter how much we may enjoy consuming delicious foods, the process of shopping, planning, and cooking may be more of a chore than a joy. Life is too valuable to spend searching the grocery aisles on a daily basis.

With that said, I include this chapter anyway because it contains an important message: At first, until you clear up any potential yeast buildup in your body, you may be prone not only to having food sensitivities, but to developing others if you eat the same foods over and over again, no matter how nutritious those foods may be. And if you have food sensitivities, making an effort to rotate what you eat may lessen the severity of your symptoms.

Many allergists now believe that eating the same thing over and over again is the hidden cause of the food addiction that leads so many Americans to be overweight.[1] Dr. Marshall Mandell explained in his *Five-Day Allergy Relief System*:

The obese person has no idea that his daily food cravings or eating habits are based on a physiologic need to stop the withdrawal symptoms caused by food addiction. All he knows is that at night he is uncomfortable until he finally yields to the need to eat the special snack he placed on the night table before retiring.... Within a few hours after eating a food to which he is both allergic and addicted (and despite the initial good effects that may have been noted), he begins to experience familiar addictive withdrawal ("hangover") symptoms that can range from slight fatigue to severe anxiety, excruciatingly painful migraine headaches, abdominal cramps, severe depression, violent anger, panic, exhaustion, asthma, arthritis, generalized itching, and very painful muscle ache.[2]

Steven Rochlitz, a physicist whose search for health led him to write about allergies and *Candida*, notes that many people eat only five to ten foods, going from one allergy-addiction to the next. He recommends a "rotary diversified diet" of nonallergenic foods as one of the best methods for not only avoiding the headache, fatigue, and depression associated with food addiction, but also for losing weight.[3]

I offer this advice about the advantages and disadvantages of a Rotary Diversified Diet:

Advantages:
    Useful when the offending foods cannot be identified or there
        are multiple food allergens;
    Intestines never receive a buildup of any one food allergen;
    Avoids buildup of single pesticides from overconsumption of
        any one food;
    Some troublesome foods may still be consumed if only eaten
        once every four days;
    Prevents the development of further food allergies;
    May be used to identify food allergies on an ongoing basis;
    Wide variety of foods contributes to better nutritional balance;
    May be used to avoid cravings associated with food addiction
        during a weight loss program;
    Diet may be less restrictive.

Disadvantages:
    Requires knowledge of food families;
    Requires planning;
    Not useful for highly sensitive patients unless most allergenic
        foods are completely eliminated;
    May fail when the specific allergen is shared in sufficient quantities by several foods of the same family.

If you'd like to rotate your diet, there are several approaches to try. The basic rotary diet requires eating a single food *only once every four days* and eating any related foods (and by that I mean any food from the same food family) *only once every two days.*[4] For example, under ideal circumstances for a basic rotation, I should eat apples once every four days and two days after I eat an apple I may choose to eat a pear, which is in the same food family.

Natalie Golos and Frances Golos Golbitz, the authors of an excellent rotation cookbook, *If This Is Tuesday, It Must Be Chicken,* include five stages for rotating, depending on the sensitivity of the individual. In Stage I you modify your diet by cutting down on sugar, salt, refined grains, junk food, and cooking. In Stage II you eliminate the worst offenders. By Stage III, you ease into a true rotation and eat foods from a single food family only every other day. Stages IV and V are for those who are the most highly sensitive. These individuals may have to restrict their diet to eating meals of one or two foods from a single food family only every four days.[5]

Here's a brief introduction to the food families of the most commonly eaten foods so you can try the basic concept of a rotary diversified diet yourself:

FOOD FAMILIES:

Apple: Apple, pear, quince
Banana: Banana, plantain
Beef: Butter, cheese, milk, beef, veal
Citrus: Grapefruit, kumquats, lemons, limes, oranges, tangerines
Composite: Artichokes, chicory, endive, escarole, head lettuce, safflower, sesame seeds, chamomile, tarragon, stevia
Crustaceans: Crab, crayfish, lobster, shrimp
Fowl: Chicken, eggs, turkey, duck, goose, pheasant, Cornish hens
Fresh-water fish: Bass, catfish, croaker, perch, pike, salmon, smelt, whitefish
Gourd: Pumpkin, squash, cucumber, cantaloupe, melons, zucchini
Grape: Grapes, raisins, cream of tartar, vinegar
Grass family: Bamboo shoots, barley, sugar cane, corn, millet, molasses, oats, quinoa, spelt, rice, rye, teff, wheat, wild rice
Legume: Beans, peas
Lily: Asparagus, chives, garlic, leeks, onions, scallions
Morning glory: Jicama, sweet potato

Mollusks: Abalone, clam, mussels, oysters, scallop
Mustard: Broccoli, Brussels sprouts, cabbage, cauliflower, collards, kale, radish, turnips, watercress
Mutton: Lamb
Nightshade: Potato, paprika, chili, eggplant, peppers, pimento, tomato, tobacco
Parsley: Carrots, celery, parsley, parsnips
Plum: Apricot, nectarine, peach, plum
Rose: Boysenberry, cherry, raspberry, dewberry, strawberry

Adapted from: James C. Breneman, *Basics of Food Allergy*; Marjorie Hurt Jones, *The Allergy Self-Help Cookbook.*

However you decide to organize it, the basic concepts behind a rotating diet include these guidelines:

Eat whole, unadulterated foods.

Diversify your diet.

Rotate what you eat.

At first eat only foods to which you are not allergic.

The good news is that if you follow a rotation diet, you may be able to consume foods to which you were previously sensitive after a period of abstaining, which may take anywhere from three months to two years.[6] In this way you may be able to incorporate more variety as long as you don't overindulge.

For those who are prone to overorganization, remember that the rotation diet is not about being perfect, it's about feeling better. You don't have to be perfect, and more than likely perfection is not a realistic option when following such a program. Just relax and do your best and see if you don't start to clear up a lot of reactions that you may not have realized were associated with your diet.

For those like me who are not prone to overorganization and who see such a prospect of rotating as totally unrealistic, just remember you have the option. And, at the very least, if you find yourself fatigued, depressed, and subject to food cravings at the same time, try the experiment of totally switching your food choices.

Action Plan

Question 29. Do you need to rotate your diet?

1. If your food sensitivities are severe, begin by dividing up the foods you can eat into food families and divide those food families over four days. For assistance in doing so, consult food rotation cookbooks. You may want to try:

> *If This Is Tuesday, It Must Be Chicken* by Natalie Golos and
>   Frances Golos Golbitz
> *Rotation Game* by Sally Rockwell
> *Rotated Allergy Recipes* by Sally Rockwell
> *The Yeast Connection Cookbook* by Marjorie Hurt Jones and
>   William Crook

2. Make a list of allowed foods for every day of your four-day rotation. Put this list in a looseleaf binder, and begin to collect recipes of foods or combinations of foods for each of your four days. I made my own recipe book when I was very sick and highly sensitive to just about everything. Organizing in this way helped me to see that there was still plenty of foods I could eat, and gave me a place to start so I could be more creative in the kitchen, which in turn helped me to stick to my nutrition plan.

3. For every day of your four-day rotation, pick a color. Then go through and mark the packages of food with a colored marker, organizing your pantry so you can quickly find the allowed foods for each particular day.

4. Even if you decide not to rotate your diet, make sure you are not eating the same thing day in and day out, which is a good way to develop food sensitivities. Go back to your food, mood, and weather diary and compare what you have been eating with the list of available food families. How many food families do you actually select from? Is there any way you could add more variety?

Question 30. Do you drink enough water and eat enough salt?

"Pathology that is seen to be associated with 'social stresses'—fear, anxiety, insecurity, persistent emotional and matrimonial problems—and the establishment of depression are the results of water deficiency to the point that the water requirement of the brain is affected." — F. Batmanghelidj, Your Body's Many Cries for Water.

"Poor adrenal functions, excessively low cholesterol levels, and a lack of salt are often overlooked as a possible cause of depression and tiredness." — William Vayda, Mood Foods.

In our search for the right drugs, the right diet, the right supplements, the right outside nutrients to prevent depression, we often overlook two of the simplest remedies of all: water and salt.

The entire central nervous system is based on electrical connections.[1] Water is an excellent conductor of electrical energy. Two-thirds of the human body is made up of water. All of the electrical and chemical connections that the brain makes are dependent upon proper hydration. When we are dehydrated, the level of energy in the brain is depleted and we feel tired and depressed.

Many experts have found that drinking water is an excellent way to reduce the severity of asthmatic and allergic reactions often found in people with a tendency toward depression. Drinking water is also a simple pain control technique, since pain may occur at a site of localized dehydration.[2]

In addition to being a substance released during an allergic reaction, the neurotransmitter histamine also plays an important role in maintaining tissue fluid balance. High histamine levels that occur naturally in cases of asthma and allergies may cause severe depression. That's why, when you're dehydrated, it's easy to feel tired and depressed. Drinking water helps to restore normal fluid balance and thus can alleviate depression.[3]

In general, experts recommend six to eight glasses of water per day over and above any other beverages to maintain adequate hydration.

Another way to think of it: drink a glass of water every hour during the working day. The amount you need may be more or less, depending on your body weight and your level of physical activity. If you'd like to find out exactly how much you should drink, start by dividing your body weight by half. If you weigh 160 pounds, for example, the number you come up with is 80. Then divide this number by 8 ounces, and you'll find out how many 8-ounce glasses of water you should start out with—in this case, ten.[4] When you exercise, you should drink an additional two glasses for every pound lost to sweat.[5]

Once you know how much to drink, the next challenge is to find what kind of water to drink—no easy task when you consider that in 1993-94, 53 million Americans, or one in five, unknowingly drank tap water polluted with feces, lead, radiation, or other contaminants, according to the Environmental Protection Agency.[6] What with filtered water, reverse-osmosis, de-ionized and distilled water, it's easy to get confused. However, start by avoiding tap water. More than 700 contaminants have been found in public drinking water, including pesticides, radioactive substances, solvents, metals, and harmful microbes.[7] Tap water may contain lead and mercury, which are known to damage the central nervous system. Not all filtering systems remove all the inorganic, organic, microbial, or radioactive substances.

Distilled water is the purest, while de-ionized water, which has had minerals removed, is next best.[8] If you purchase a filter to hook up to your kitchen sink, find out if it has a useful life, and replace it when necessary. Filters do not remove all bacteria, and the bacteria that the filters do trap provide excellent breeding ground for yet more.

As part of your effort to remain properly hydrated, do not cut back on sodium unless advised to do so by your doctor. Sodium, potassium, and chloride assist in maintaining the body's proper water balance and blood chemistry. While many people are trying to reduce the amount of sodium chloride—table salt—in their diets in an effort to reduce high blood pressure, if you are constantly tired and depressed, you may do well to include it in your diet.

Recent studies of patients with chronic fatigue have found that those with low blood pressure have been helped by eating table salt. In addition, many stressed-out, depressed people who have exhausted their adrenal glands tend to lose salt and retain potassium. If anything, a constant craving for salt may well be an indication of adrenal stress. Salt is needed for heart action, to make hydrochloric acid in the stomach, and for the fluid around the cells. The nerve cells of the brain, and consequently all our emotions, are affected by our salt level.[9]

Of course, the average American consumes between 2,300 to 20,000 milligrams of sodium every day, while the estimated minimum requirement is somewhere between 200 and 500 milligrams a day.[10] However, it is worth mentioning that those who find themselves depressed may actually want to experiment with increasing the amount of salt in their diets in an effort to raise their blood pressure and beat fatigue and depression. You may want to gradually increase your salt intake by ½ to 1 teaspoon a day until you find the amount that helps you feel better.[11]

Action Plan

Question 30. Do you drink enough water and eat enough salt?

1. Figure out how many glasses of water you drink every day.
My body weight _____ divided by 2 = _____ divided by 8
oz. = _____ number of glasses

2. Get a water bottle and carry it with you throughout the day. Plan to drink half the water you need by lunch time, and the other half throughout the afternoon and evening. When you are exercising, carry your water bottle with you and stop to drink whenever you feel thirsty.

3. If you decide to purchase bottled water, ask the company for information about the source of your water and find out what kind of pollutants have been filtered out. If you purchase a water filter, find out how often the filter needs to be replaced.

4. If you are on a salt-restricted diet, ask your health care professional or a nutritionist to reevaluate. If you crave salt and have been under a great deal of stress, ask your doctor if you need a test of your adrenal function (see Question 19).

PART V

VITAMINS, MINERALS, AND OTHER SUPPLEMENTS

31. Does your body properly absorb vitamins and minerals?

32. Do you have symptoms that might indicate a deficiency of B vitamins?

33. Are you deficient in Vitamin C?

34. Do you absorb a balanced ratio of calcium and magnesium?

Question 31. Does your body properly absorb vitamins?

"No two people have exactly the same inherited characteristics carried in his or her body's estimated 100,000 genes. Therefore, no two people have the same nutrient needs.... In short, there are many people who should not attempt self-help, and there is no way for a doctor to know who these people are unless he examines them." — William H. Philpott and Dwight K. Kalita, *Brain Allergies: The Psychonutrient Connection.*

Although mental illness can result from vitamin deficiencies,[1] it pays to take a rational approach to supplementation. When it comes to vitamin pills, however, I frequently see two extremes.

On the one hand, there's the approach taken by the American Council on Exercise, which certified me in aerobics and personal training. Vitamin and mineral supplements are not good "health insurance," according to the A.C.E. manual for aerobics instructors. "Other misguided reasons for taking supplements include inadequate sleep, crash diets, overtraining, chronic stress, frequent fast food meals, and fasting," A.C.E. maintains in its official position statement on vitamins. "There is no pill or tablet that can restore an out-of-balance lifestyle. [However,] there is no harm in taking a single multivitamin-mineral supplement that supplies no more than 100 percent of RDAs (Recommended Daily Allowance of vitamins and minerals)."[2]

A.C.E. says there are certain situations where supplements would be appropriate, and these are, in brief, anyone on a restricted calorie diet, pregnant or lactating women, vegetarians, anyone with chronic illness, heavy smokers or drinkers or—you may have guessed—anyone who is "allergic to or intolerant of" certain foods. "People who cannot eat certain types of foods, such as wheat, fruits and milk products, may miss out on some important nutrients," A.C.E. says. "Note: the calcium provided in a multivitamin-mineral tablet may not be adequate for an individual who is lactose intolerant (unable to digest milk sugar, most common among blacks, Hispanics and Asians) and entirely avoids milk products."[3]

Contrast this conservative approach with people whom I call M&M vitamin junkies, who treat multicolored vitamins as if they're choosing one orange, two red, and four green M&Ms for the day. Market research now shows that one of the top seven reasons Americans take vitamin or mineral supplements is to fight depression.[4]

Although during the course of my recovery I had an entire lunch sack of vitamin and mineral bottles with which I was supposed to supplement my diet, I never considered nutritional supplements a substitute for psychiatric drugs. Instead, I used them to correct underlying deficiencies due to chronic malabsorption problems I had.

The National Academy of Sciences sets the Recommended Dietary Allowances (RDAs) to cover 98 percent of all normal, healthy persons in the United States. However, the RDAs contain a margin of safety. You can consume 67 percent of the RDA and still be adequately nourished. The RDAs do not, however, cover people with illness or chronic disease, and that's where supplementation may be appropriate.

During the early writing of this book, I was alarmed when a friend with chronic depression borrowed my manuscript and immediately went out and bought the very same vitamins and minerals I had been taking. Do not assume that what is right for me or anyone else will necessarily be your magic bullet. Before you embark on any serious attempt to use nutritional supplements to treat depression, I strongly recommend that you seek the advice of a medical professional—your family physician, a nutritionist, a kinesiologist, or other knowledgeable person other than the friendly salesman at your corner health food store.

A word here on the term *nutritionist.* According to Paul Goldberg, a professor of clinical nutrition at Life College in Marietta, Georgia, there is no legal definition for those who call themselves nutritionists. One person might read a book on a dietary topic and begin to preach it. Others call themselves nutritionists in order to market their products. Be careful that the person you consult about vitamins, minerals, and other supplements has appropriate training, which may include a degree in chiropractic, allopathy, naturopathy, osteopathy, and/or advanced degrees in biochemistry, public health epidemiology, or preventive medicine. Registered dietitians are not primarily health care practitioners nor are they natural practitioners. They may work in conjunction with a medical doctor.

The reason you need to be careful about whom you consult and what supplements you choose is simple. Vitamins and minerals exist in your body in a delicate balance. Oversupplementation with any single one can cause a corresponding underrepresentation in another key element. Also, some fat-soluble vitamins, notably A, D, E, and K, may build up in your liver, ultimately reaching toxic levels if you take too much on a regular basis. Less of a concern than your health, but still important, is your pocketbook. If you take too many of the water-soluble vitamins, you excrete what your body doesn't need so you are simply wasting your money.

Even though I have spent years researching the topic, I still consult my doctor about all supplements. Invariably, when I go to the health food store and purchase whatever seems to look good at the time, I end up buying something that doesn't agree with me and throwing myself off balance again. Even when I need a basic vitamin, such as E, for example, I have been so sensitive that one brand or one preparation may agree with me, and another one won't.

Ask your doctor whether you should supplement your diet with B vitamins, vitamin C, magnesium and calcium, or other essential nutrients. Tests are available that will be able to show how well your body is absorbing particular nutrients, and he or she can use this information to make sound recommendations.

Action Plan

Question 31. Does your body properly absorb vitamins?

1. Get professional advice. Ask your health care professional, nutritionist, or a nutritionally-oriented kinesiologist which nutritional supplements you need. Blood tests can show whether or not you are absorbing what you need. Qualified kinesiologists can tell you which particular supplements are most helpful to your particular body.

2. Ask the professional you consult how long you need to take these supplements. How will he or she know if your nutritional needs change?

3. If you take the fat-soluble vitamins, A, D, E, or K, ask the consulting health care professional to give you a limit so you don't overdose. Get a written plan of which supplements to take at which particular times of the day. Stick to the plan he or she recommends, doing your best to make sure you get the same amounts of the same supplements at the same time of day every day.

4. Monitor all side effects to nutritional supplements, including vitamins, minerals, and all herbs, just as you would if you were taking prescribed medication. If you have an adverse reaction to any supplement, take it back to your doctor and ask him to reevaluate.

5. If you need high doses of nutritional supplements, ask your doctor why your body is not properly absorbing what it needs. Go back to Question 10. Do you have digestive disorders?

6. Find out if the health care professional who is advising you will make a commission on the supplements he or she sells to you. There is nothing wrong with a doctor making a reasonable profit, but you may be able to purchase the same vitamins and minerals by mail, or order directly from the company.

7. If you have food sensitivities, make sure your nutritional supplements are allergy free. You can find vitamins made without corn, sugar, yeast, or other known allergens. Read the labels on all supplements. You may be surprised to find that in many vitamins, including some of the ones sold by multi-level marketing companies, the first ingredient listed is sugar.

Question 32. Do you have symptoms that might indicate a deficiency of B vitamins?

"Mental illness, and an assortment of physical diseases, can result from a low concentration in the brain of any one of the following vitamins: thiamine (B-1), niacin (B-3), pyridoxine (B-6), hydroxocobalamin (B-12), pantothenic acid, folic acid and ascorbic acid (Vitamin C)." — William H. Philpott and Dwight K. Kalita, *Brain Allergies: The Psychonutrient Connection.*

Optimal amounts of B vitamins especially can do wonders for improving your mood.

B VITAMINS AND THEIR DEFICIENCY SYMPTOMS

B-1 (Thiamine): Loss of appetite, irritability depression, confusion, loss of memory, inability to concentrate, fear of impending doom, sensitivity to noise, insomnia, tension.

B-2 (Riboflavin): Degeneration of nerve tissue, sensitivity to bright light, cracks at corners of mouth.

B-3 (Niacin, naicinamide, and nicotinic acid): Anxiety, depression, chronic fatigue, pellagra, headaches, loss of appetite, insomnia.

B-5 (Pantothenic acid): Irritability, depression, dizziness, tension.

B-6 (Pyridoxine): Irritability, fatigue, restlessness, itchy skin, hair loss.

B-12 (Cyanocobalamin) and B-12B (Hydroxocobalamin): Poor concentration, depression, manic depression, agitation, hallucinations, pernicious anemia, immune disorders, fatigue, disturbed carbohydrate metabolism, spinal cord degeneration, pale skin, dandruff.

Biotin: Fatigue, depression.

Folic acid: Depression.

Sources: William H. Philpott and Dwight K. Kalita, *Brain Allergies: The Psychonutrient Connection;* Carl C. Pfeiffer, *Nutrition and Mental Illness;* Lloyd Rosenvold, *Can A Gluten-Free Diet Help?;* "X-Linked Dominant Manic-Depressive Illness," *The Journal of Orthomolecular Psychiatry;* and H.L. Newbold, *Dr. Newbold's Nutrition for Your Nerves.*

There may be a wide variety of reasons for deficiency of B vitamins, including:

    Vegetarianism or alcoholism
    Drugs, including oral contraceptives, neomycin, methotrexate
    Liver, pancreatic, or kidney disease
    Protein malabsorption
    Metabolic disorders
    Lack of other vitamins, especially A, C, or E
    Gastrointestinal disorders
    Gluten intolerance
    High-sugar diets
    Antibiotics and sulfa drugs that destroy intestinal bacteria
    Stress

If you decide to supplement your diet with B vitamins, consult a doctor or nutritionist. Overdosing with B vitamins can cause a whole other set of problems. Overuse of B-6, for example, has been associated with numbness in the hands and feet.[1] Niacinamide, one of the forms of vitamin B-3, may make some people tired and depressed. Other overdose symptoms associated with B-3 have included nausea, vomiting, and activation of peptic ulcer. High doses of B-6 may make you nervous, irritable, or slightly nauseated[2] or produce numbness in your toes.[3] B-12, or cyanacobalamin has been reported to be toxic for some people suffering from dimness of vision.[4]

Even though B vitamins are water soluble and easily excreted by the body, too much of one B vitamin may result in a deficiency of the other. For this reason, if you decide to supplement on your own, it is advisable to use a B complex vitamin rather than to supplement with individual B vitamins.

FOOD SOURCES OF B VITAMINS:

    B-1: Breads, cereals, oatmeal, rice, ham, pork, Brazil nuts, fish, peas, pumpkin, wheat
    B-2: Liver, breads, and cereals
    B-3: Chicken breast, mackerel, swordfish, veal chops, anchovies
    B-5: Avocados, meat, poultry, seafood, peanuts, pineapple, soybeans

B-6: Oatmeal, plantains, bananas

B-12: Meat, poultry, dairy products, and seafood, especially liver, sardines, mackerel, red snapper, salmon, Swiss cheese, and egg yolks

Biotin: Liver, kidney, egg yolks, and yeast

Folic acid: Yeast, almonds, asparagus, legumes, peanuts, turkey, walnuts, mackerel, cottage cheese

Sources: William Vayda, *Mood Foods*; Jean Carper, *Food—Your Miracle Medicine*; and Maureen Salaman, *Foods That Heal.*

Action Plan

Question 32. Do you have symptoms that might indicate a deficiency of B vitamins?

1. List any symptoms you have that may indicate a deficiency of B vitamins:

2. List any health problems you have that may contribute to a deficiency of B vitamins:

3. Look over the natural food sources of B vitamins, and plan to include more of them in your diet.

4. Ask a qualified health professional not only if you need to supplement with B vitamins, but also how much and which particular ones.

Question 33. Are you deficient in Vitamin C?

*"Mental disturbances, I found, are also associated with defi-
ciencies of vitamin C (depression), vitamin B-1 (depression),
vitamin B-6 (convulsions), folic acid, and biotin, and there is
evidence that mental function and behavior are also affected
by changes in the amounts in the brain of any of a number of
other substances that are normally present."* — Linus Pauling, *How to Live Longer and Feel Better.*

Despite all the fame and glory he received during his lifetime as a
two-time winner of the Nobel prize, Linus Pauling may be most
remembered as the man who explained to the general public why vitamin C can help the common cold. But his work about vitamin C also
made a huge contribution to the understanding of the common cold of
mental illness—depression.

SYMPTOMS OF VITAMIN C DEFICIENCY:
 Chronic infections, viral diseases, and disorders of the immune
     system
 Rheumatoid arthritis and aching joints
 Allergies
 Emotional stress
 Tooth decay, bleeding gums
 Constipation
 Heart attacks, hemorrhage, strokes, hemorrhoids, and other vas-
     cular diseases
 Impaired ability to heal, excessive scarring, tendency to bruise
     easily
 High levels of copper in the body, which may lead to anxiety and
     phobias

Sources: Linus Pauling, *How To Live Longer and Feel Better;* Carl C. Pfeiffer, *Nutrition and Mental Illness;* H.L. Newbold, *Mega-Nutrients for Your Nerves.*

There may be a wide variety of reasons for deficiency of vitamin C, including:
Stress
Environmental pollution
Allergies
Illness
Use of tobacco products
High levels of copper in the body

Source: H.L. Newbold, *Mega-Nutrients for Your Nerves.*

Like B vitamins, vitamin C is water-soluble, so the body generally excretes what it doesn't need, rather than storing it as it does, for instance, with vitamin A. Even though you need to constantly replenish this vitamin, you should also consult your doctor about how much your body needs for optimal health, especially if you are considering taking 1,000 mg. or more.

Possible side effects of taking too much vitamin C include kidney stones, gas, loose bowels, and abdominal pains.[1] Because too much vitamin C can upset your stomach, an onset of diarrhea is a sign that you are getting too much.

FOOD SOURCES OF VITAMIN C:

Fruits and vegetables, rose hips, acerola cherries, guavas, black currants, parsley, green peppers, watercress, chives, strawberries, persimmons, spinach, oranges, cabbage, grapefruit, papaya, elderberries, kumquats, dandelion greens, lemons, cantaloupe, green onions, limes, mangoes, loganberries, tangerines, tomatoes, squash, raspberries, romaine lettuce, and pineapple.

Source: Maureen Salaman, *Foods That Heal.*

Action Plan

Question 33. Do you have symptoms that might indicate a deficiency of vitamin C?

1. List any symptoms you have that may indicate a deficiency of vitamin C:

2. List any health problems you have that may contribute to a vitamin C deficiency:

3. Look over the natural food sources of vitamin C, and plan to include more of them in your diet.

4. Ask a qualified health professional not only if you need to supplement with vitamin C, but also how much you need to take. As you begin to supplement with vitamin C, monitor your gastrointestinal symptoms. If you develop diarrhea, kidney stones, gas, or abdominal pains, you may need to cut back on your dosage or switch to a variety that is manufactured from another food source.

Question 34. Do you absorb a balanced ratio of calcium and magnesium?

"The results of these experiments show a beneficial effect of calcium on mood and suggest a possible use for the treatment of depressive disorders." — "A Beneficial Effect of Calcium Intake on Mood," *Journal of Orthomolecular Medicine.*

"...psychotic behavior, including auditory and visual hallucinations, has been reported in 50 percent of the subjects with low magnesium levels in their blood." — "Seventy-Two Percent of Americans Are Magnesium-Deficient," *Better Nutrition for Today's Living.*

While you are asking your doctor about tests to determine if you are absorbing enough vitamins, be sure to ask to see if you need to supplement your diet with calcium and magnesium. These two important minerals regulate electrical impulses in the central nervous system and surveys show that large numbers of Americans are deficient in both.

MINERAL AND DEFICIENCY SYMPTOMS
   Calcium: Depression, osteoporosis, leg cramps
   Magnesium: Hallucinations, high blood pressure, heart attacks, hardening of the arteries, fatigue, PMS, insulin resistance, impaired glucose metabolism, migraines, alcoholism, depression, poor muscle coordination, nervousness, schizophrenia, hypoglycemia, and dementia

Sources: "Magnesium and Health," *Vitamin Research Products Nutritional News*; William H. Philpott and Dwight K. Kalita, *Brain Allergies: The Psychonutrient Connection*; and Smart Basics, Inc., "Smart Basics Minerals Glossary."

There may be a wide variety of reasons for calcium and magnesium deficiency or imbalance, including:

High-protein diets
Hormone imbalances
Alcoholism
An abnormal acid-alkaline body chemistry
High-sugar diets
Alcohol and caffeine
Consumption of large amounts of foods high in oxalic acid, such
    as cocoa, spinach, kale, rhubarb, almonds, and whole wheat
Use of vitamin C supplements
Inadequate amounts of vitamin D
Use of antibiotics or antacids containing aluminum

Sources: H.L. Newbold, *Dr. Newbold's Nutrition for Your Nerves*; William H. Philpott and
Dwight K. Kalita, *Brain Allergies: The Psychonutrient Connection*; Nancy Appleton, *Lick the
Sugar Habit*; Smart Basics, Inc., "Smart Basics Minerals Glossary."

Both minerals have been used to treat depression, but before supplementing, ask your doctor for advice. As with vitamins, excessive
intake of one mineral may lead to imbalances in others, and calcium
and magnesium work together in the body.

Overdosing with magnesium may cause diarrhea. Magnesium
should be avoided by patients with impaired kidney function.[1]

FOOD SOURCES OF CALCIUM:

Dairy products, sardines, kelp, egg yolks, yeast, parsley, brazil nuts,
lentils, walnuts, green leafy vegetables, and seafood.

FOOD SOURCES OF MAGNESIUM:

Sesame seeds, nuts, tofu, fish, dairy products, lean meat, and whole
grains.

Sources: "Seventy-Two Percent of Americans Are Magnesium-Deficient," *Better Nutrition for
Today's Living*; and Maureen Salaman, *Foods That Heal*.

Action Plan

Question 34. Do you absorb a balanced ratio of calcium and magnesium?

1. List any symptoms you have that may indicate a deficiency of calcium or magnesium:

2. List any health problems you have that may contribute to a calcium or magnesium deficiency:

3. Look over the natural food sources of these minerals, and plan to include more of them in your diet.

4. Ask a qualified health professional not only if you need to supplement, but also how much you need to take. Ask him or her specifically what ratio you need of calcium to magnesium, as these two minerals work in balance in the body.

5. If you have trouble falling asleep at night, ask your health care professional if you should supplement with liquid magnesium, a natural alternative to tryptophan, which is a neurotransmitter no longer sold separately on the U.S. market.[2]

PART VI

HABITS OF MIND

35. Do you get enough exercise to relax your mind?

36. Should you learn new techniques to balance your mind and body?

37. Do you think positively to create the reality you want?

38. Have you learned what your depression has to teach you?

Question 35. Do you get enough exercise?

"...aerobic exercise is more effective than placebo and no treatment, and it is as effective as group psychotherapy, individual psychotherapy or meditation/relaxation." — Siegfried Weyerer and Brigitte Kupfer, "Physical Exercise and Psychological Health," *Sports Medicine.*

It may seem that I, being a personal trainer, have a bias in favor of physical exercise. That's quite true. But I can also cite you chapter and verse from my own experience and from medical literature why getting off your duff may be the best thing you ever did to get over your depression.

In my early thirties, when I went off my medication so that I could try to get pregnant, the only relief I found was at the gym, on a hiking trail, or even out in my garden digging in the dirt. Over the years, my depression would have been much worse had it not been for biking, skating, jogging, aerobic dance, swimming, weight lifting, hiking, and yoga. In fact, the entire reason I joined the fitness industry was to find a way to supplement my income while doing what I needed to do to manage my depression on a regular basis.

There are several key reasons that exercise lifts your mood:

❖ Physical activity relieves stress, a major contributor to depression.

❖ Endorphins released into the brain during a good workout lift the mood.

❖ According to Eastern tradition, exercise cools the liver and assists in detoxifying the body of substances that might interfere with the functioning of the brain.

❖ Exercise improves self-confidence and a feeling of mastery over one's body.

❖ Deep breathing during exercise can provide a form of meditation.

❖ Regular workouts reinforce the importance of nurturing yourself.

Physical activity is often divided into two types: aerobic or large-muscle exercises such as swimming, biking, hiking, jogging, or walking that boosts the heart rate; and anaerobic activities such as weight training. Many Americans believe you must already be fit and in beautiful shape to get anything out of a regular workout, but that is a mistaken notion. Only about 20 percent of the population get enough aerobic exercise at a level to benefit their cardiovascular systems.[1] The good news is that you don't have to do only aerobic activities that accelerate the heart rate over a long period of time to benefit psychologically. In fact, one group of researchers found that men who practiced yoga had lower levels of tension, fatigue, and anger than those who swam regularly.[2] One survey of the effects of the gentlest mind-body exercises such as Feldenkrais, Tai Chi, yoga, the Alexander Technique, Pilates, and Qigong found demonstrable decreases in participants' anxiety levels and even dramatic improvements in body chemistry, such as improved glucose tolerance and reduced responsiveness to stress hormones.[3]

Study after study has found that the most sedentary, even obese, and even wheelchair-bound individuals can benefit from some kind of regular program whether or not they improve their overall physical fitness. Anyone who has ever bothered to go for a walk after a rough day at the office will know what I'm talking about but may not be able to explain how exercise can affect the emotions. The best explanation I've found comes from Moshe Feldenkrais, a brilliant physicist who found himself in the unlikely role of inventing a whole new system of movement when he became confined to a wheelchair.

Feldenkrais observed that four components make up every waking state: sensation, feeling, thought, and movement.[4] In other words, for every state of mind, there will be corresponding patterns of spatial and rhythmic changes in the body, including changes in breathing, eating, speaking, blood circulation, and even digestion. Actors demonstrate this principle when they evoke certain emotional states simply by mimicking the gestures and habits typically associated with each state of mind.

The motor cortex of the brain, where patterns activating the muscles are established, lies only a few millimeters above the brain structures that process and associate emotions. "Owing to the close proximity to the motor cortex of the brain structures dealing with thought and feeling, and the tendency of processes in the brain tissue to diffuse and spread to neighboring tissues, a drastic change in the motor cortex will have parallel effects on thinking and feeling," Feldenkrais wrote in his book *Awareness Through Movement.*[5]

In other words, to change how you feel, change what you are doing with your body.

If these explanations are not convincing enough, I offer this warning: If you don't exercise, you will be at significantly higher risk for developing depression or increasing the severity of any depression you already have. Men who don't exercise are more than twelve times more likely to be depressed than those who do.[6] Although similar figures aren't available for women, lack of physical activity has been found to be a significant predictor for depressive symptoms for all sorts of people. And from years of teaching and training, I know that women who don't exercise have lower self-esteem and are less likely to take care of themselves—mentally or physically—than those who do.

A more pressing question may be how much activity you need to combat depression. Here the research is unclear, but in my personal experience I have observed that the amount of exercise you need will vary with your stress level but not necessarily with your perceived state of physical wellness. Even those who find themselves sick and tired may benefit from an easy walk around the block. I personally recommend—as does the U.S. Surgeon General—some kind of physical activity every day, even if it's just going for a thirty-minute walk to take a breath of fresh air. The key elements are balance and joy in movement.

To answer for yourself how much activity you need, refer back to your food, mood, and weather diary. Keep track of how much and what kind of exercise you undertake, and how you feel before and after each workout.

Action Plan

Question 35. Do you get enough exercise?

For the next week, use your health diary to focus on exercise.

Whatever you do, pick an activity you like to do; you're more likely to improve your mood if you choose something you enjoy. Working out on gym equipment or joining an aerobics class is great. But so is bicycling, walking briskly, rollerblading, or dancing to favorite energetic music.

Make the following commitment to yourself:

For the next week, I make a commitment to myself to do the following kind of exercise: _____.
(But feel free to switch mid week; the important thing is to do *something*.)

I choose to exercise at the following time: _____.

I will exercise _____ days this week.

When I work out, I will continue for _____ minutes.

I, _____ deserve to nurture my mind and body by taking the time to exercise. If I haven't been using my body in any regular activity, I realize it may take time to feel completely comfortable, but I'm going to give this my best shot. Even if I don't enjoy myself at first, if I feel better mentally after at least three exercise sessions, I commit myself to continue at least through the rest of the week.

Then, each day, make notes on a chart like this:

	Before*	During†	After‡	What I did & how long
Day 1				
Day 2				
Day 3				
Day 4				
Day 5				
Day 6				
Day 7				

* Before: On a scale of 0 to 10, with 0 being stressed out, fatigued, and down-in-the dumps and 10 being radiantly joyous, rate how you felt before your workout. Notice also what you were thinking about—the content of your thoughts—as in, "I was a 4. Stressed out after a hard day at the office. Angry at X. Frustrated about Y…"

† During: Rate the intensity level of your exercise on a scale of 1-10, with 1 being no strain at all, 6-8 being a fat-burning range where you were breathing heavily and sweating but still able to carry on a conversation, and 10 being out of breath.

‡ After: Most importantly, record how you felt after you exercised. Rate your mood again, and notice if it improved. Also, notice if the content of your thoughts changed. Even more helpful would be to make more extensive entries, for example: "Once I got into the rhythm of pedaling on my bicycle, I lost track of how discouraged I felt, and by the time I returned home half an hour later I was calm and at peace. For an hour, I forgot all about my ex-husband, my bills, and how desperate my life had become. I felt much more centered and was able to go home and appreciate my family."

At the End of the Week:
    Reflect on the overall effect the exercise had on the rest of your life.
    ıf and take time to appreciate any changes in your physical
    nost importantly reflect on your mental and spiritual state.

Question 36. Should you learn new techniques to balance your mind and body?

> *"Many of us have come to accept limitations in our lives as inevitable, and may fail to find the benefits that positive stress can bring. The Brain Gym movements are a natural, healthful alternative to tension that we can use and teach others to use when challenges present themselves."* — Paul and Gail Dennison, *Brain Gym Teacher's Edition.*

When I first shared this manuscript, several friends advised me against discussing the exercises I had learned to balance my mind and body. For those accustomed to solving all problems with a pill, they argued, even the wonders of what nutrition can do might seem a stretch—these exercises might be going too far. But, after careful consideration, I decided to retain this information. Had I not been convinced by experience, I too would have dismissed the potential of Touch for Health and Brain Gym as too incredible.

First, a little background. In 1964, when chiropractor John Thie was first exposed to George Goodheart's technique of manual muscle testing, he quickly recognized the potential of this kind of biofeedback. Today the body of knowledge that Goodheart developed is known as Applied Kinesiology, and it has been employed literally around the world in a variety of different disciplines. In 1973, the first edition of Thie's book, *Touch for Health,* was published to teach the general public how to combine modern kinesiology with ancient Oriental health techniques.

Paul Dennison, an educator, developed what is now known as Educational Kinesiology. Just as Touch for Health establishes a new balance between the muscles and energy system of the body, Educational Kinesiology specializes in balancing the function of the brain. Dennison calls his exercises Brain Gym™ because they literally balance the brain. And what could be more appealing to someone who wants to overcome mood swings?

After seeing the profound changes that Touch for Health and Brain Gym had brought to my health and mental outlook and after researching the field of kinesiology, I became certified in these disciplines and continue to use them with my personal training clients. I've used them with professional athletes, artists and musicians, students and salesmen, and, closer to home, clients who want to develop a more positive outlook for any number of different goals.

Touch for Health is based on a complex system that strengthens and energizes forty-two muscle groups in the body. If you are interested in receiving a Touch for Health muscle balancing session or finding classes in your area, you can contact the Touch for Health Association of America at 3223 Washington Blvd., Suite 201, Marina del Rey, CA 90292 or call 800-466-8342. Although some of the techniques in Brain Gym are complex, this system contains delightfully simple movements you can include in your daily routine to manage stress and dramatically alleviate negative moods.

Before I explain how you can benefit from Brain Gym, I must first relate a personal story. Several years ago, I was supporting myself as a tutor and an aerobics instructor while I pursued my dream of writing plays. Although I was a pretty good tutor, there was one little boy in particular whose predicament challenged me to dig deeper. In private, I had a nickname for him: Hard Core. For years, Hard Core had been relegated to classes for those with behavioral disorders and learning disabilities. I prided myself on the turnarounds my students made. But I had tutored Hard Core for about a year and had tried just about everything I knew with him, and still he was getting thrown out of school every other month and not reading very well. About that time a friend convinced me to learn Brain Gym. I tried using it on this little boy, and within weeks of using the techniques, Hard Core had become the teacher's pet and had made a dramatic turnaround in his schoolwork. Frankly, I was so impressed I decided I needed to learn more about Brain Gym so I could help myself.

So what is Brain Gym and why does anybody need it? Brain Gym is a collection of physical exercises that can be used to access more of the power of our minds. On a good day, most of us use maybe 10 percent of our brain capacity. Stress shuts off a lot of our potential, and we move through life on automatic pilot, relying on old patterns to guide us without thinking.

When we become depressed, we frequently use mostly one side of the brain or the other, usually the right side. Thinking in general and positive thinking in particular is a lot more difficult than if we had easy access to our whole brain. Even environmental exposures, such as chemicals that disrupt our hormones, affect the midbrain and thereby our emotions, directing the quality of choices we make.

Although they were not originally invented to alleviate depression, I have found these movements to be invaluable in my own recovery. Dennison, the author of twelve books on the subject and the head of the Educational Kinesiology Foundation of Ventura, California, has given me permission to share a few of the basic movements with you:

1. Before starting any of the exercises, get in PACE. PACE stands for positive, active, clear, and energetic, which is how you will feel once you finish this warmup.

First, drink water.

Second, put one hand on the belly button. Put the fingers of the other hand under the collarbone, on either side of the breastbone. You'll feel a soft spot here. Rub this spot as you hold your belly button with the other hand.

Third, *cross crawl.* Lift the right knee and bring your left hand across the body to touch it. Repeat on both sides about 25 times.

Fourth, *hook up.* Cross one foot over the other. Cross one arm over the other and clasp your hands. As you inhale, bring the tongue to the roof of your mouth. As you exhale, bring the tongue down. If you'd like, you may shut your eyes as you relax and breathe. When you feel completely relaxed, uncross your arms and legs and keep breathing as you were, bringing your fingertips together.

One Brain Gym enthusiast, Jan Irving, wrote an entire doctoral thesis at Oregon State University about the dramatic effects of these four simple exercises. After studying a group of nursing students in 1995, she found that six minutes of PACE led to a 69.5 percent reduction in self-reported anxiety and an 18.7 percent increase on tests of fourteen different motor skills.[1] I find it useful to get in PACE every morning and again before facing any stressful situation.

2. For seeing. This exercise improves your vision and accesses different parts of your brain. Make a Lazy 8 by extending your left arm in front of your body, thumb up as in an "All O.K." sign. With your thumb, draw, in the air, a large horizontal figure-8 (∞). First, move your thumb up to the left and then down and around, coming up the midline of the body, then over and up to the right and around. As you move your thumb, keep your head straight and let your eyes follow along. Repeat with your right arm, and then bring both arms and thumbs together to make a Lazy 8.

3. For listening. Put on your Thinking Caps by placing the thumb of each hand behind the top of each ear. Use the fingers to roll your ears backwards. In the process, you'll be stimulating a series of acupressure points. The Thinking Cap affords you a better range of hearing, relaxes your jaw, tongue, and facial muscles, allows you to focus and pay attention, and is also a great remedy for calming states of shock.

4. For a positive attitude. Hook up and breathe as you did in the fourth step of the warmup, except bring your hands to your forehead. Hold two points called your Positive Points on the bony prominence, each one just above the middle of your eye. Think of a stressful situation as you are holding your Positive Points until you feel relaxed. Hold these points until you feel a strong pulse and the pulses synchronize.

Brain Gym is experienced in two ways: in courses and in private sessions. Either way, your certified Brain Gym instructor will lead you through a process called a *balance*. You start a balance by choosing a goal—something you wish to accomplish or some potential within yourself that you would like to develop. Your instructor will then guide you through a series of Brain Gym activities that are chosen to meet your specific needs. These activities help you access the skills and abilities that your goal requires, allowing you to easily and enjoyably fulfill dreams that once may have seemed unreachable.

For more information about finding a certified Brain Gym teacher near you, contact the Educational Kinesiology Foundation at P.O. Box 3396, Ventura, CA 93006, or you may call 800-356-2109 or 805-658-7942.

Although Brain Gym and Touch for Health have worked best for me, there are many other mind-body techniques—such as Rolfing, Core Energetics, yoga, meditation, and massage, to name just a few—that you may want to try to relieve stress and maintain a healthy equilibrium.

...on 36. Should you learn new techniques to balance your mind and body?

1. Every morning, get in PACE. Spend six minutes doing the four Brain Gym exercises. Notice how you feel before and afterwards. You should feel positive, active, clear, and energized.

2. Any time during the day when you start to lose your emotional balance, go back and get in PACE. If you don't have time to do all four PACE exercises, do hook-ups or cross crawl. This is one of my top recommendations. Of all the things you can do to reduce your depression and anxiety, getting in PACE and repeating the PACE exercises can be one of the most powerful things you can do for yourself. If you can access both sides of your brain, you will be less likely to be emotionally overwhelmed and more likely to approach any challenge with equanimity. Brain Gym exercises can alleviate major emotional upheavals in a matter of minutes.

3. Call the Educational Kinesiology Foundation and find out about classes in your area, or schedule an appointment with a Brain Gym consultant near you to have a private balance.

4. Especially if you have chronic pain in addition to your depression, call the Touch for Health Foundation and find out about private classes to learn the foundation's powerful self-help techniques. Find a Touch for Health practitioner near you and ask him or her to teach you how to give yourself a neurolymphatic massage to use as part of your detoxification program (see Question 18). Many massage therapists and doctors use Touch for Health as part of their regular routine. Treat yourself to a private Touch for Health balance and enjoy feeling pain-free and relaxed.

Question 37. Do you think positively to create the reality you want?

"If one asks for success and prepares for failure, he will get the situation he has prepared for." — Florence Scovel Shinn, *The Wisdom of Florence Scovel Shinn.*

So-called New Age literature is replete with the message that we create our own reality. But so is what I call Old Age literature—the scriptures. After all, it was Jesus who said, "If two of you shall agree on earth as touching any thing that they shall ask, it shall be done for them of my Father, which is in heaven."[1] Even now, science is beginning to back up what prophets have been telling us for aeons.

Martin E.P. Seligman, an academic who has studied the phenomenon, attributes the ten-fold increase in the incidence of depression this century to what he calls "an epidemic of learned helplessness." He believes that a pessimistic style of self-talk is at the core of all kinds of depression, be they of the short-term or long-term variety. "A negative concept of the future, the self, and the world stems from seeing the causes of bad events as permanent, pervasive, and personal, and seeing the causes of good events in the opposite way," Seligman argues.[2]

Although I had always heard about the power of positive thinking, I had the opportunity to put the issue to the test when I first became ill with Chronic Fatigue Syndrome. As luck may have had it, a friend recommended I take a class on positive thinking.

At first, it was not immediately clear to me why I should be sitting in a class making lists of my good and bad traits and talking about prosperity charts—basically collages of all we hoped to will into our lives. *This is stupid,* I commented to myself the first evening we were all assembled. *Everybody knows you should think positively. Why am I here?*

The very next day, the doctor gave me the diagnosis, and I was devastated. I was frightened, angry, and upset. I had read that people with Chronic Fatigue Syndrome are sick an average of two and a half years, and many linger on with the disease indefinitely. I did not want to spend another month, let alone the years to come, alone in my living room with my feet propped up on the couch, unable to write or exercise or live with the joy I had longed to experience. *Oh*, I realized, *that's why I'm in that class!*

So, while slouching on my couch, I came up with my own affirmation: *I'm going to be well by January 1* (which was a mere two and a half months away). At the time I was still very tired, depressed, and constantly battling infection. As January 1 came and went, I began repeating to myself, *I am radiantly healthy.* It didn't matter that I lost seven pounds in a weekend. I kept telling myself that I believed I was already radiantly healthy.

A full six months later, I had completed nine months of withdrawal from my psychiatric drugs and my energy had come back. I knew I had been very blessed.

One strategy to promote positive thinking is to use these affirmations:

❖ I am content and all my needs are satisfied.

❖ I live in harmony with the flow of life.

❖ I relax, do my best, and the world is beautiful.

❖ I release my fears and connect with a higher power.

❖ I let go of the past to allow new joy to enter.

❖ I allow only the most positive energy to enter my body, mind, and spirit.

❖ I convert all energy that comes to me into gifts of love for myself and others.

❖ I flow with joy.

Although you can repeat affirmations to yourself, one way to make them more effective is to couple them with movements, particularly the Brain Gym exercises discussed in Question 36. In this way, by including movement, you will be literally changing your emotional energy and recruiting more of the midbrain, where your feelings are processed. One faculty member of the Educational Kinesiology Foundation, Don Wetsel of Raleigh, North Carolina, recommends using the Thinking Caps, Cross Crawl, and Lazy 8s while repeating your daily affirmations.

Other strategies:

❖ Begin each day by writing a page of positive affirmations in your journal.

❖ Devote commuting time to work for silent prayers of thanksgiving.

❖ Take note of your prayers and how each one is answered.

❖ Record every compliment you receive and take it seriously.

❖ Conclude every day by noticing all the ways you have been blessed.

Very often, when we become depressed, we believe our lives are not working according to plan. We think we—or others—have erred, that there is some inherent unfairness in life, or that some higher power has overlooked us. In fact, even our illnesses and the very worst of the emotional suffering we feel may be a perfect part of some unseen order.

One of the worst things we can do, I think, is to believe that we are ill because we have not practiced positive thinking. Very often, as in my case, illness is the greatest spiritual teacher. Allow yourself to see the perfection in even the most disastrous life events, and you will be able to find it. Even if you can't see the divine perfection at first, allow that you may later comprehend what it is, and the insight will indeed come to you.

Although I had read what seemed like half a library of books about positive thinking, I needed to become sick to learn this important lesson. Every time I became anxious, even over some minor event like driving in rush hour traffic, my physical symptoms became worse— my fatigue would deepen, my sore throat would become more hoarse. Once I accepted the perfection in what seemed before like a chaotic, cruel, and uncaring world, disappointments that might have previously caused me worry dropped by the wayside and I was able to appreciate more of the beauty of my life.

Moreover, I have found over and over again that my worst difficulties always prove to be my greatest blessings. Had I not become very ill, for example, I would never have had the courage to try a nutritional approach to treating my depression. Had I been faced with the choice, I might have taken the coward's way out and avoided the very recovery I was destined to enjoy. Had I not had a difficult student, I might not have learned Brain Gym. Had I not been so harshly judged by others about being a manic depressive—over and above the pain of the illness itself—I might not have done my best to overcome it. In nearly every case, as I reflect, I am able to see the gift in each adversity.

If you neglect to make this choice, to choose to think positively about the wisdom of what happens in your life, you may never recover from depression.

According to Kenneth B. Matheny and Richard J. Riordan, authors of *Stress and Strategies for Lifestyle Management,* depression often occurs as a result of neurotic thinking patterns.[3] We are more likely to hear criticisms and perceive hurts, so many times positive thoughts have little chance of literally turning the tide of the nerve connections in our brains.

"While antidepressive medications often smooth out the neuronal misfiring, the negative thinking patterns may remain to single-handedly maintain the depression," Matheny and Riordan have observed. "It is a well-known fact that persons suffering from depression are best helped early in the disease—probably because early intervention interrupts the consolidation of such neurotic beliefs. Biochemical remedies that typically work well are not always effective for the hardened depressed patient."[4]

Which brings me back to an important point: I believe the strategies I suggest in this book may work equally well for both those with long-term depression and those with short-term depression. To overcome depression, you must learn to nourish yourself on all levels—physical, emotional, and spiritual. If you rely totally on some outside agent, especially drugs, to do it for you, you may never comprehend the limitless joy that already resides inside you.

Action Plan

Question 37. Do you think positively to create the reality you want?

Purchase a journal to house your private thoughts. As a writer, I keep a hard-bound journal with acid-free paper and carry it with me everywhere. However, your journal need not be expensive—even a spiral-bound notebook from the dime store will do. Or, if you'd rather, you may want to use pages in your mood, food, and weather diary. The form is not important—what is important is that you have a place to keep your thoughts and that you feel comfortable keeping it in a private place for your own reflection.

Set aside a few hours when you can rest and relax, and make headings at the top of each page. You will want to have a heading for each of these categories:

MY WORK
MY FAMILY
MY LOVE LIFE
MY BODY
MY SPIRITUALITY
MY MIND

Also include headings for any other subject that seems important to you.

Use these pages to get in touch with the true nature of your beliefs and then use the knowledge you gain from this self-understanding to transform negative beliefs into positive ones.

On the front of each page, write "What I really believe" and list, as thoughts come to you, your core beliefs. Don't censor your thoughts. Allow the darkest corners of your mind to come to the light.

On the back of each page, write "What I would like to believe," and reframe your experience.

For example, if, in your journal page for MY FAMILY, you note, "My family has always treated me as the scapegoat. They have never really loved me," you have done yourself the favor of identifying the limiting belief that may hold you back from healing your relationships, no matter how hard you may try to pretend otherwise. Begin to see the positive possibilities, and use this vision to create personal affirmations. Begin with a realistic possibility. You may write "My family is capable of understanding who I really am." Then, stretch toward a greater vision of what you want, such as "As I heal myself, my new well-being brings light and love to everyone."

Or, under your page marked, MY MIND, if you wrote "I have spent my whole life in depression. I don't even know what happiness is," you may affirm "I can learn to be happy. I want to learn to be happy. Happiness is my right and true nature. As I heal myself, I will discover the higher spirit within that longs to be free."

If you are artistically inclined, you may want to include drawings. Draw the reality of how you feel now. Then take your most gorgeous colored markers and draw the panorama of what you most want to bring into your life.

Make your personal creed: From this vision, write a list of personal affirmations that you can revisit on a daily basis. If there are any that you find particularly challenging, you may want to rewrite them or say them aloud throughout the day.

It may sound silly, but it will work. When I got out of the mental hospital, I realized that as long as I continued to hate myself, I would still want to end my life. So I walked around for weeks afterwards, repeating silently, *I like myself, I LIKE myself!* It seemed like a total lie at first. No psychotherapist told me to do this; it was something I knew instinctively. Even though I felt suicidal for years afterwards, I managed to make it through. Never again did I even attempt to carry through on my most morbid thoughts.

Periodically revisit your core belief pages. Note what beliefs have changed and what have remained. Where you have been able to convince yourself of a truly positive thought, put a star! Take yourself to lunch. Reward yourself. Then dream up new affirmations. Your spirit will never be limited as long as your mind is free to dream.

Question 38. Have you learned what your depression has to teach you?

"There is no antidepressant that will cure a depression which is spiritually based, because the malaise does not originate from brain dysfunction but from an accurate response to the desecration of life. The body is the reflection of the spirit in its physical expression, and its problems are the dramatization of the struggles of the spirit which gives it life. A belief that we ascribe to 'out there' has its effect 'in here.' Everyone dies by his own hand. That is a hard clinical fact, not a moral view."
— David R. Hawkins, *Power Vs. Force: An Anatomy of Consciousness.*

As I researched, I became more and more impressed by the complexity of depression. There is no doubt in my mind that depression is an illness that afflicts mind, body, and spirit, and that any successful approach to eradicate it must address all three components.

But I am still baffled by a fundamental question: What causes depression?

Is it an overreaction to what's out there, in the environment, as in hypersensitivity to dust, pollen, chemicals, even foods?

Is it an imbalance of the hypothalamic-pituitary-adrenal axis, or the endocrine system?

Is it an emotional reaction to a physical overgrowth in the body, such as the yeast *Candida albicans?*

Is it a roller coaster ride caused by the ups and downs of low blood sugar?

Is it a negative thought pattern that originated in childhood, growing up in the larger context of a dysfunctional family?

Is it a difficulty in nourishing ourselves caused by a digestive disorder?

Is it really an immunological problem caused originally by a virus, as some researchers are now beginning to believe?

And does it start out there, in the larger context of the world we perceive through our own eyes and our own biased senses, or does it begin from within?

In short, is it out there or in here?

I leave these questions up to the experts, but one thing I know: depression is a teacher. Throughout all forms of our education, some teachers are crotchety and others are gentle and dote on us; but, whether or not we appreciate the messenger, we are here to grow and learn.

Although philosophers have debated for aeons why suffering exists in the world, I choose to believe that everything exists and everything happens for the total benefit of our spirits. Maybe not *our* spirits even. Maybe somebody else's spirit. In a dimension that we on earth may not be able to comprehend, selfless spirits may choose to perform certain tasks on earth that appear unappealing in terms of the way we judge, but which may result in spiritual blessings for many. If we accept our task of learning and stop judging whether the way we're learning is fun or difficult, we can make great progress toward getting on, moving on, and even letting go.

At first, the question "Why am I depressed?" may seem like a nuts-and-bolts question similar to what a judge might ask about the background for a lawsuit. You could answer, "He/she did this/that/the other and as a result I feel..." But the past is past. Before we can accept the present—the actual gift in the present—we must let go. None of us are perfect—and neither are our families. If we take the approach of learning and welcoming the knowledge that life bestows upon us, then we do not need to be weighed down and depressed by anything that happens. Enlightened people with depression will quickly learn that the first answer to the question "Why am I depressed?" may indeed be "Because there's still something out there I haven't quite figured out yet."

Psychologists, psychiatrists, and other trained counselors may be able to help you get to the bottom of this question. Therapy is not something to be ashamed about. Understanding ourselves is a key to spiritual growth, and many people haven't even begun to fathom the priceless wisdom within themselves. But do your best to avoid spending $100 an hour wallowing in what I call "awfulizing." If you need to plan a pity party, go ahead, let it out in whatever ways seem to you most cathartic and, at the same time, socially responsible. But then get on with the meat of the question: "Why am I depressed?"

Victor Frankl, a psychiatrist who survived the Nazi death camps, believed that happiness lies not so much in a life of ease but in a life of purpose. In his great work, *Man's Search For Meaning*, Frankl wrote,

"Ultimately, man should not ask what the meaning of his life is, but rather that it is he who is asked. In a word, each man is questioned by life; and he can only answer to life by answering for his own life; to life he can only respond by being responsible."[1]

I came to believe that the more I fathomed the lessons depression had to teach me, the less I would have to suffer. The more I accepted myself and saw the meaning of my suffering, the more quickly I could adapt so the pain would eventually abate or even disappear.

I came to believe first of all that I had had lifelong depression as a means of developing my meager faith. That is, faith in my Heavenly Father, faith in myself, even faith in a world I once viewed as frightening, hostile. I figured I needed to learn great spiritual confidence because anybody can have faith when all is going well. I needed to be able to connect with a higher power even when my mind was going nuts. I saw that even the talents I had been given and my chosen profession, writing plays in a world where so few get produced, required me to learn to trust in a force greater than myself.

Second, I realized I had been too quick to absorb what I call negative energy. Anybody within 300 miles who had a problem, it seemed, well, that was my problem too. At first I thought I was being empathetic, being kind, but really I took on blame and pain without providing much of a solution. I was the scapegoat in my family and the scapegoat everywhere else.

For thirty-six years I wished everybody else would change, and then I changed myself. I learned that by healing myself I could heal everyone around me. It's funny—as soon as I realized these lessons, my severe depression was ready to slip away.

Perhaps you too will be ready to let go of your depression if you take the time to find out what it is you were supposed to learn from it. Do not be afraid. The answer you find will lead to greater joy.

Action Plan

Question 38. Have you learned what your depression has to teach you?

Plan ahead to set aside an appropriate time—alone, with a friend or loved one, or with a counselor. If you know ahead of time that you are going to face this question on a specified date, at a prescribed time, and at a given place, your mind will find the space in your daily life, perhaps while dreaming or even driving, to produce the answers.

At the designated time, complete the following thoughts:

If there is a specific situation that troubles me, I could feel better about this situation if I realized_____
_____.

If I realized _____
I would feel_____.

Overall, my depression has benefited me in the following ways:
_____
_____.

If I agree to gain the knowledge of what depression has to teach me, I can let go of my own suffering by_____
_____.

I needed to be depressed in the past because _____
_____.

I am ready to accept the light and love of a power greater than myself because I realize _____
_____.

I know I really want to be happy because _____

_____.

To me, the difference between depression and happiness is _____

_____.

I am thankful for having been depressed because I learned _____

_____.

If I do/think/choose_____,
I will be able to let go of this depression and embrace the goodness
that life has to offer me.

This is how I feel about my life now: _____

_____.

This is how I want to feel: _____

_____.

I have a spirit with a free will. Even though I am suffering now, I know
that I can choose to find a path that will lead me to greater peace and
joy because _____

_____.

If I am unable to change any physical circumstance in my life, I know
that my spirit will always be free and I can choose to think _____

_____.

It has now been nearly two years since I took my last dose of lithium and two and a half years since I took my last antidepressants. I am happier, healthier, and more balanced and blessed than ever before.

Changes have taken place in my family, as well. In the beginning, when I first told them of my holistic approach, my mother, father, and brother telephoned me regularly to warn me of the path I was taking. "Are you still on that dumb asparagus diet?" they would ask. That's the term they came up with when I tried to explain what I was doing— "the dumb asparagus diet." The doctors in my family, experts in their fields, didn't believe that changing what you eat, going to an alternative practitioner, or anything else I was doing could possibly do anything other than waste money. Although I understood their fears, the improvements in my mind and body convinced me that I was taking the right course of action. And, as the months passed, they gradually quieted down.

Today, nobody has to prove who was right. They were right to be concerned. I was blessed to find this path, and most of all I believe that my recovery was not about proving anything to anybody, but about bringing myself and even my entire family a little further into the light.

Recently I had a new play produced in New York City. On this very special night, my family all showed up at the same performance to watch a play I had written about another, imaginary family. And they laughed. I sat in the audience and watched them laugh and afterwards I was immensely grateful—for the play production, for having all my family together, and, most of all, for having healed myself and in the process managing to heal a little bit of everyone around me.

Over the past year, I have gathered courage to tell my story. I was very afraid to tell what had happened to me; I understood that stepping forward to offer hope to others would mean opening myself up to questions about my past, and I am not now nor have I ever been a perfect person. And then about a year ago I had the great fortune of being able to give a lecture to a group of nutritionists at a chiropractic college. My fears fell away when, instead of looking down on me, the students in the class responded with respect, and even awe. When I spoke of the difficulties I had been through, they understood, and they began to tell me of friends, patients, and relatives who were struggling in a similar, desperate fashion.

I pray all the time that I will be able to offer hope to others, and even to show them a path that they might not have been aware existed. When the time seems appropriate, I discuss what I have done with clients at the gym, friends who get discouraged, anyone I meet who seems to want to understand. So far, no one I know has been inspired to take all the steps that I have taken, but many have taken small steps, even big ones, toward their own path of recovery. I can't begin to express how I feel when someone calls to say, "I feel so much happier!"

Whenever people ask me for advice on withdrawing from medication or about specific vitamins, I quickly refer them to a doctor who can offer an objective and scientific appraisal. I am very aware that the path for each of us will be our own. The important thing to know is that a path does, in fact, exist, and that this path by definition leads to healing not only the body and the mind, but also, most important, the spirit.

There is do doubt in my mind that I have been guided by God, and that this work is divine work. I believe that our Father in heaven, the great force of love that permeates the universe (however, or whatever, you may call the Great Creator), definitely wants all of us to grow spiritually from our challenges, not just mask them with drugs that can never lead anyone to true happiness. I have no regrets about what has happened to me. I believe, in a funny way, that God gave me an extensive case of depression, short of alcoholism or drug addition, because He knew that I would be tenacious enough to find my way back and explain the broadest possible ramifications of what it means to heal body, mind, and spirit. For this, I feel incredibly humble. I pray all the time for the ability to comprehend His will because His will is so good, and so much wiser than my own.

Along the way, I have met plenty who doubted me. One woman I consulted said she thought I had written this book for myself—but she was wrong. It was very difficult for me to do the research necessary, to decide to tell my personal story, and to organize the complex medical material into a form I thought might be helpful to the average reader. I am the sort who would rather forget. And that is one comforting thing about pain in general—it is possible to put it all behind you.

But in my dedication to put this book together I have also had plenty of encouragement. Oftentimes I would be in the library and an unexpected resource would turn up, misfiled, placed there seemingly to wait for me. A woman who began to write to me on the Internet about similar health problems turned out to be a former medical editor, and she corrected my manuscript for free. Among the several agents who wanted to sell my book, I found one who not only has a degree in psychology, but who had been able to go off antidepressants himself by following a similar path. "I am reading this book not just as an agent, but to help me personally," he told me.

At every step I have been motivated by the memory of those who suffered fates similar to mine. A former copy editor who ended his life after desperately trying drug after drug and even allowing doctors to perform a lobotomy. Another playwright who has gone into deep isolation as his last means of maintaining emotional balance. A friend who lost one sister to suicide while another still battles manic depression. My beloved grandmother. Even the great-grandmother for whom I was named.

There is no doubt in my mind that I have left my life of depression behind forever, but I cannot forget others who are stilling rolling their own stones up a hill, only to be flattened time after time.

As I conclude my story, I am relieved to be nearing completion of this part of my life's work. "Let me leave an arrow in the woods for others, then let me slip away to the peace and silence of my writing," I ask God.

As I write these words, I am struggling with my most recent play, *Blue Rose, Blue Moon*. My orange cat, a constant companion during fourteen years of various minor literary endeavors, is scratching on my desk and drooling on my open journal. I do not approve of his behavior, but he looks too content to bother. My office window is open to the cool night air, and I look out into the darkness and wait for the words to come. It is the intimacy of this moment that is, for me, what success is all about.

Overcoming depression has given me the peace I need to be able to face myself with courage—the ultimate task of a writer, of one who must look into her own heart in order to make something new and beautiful. I offer this book—and share my story—hopeful that my journey will provide the inspiration and the guidance for others to find *their* peace and learn to make *their* lives new and beautiful.

I am blessed with a loving husband, a comfortable home, a garden that needs weeding but that bears many radiant flowers, and now a family much more at peace. Above all I now have what I always wanted—a free and easy spirit without drugs.

I know these blessings are meant for each of us, in our own way, in our own time, when we are ready to accept them.

Introduction

1. "Critical Issues in the Treatment of Affective Disorders," *Depression* 3 (1995), pp. 187-198.

2. "How Much Does Depression Cost Society?" *Harvard Mental Health Letter*, Oct. 1994.

3. "Critical Issues in the Treatment of Affective Disorders," p. 194.

4. Ibid., pp. 187-198.

5. Ibid.

6. Ronald F. Bourne, "Serotonin: The Neurotransmitter for the '90s," *Drug Topics*, October 10, 1994, p. 108.

7. "Lithium-Thyroid Interactive Hypothesis of Neuropsychological Deficits: A Review and Proposal," *Depression* 1 (1994/1995), pp. 241-251.

8. Peter C. Whybrow, "Sex Differences in Thyroid Axis Function: Relevance to Affective Disorder and Its Treatment," *Depression* 3 (1995), pp. 33-42.

9. "How Much Does Depression Cost Society?" p. 7.

10. Lawrence H. Price and George R. Heninger, "Lithium in the Treatment of Mood Disorders," *The New England Journal of Medicine*, Sept. 1, 1994, pp. 561-624.

11. Whybrow, "Sex Differences in Thyroid Axis Function," p. 36.

Question 1. Do you have a trusting relationship with a health care professional who is capable of directing the care of both your mind and your body?

1. "The Treatment of Depression: Prescribing Practices of Primary Care Physicians and Psychiatrists," *The Journal of Family Practice* 35, no. 6 (1992), p. 628.

2. Peter R. Breggins, *Toxic Psychiatry: Why Therapy, Empathy, and Love Must Replace the Drugs, Electroshock, and Biochemical Theories of the "New Psychiatry"* (New York: St. Martin's Press, 1991), p. 145.

Question 5. Do you have physical health problems that may be contributing to your depression?

1. Robert G. Robinson and Peter V. Rabins, *Aging and Clinical Practice: Depression and Coexisting Disease* (New York: Igaku-Shoin, 1989), p. 83.

2. Kathleen D. Friend and Carol L. Alter, "T4 Therapy in Depression and Hypothyroidism," *Depression* 2 (1994/1995), p. 280.

3. Irl Extein and Mark S. Gold, eds., *Medical Mimics of Psychiatric Disorders* (Washington, DC: American Psychiatric Press, 1986), p. 113.

4. Ibid., p. 15.

5. "Update on Mood Disorders," *The Harvard Mental Health Letter*, Dec. 1994.

6. "Schizophrenia and Bipolar Disorder May Be On a Continuum," *The Schizophrenia-Bipolar Interface: Current Research and Future Directions,* presented at the 1995 International Stanley Foundation Satellite Symposium, organized by Dr. E. Fuller Torrey, Stanley Foundation Web Site, http:/www/nami.org/about/stanley.htm.

Question 6. Are you on any form of medication that may be destabilizing your emotions?

1. William G. Crook, *The Yeast Connection and the Woman* (Jackson, TN: Professional Books, 1995), p. 604.

2. "The Risks of Excessive Drinking," The Coalition for Consumer Health and Safety Web Site: Hidden Hazards, http://www.essential.org./cchs.hh .html#Alcohol.

3. Jonathan Brostoff and Linda Gamlin, *The Complete Guide To Food Allergy and Intolerance* (New York: Crown Publishers, 1989), pp. 152-153.

4. "Alcoholism," *Mastering Food Allergies* 5, no. 1 (December-January 1990), p. 3.

Question 7. Do you have environmental allergies?

1. George J. Siegel, Bernard W. Agranoff, R. Wayne Albers, Perry B. Molinoff, eds., *Basic Neurochemistry: Molecular, Cellular, and Medical Aspects*, 4th ed. (New York: Raven Press, 1989), p. 256.

2. Carlton Fredericks, *Carlton Fredericks' New Low Blood Sugar and You* (New York: Putnam Publishing, 1985), p. 213.

3. "Significantly Increased Expression of T-Cell Activation Markers in Depression: Further Evidence for an Inflammatory Process During That Illness," *Progress in Neuro- Psychopharmacology and Biological Psychiatry* 17 (1993), pp. 241-253. Also, "Investigations of the Cellular Immunity During Depression and the Free Interval: Evidence for an Immune Activation in Affective Psychosis," *Progress in Neuro-Psychopharmacology and Biological Psychiatry* 17 (1993), pp. 713-727.

4. "Investigations of the Cellular Immunity During Depression and the Free Interval," p. 713.

5. "Emotions Impact on Allergies," *Mastering Food Allergies* 9, no. 4 (July-August 1994), p. 2.

6. Martha Sanbower, "Recognition and Treatment of Physical Factors in Psychotherapy Clients," *Journal of Orthomolecular Medicine* 5, no. 2, pp. 79-90.

Question 8. Are you exposed to chemicals that may contribute to your depression?

1. Bryan Ballantyne, Timothy Marrs, and Paul Turner, eds., *General and Applied Toxicology*, Vol. I (New York: Stockton Press, 1993), p. 195.

2. William H. Philpott and Dwight G. Kalita, *Brain Allergies: The Psychonutrient Connection* (New Canaan, CT: Keats Publishing, 1980), pp. 100-101.

3. William J. Rea, *Chemical Sensitivity: Principles and Mechanisms* (Boca Raton, FL: Lewis Publishers, 1992), p. 487.

4. Ibid., p. 482.

5. Ibid., p. 30.

6. Ibid., p. 32.

7. Linus Pauling, *How To Live Longer and Feel Better* (New York: Avon Books, 1987), p. 104.

8. "The Detoxification Supplementation Therapy: A Shortcut to the Recovery of the Mental and Degenerative Diseases," *The Journal of Orthomolecular Medicine* 9, no. 4 (fourth quarter, 1980).

9. Sherry Rogers, *The E.I. Syndrome* (Syracuse, NY: Prestige Publishers, 1986), pp. 128-132.

10. "Health Risks of the 21 Most Common Chemicals Found in 31 Fragrance Products by a 1991 E.P.A. Study," immunerequest@weber .ucsd.edu.

11. Adrienne Buffaloe, "Chemical Sensitivity: It's a Serious Problem More Often Than You Think," http://www.accessnewage.com/articles/ health/chemical.htm.

Question 9. Do you have toxic metals in your body?

1. Hal A. Huggins, *It's All in Your Head* (Garden City Park, NY: Avery Publishing Group, 1993); H. Richard Casdorph and Morton Walker, *Toxic Metal Syndrome: How Metal Poisonings Can Affect Your Brain* (Garden City Park, NY: Avery Publishing, 1995); Robin B. Kanarek and Robin Marks-Kaufman, *Nutrition and Behavior* (New York: Van Nostrand Reinhold, 1991), pp. 102-126.

2. Huggins, *It's All in Your Head,* p. 128.

3. Philpott and Kalita, *Brain Allergies,* p. 107.

4. Sam Ziff and Michael F. Ziff, *Dentistry Without Mercury* (Orlando, FL: Bio-Probe Inc., 1993), p. 15.

5. Alfred V. Zamm, "Removal of Dental Mercury: Often an Effective Treatment for the Very Sensitive Patient," *The Journal of Orthomolecular Medicine* 5, no. 3 (third quarter 1990), pp. 138-139.

Question 10. Do you have digestive disorders?

1. Sandra Blakeslee, "Brain in the Gut Makes Gut Reactions," *The New York Times,* Jan. 23, 1996.

2. Lloyd Rosenvold, *Can A Gluten-Free Diet Help* (New Canaan, CT: Keats Publishing, 1992), p. 20.

3. Carl C. Pfeiffer, *Nutrition and Mental Illness* (Rochester, VT: Healing Arts Press, 1987), p. 31.

4. Steven Rochlitz, *Allergies and Candida With the Physicist's Rapid Solution* (New York: Human Ecology Balancing Sciences, 1989), p. 80.

5. "Leaky Gut: A Common Problem with Food Allergies," *Mastering Food Allergies* 7, no. 5 (Sept.-Oct. 1993), pp. 1-3.

6. Harold Edwin Himwich, *Biochemistry, Schizophrenia and Affective Illnesses* (Baltimore: Williams and Wilkins, 1971), p. 351.

7. "Plasma Concentrations of Gamma-Aminobutyric Acid (GABA) and Mood Disorders: A Blood Test for Manic Depressive Disease?" *Clinical Chemistry* 40, no. 2 (1994), pp. 296-302.

8. "Relationship Between Irritable Bowel Syndrome and Double Depression," *Depression* 3 (1996), pp. 303-306.

Question 11. Do you metabolize carbohydrates normally?

1. Himwich, *Biochemistry, Schizophrenias and Affective Illnesses*, pp. 351-353.

2. Ibid., p. 351.

3. Frederick J. Vagnini, "What's Wrong With Pasta," *Cardiovascular Newsletter*, http://www.holistic.com/essays/insuln01.html.

4. Richard J. Wurtman and Judith J. Wurtman, "Carbohydrates and Depression," *Scientific American*, Jan. 1989, pp. 68-75.

5. Ibid., p. 68.

6. Phyllis Avery, *Stop Your Indigestion: Causes, Remedies, Recipes* (Vista, CA: Hygeia Publishing Co., 1993), pp. 16-19.

Question 12. Are your amino acid levels adequate and balanced?

1. Robert Erdman, *The Amino Revolution* (New York: Simon and Schuster, 1987), p. 90.

2. "Plasma Tryptophan Levels and Plasma Tryptophan/Neutral Amino Acids Ratio in Patients with Mood Disorder, Patients with Obsessive-Compulsive Disorder, and Normal Subjects," *Psychiatry Research* 44, no. 2 (1992), pp. 85-91.

3. "Plasma Ratios of Tryptophan and Tyrosine to other Large Neutral Amino Acids in Manic Depressive Patients," *Journal of Psychiatry & Neurology* 46, no. 3 (1992) pp. 711-20.

4. "Plasma Concentrations of Gamma-Aminobutyric Acid (GABA) and Mood Disorders: A Blood Test for Manic Depressive Disease?" *Clinical Chemistry* 40, no. 2 (1994), pp. 296-302.

5. "CSF 5-HIAA Predicts Suicide Risk After Attempted Suicide," *Suicide & Life-Threatening Behavior* 24, no. 1 (1994), pp. 1-9.

6. Priscilla Slagle, *The Way Up From Down* (New York: St. Martin's Paperbacks, 1992), p. 301.

7. Philpott and Kalita, *Brain Allergies*, p. 60.

8. Smart Basics, Inc., "Smart Basics Glossary: Amino Acids," http://www/vrcreations.com/index.html, 1996.

9. Slagle, *The Way Up From Down*, pp. 304-06.

10. Erdman, *The Amino Acid Revolution*, pp. 114-15.

11. Arnold Fox and Barry Fox, *DLPA To End Chronic Pain and Depression* (New York: Pocket Books, 1985).

Question 13. Do you have food allergies or food sensitivities?

1. John Bartlett, ed., *Familiar Quotations* (Boston: Little Brown and Co., 1882), p. 114.

2. Jonathan Brostoff and Stephen J. Challacombe, *Food Allergy and Intolerance* (London: Bailliere Tindall, 1987), p. 688.

3. John N. Hathcock, *Nutritional Toxicology*, Vol. I (New York: Academic Press, 1982), p. 490.

4. John N. Hathcock, *Nutritional Toxicology*, Vol. II (Orlando, FL: Academic Press, 1987), p. 177.

5. Ibid., p. 174.

6. Ibid., p. 186.

7. Ibid., p. 190.

8. J.O. Hunter, "Food Allergy or Enterometabolic Disorder?" *Lancet* 338 (Aug. 1991), pp. 495-496.

9. Hathcock, *Nutritional Toxicology*, Vol. II, p. 193.

10. Breggins, *Toxic Psychiatry*, p. 160.

11. T.J. David, *Food and Food Additive Intolerance In Children* (London: Blackwell Scientific Publications, 1993), p. 427.

12. Lynn Lawson, *Staying Well in a Toxic World* (Chicago: Noble Press, 1993), p. 267.

13. "Cerebral Allergies," *Mastering Food Allergies* 3, no. 5 (May 1988).

14. Hathcock, *Nutritional Toxicology*, Vol. II, pp. 180-82.

15. Rogers, *The E.I. Syndrome*, p. 225.

16. Harvey M. Ross, *Fighting Depression* (New Canaan, CT: Keats Publishing, 1992), p. 116.

17. Carl C. Pfeiffer, *Mental and Elemental Nutrients* (New Canaan, CT: Keats Publishing, 1975), p. 369.

18. "Leaky Gut: A Common Problem with Food Allergies," p. 2.

19. Brostoff and Challacombe, *Food Allergy and Intolerance*, p. 873.

20. Ibid.

21. Ibid.

Question 14. Should you try various home tests to identify your food sensitivities?

1. Rogers, *The E.I. Syndrome*, p. 224.

2. Ibid., p. 228.

3. Arthur F. Coca, *The Pulse Test: Easy Allergy Detection* (New York: Arco Publishing, 1982), p. 143.

Question 15. Do you have a yeast infection?

1. Malcolm D. Richardson and David W. Warnock, *Fungal Infection: Diagnosis and Management* (Boston: Blackwell Scientific Publications, 1993), p. 103.

2. F.C. Odds, *Candida and Candidosis* (Baltimore: University Park Press, 1979), p. 1.

3. Martha Sanbower, "Manic Depression: An Alternate Treatment," *Journal of Orthomolecular Medicine* 2, no. 3, p. 155.

4. Gary Null, *No More Allergies* (New York: Villard Books, 1992), p. 59.

5. Rochlitz, *Allergies and Candida with the Physicist's Rapid Solution,* p. 80.

6. Odds, *Candida and Candidosis,* p. 77.

7. Ibid., p. 195.

Question 16. Is your thyroid functioning normally?

1. Richard A. Depue, *The Psychobiology of the Depressive Disorders* (New York: Academic Press, 1979), p. 427.

2. Extein and Gold, *Medical Mimics of Psychiatric Disorders,* p. 103.

3. "Hypothyroidism: A Missed Diagnosis," *The Felix Letter, A Commentary on Nutrition* 42 (1988), p. 1. Also, Crook, *The Yeast Connection and the Woman,* pp. 547-55.

Question 17. Are you hypoglycemic?

1. D. Andreani, P.J. Lefebvre, V. Marks, and G. Tamburrano, eds., *Recent Advances in Hypoglycemia* (New York: Raven Press, 1992), p. 32.

2. "Hypoglycemia: The Modern Holistic Approach: A Talk By Mark S. Smith," *Hypoglycemia Association Bulletin* 185 (n.d.).

3. Fred D. Hofeldt, *Preventing Reactive Hypoglycemia* (St. Louis: Warren H. Green, Inc., 1983), pp. 13, 116.

4. Martin L. Bud, *Low Blood Sugar (Hypoglycemia): The 20th-Century Epidemic?* (New York: Sterling Publishing Co., 1983, p. 13.

5. Rochlitz, *Allergies and Candida With the Physicist's Rapid Solution*, p. 35.

6. Ibid., p. 70.

7. Kanarek and Marks-Kaufman, *Nutrition and Behavior*, p. 179.

8. Brostoff and Gamlin, *The Complete Guide To Food Allergy and Intolerance*, p. 149.

9. Pfeiffer, *Mental and Elemental Nutrients*, p. 383.

10. Hofeldt, *Preventing Reactive Hypoglycemia*, p. 116.

11. Lawson, *Staying Well in a Toxic World*, p. 307.

12. Carlton Fredericks, *Carlton Fredericks' New Low Blood Sugar and You* (New York: Putnam Publishing, 1985), pp. 211, 214.

Question 18. Do you need to detoxify your body?

1. "The Detoxification Supplementation Therapy: A Shortcut to the Recovery of the Mental and Degenerative Diseases"; and Jeffrey S. Bland, "A Functional Approach to Mental Illness: A New Paradigm for Managing Brain Biochemical Disturbances," *Townsend Letter for Doctors*, Dec. 1994, pp. 1335-41.

2. Bland, "A Functional Approach to Mental Illness," p. 1336.

3. "Detoxification," *Nutritional Pearls* 24 (Marietta, GA: Metagenics, n.d.).

4. "Biodetoxification," *Mastering Food Allergies* 35 (1989), p. 6.

5. "One Reason You May Fail To Get Well—Even On Best Diet," *Mastering Food Allergies* 42 (1990), p. 2.

Question 19. Do you have high levels of cortisol in your body?

1. Cuthbert L. Cope, *Adrenal Steroids and Disease*, 2d ed. (Philadelphia: J.B. Lippincott Co., 1972), p. 151; Lorraine Dennestein and Ian Fraser, eds., *Hormones and Behavior* (New York: Excerpta Medica, 1986), p. 485; and Erwin K. Koranyi, ed., *Physical Illness in the Psychiatric Patient* (Springfield, IL: Charles C. Thomas Publisher, 1982), p. 53.

2. Cope, *Adrenal Steroids and Disease*, p. 148.

3. F. John Service, *Hypoglycemic Disorders* (Boston: G.K. Hall Medical Publishers, 1983), p. 14.

4. Cope, *Adrenal Steroids and Disease*, pp. 559, 313-314.

5. Jay Schulkin, ed., *Hormonally Induced Changes in Mind and Brain* (San Diego: Academic Press, 1993), p. 270; and Robinson and Rabins, *Aging and Clinical Practice: Depression and Coexisting Disease*, pp. 85, 97.

6. Blair Justice, *Who Gets Sick?* (New York: Tarcher, 1988), p. 102.

7. G.E.W. Wolstenholme and Ruth Porter, *The Human Adrenal Cortex: Its Function Throughout Life* (Boston: Little, Brown and Co., 1967), p. 98.

8. "Steroid Hormones, Clinical Correlates," Diagnos-Techs Inc. Seminar in Atlanta, Ga., October 1995.

9. Pfeiffer, *Mental and Elemental Nutrients*, p. 393.

10. "Steroid Hormones, Clinical Correlates," Diagnos-Techs Inc. Seminar.

11. Ibid. Also, Carla Hannaford, *Smart Moves: Why Learning Is Not All In Your Head* (Arlington, VA: Great Ocean Publishers, 1995), p. 162.

12. Robinson and Rabins, *Aging and Clinical Practice*, p. 85.

13. George J. Siegel, et al, *Basic Neurochemistry*, p. 884.

14. Kenneth B. Matheny and Richard J. Riordan, *Stress and Strategies for Lifestyle Management* (Atlanta: Georgia State University Business Press, 1992), p. 12.

15. Dina Nerozzi, Frederick K. Goodwin, and Erminio Costa, eds., *Hypothalamic Dysfunction in Neuropsychiatric Disorders* (New York: Raven Press, 1987), pp. 165-177.

Question 20. Do you need to lower your stress level?

1. Schulkin, *Hormonally Induced Changes In Mind and Brain*, p. 254.

2. M.J.A.J.M. Hoes, "Stress and Strain: Their Definition, Psychobiology, and Relationship to Psychosomatic Medicine," *The Journal Of Orthomolecular Medicine* 1, no. 1 (first quarter 1986), p. 30.

3. Koranyi, *Physical Illness in the Psychiatric Patient*, p. 54.

4. Ibid.

5. "Steroid Hormones, Clinical Correlates," Diagnos-Techs Inc. Seminar.

6. Doc Lew Childre, *Freeze Frame: Fast Action Stress Relief* (Boulder Creek, CA: Planetary Publications, 1995), pp. 48-49.

Question 21. Do you have an adequate stress management program?

1. Cope, *Adrenal Steroids and Disease*, p. 151; Dennestein and Fraser, *Hormones and Behavior*, p. 485; and Koranyi, *Physical Illness in the Psychiatric Patient*, p. 53.

Question 23. Do you need to adopt dietary and lifestyle changes to stabilize your blood sugar?

1. Nancy Appleton, *Lick the Sugar Habit* (Garden City Park, NY: Avery Publishing Group, 1988), pp. 12-20.

2. Philpott and Kalita, *Brain Allergies*, pp. 120-21.

3. Pauling, *How To Live Longer and Feel Better,* p. 289.

4. Dorothy R. Schultz, "The Information Super Highway," *Hypoglycemia Association Bulletin* 197 (Oct.-Dec. 1995).

5. "Nicotine Addiction and Schizophrenia," *The Journal of Orthomolecular Medicine* 5, no. 3 (1990), p. 181.

6. Gary Null, *Nutrition and the Mind* (New York: Four Walls Eight Windows, 1995), p. 44.

7. Marge Smith, "Feeding Yourself In All Sorts of Circumstances," *Hypoglycemia Association Bulletin* 164 (Sept. 1995).

8. "An Adequate Breakfast," *Hypoglycemia Association Bulletin* 95 (July-Aug. 1977).

9. Justice, *Who Gets Sick?* p. 107.

10. "Steroid Hormones, Clinical Correlates," Diagnos-Techs Inc. Seminar.

11. Fredericks, *Carlton Fredericks' New Low Blood Sugar and You,* pp. 218-219.

12. "Steroid Hormones, Clinical Correlates," Diagnos-Techs Inc. Seminar.

13. Ibid.

Question 25. Are you willing to give up the 10 kinds of foods most likely to aggravate depression?

1. Michael F. Jacobson, Lisa Y. Lefferts, and Anne Witte Garland, *Safe Food: Eating Wisely in a Risky World* (New York: Berkeley Books, 1993), p. 153.

2. Health ResponseAbility Systems, Inc., "Preventing Food-Borne Illness," HRS Health Knowledge Center, AOL Health and Medical Forum (America Online), 1995.

3. Bud, *Low Blood Sugar (Hypoglycemia),* p. 66.

4. Brostoff and Gamlin, *The Complete Guide to Food Allergy and Intolerance,* p. 193.

5. Richard J. Wurtman and Judith J. Wurtman, *Nutrition and the Brain,* Vol. 4 (New York: Raven Press, 1979), pp. 161, 191-93.

6. Huggins, *It's All in Your Head,* p. 154.

7. Brian MacMahon and Takashi Sugimura, *Banbury Report, Coffee and Health* (Cold Spring Harbor, NY: Cold Spring Harbor Laboratory, 1984), p. 49.

8. Hathcock, *Nutritional Toxicology,* Vol. I, p. 480.

9. Slagle, *The Way Up From Down,* p. 143.

10. Bud, *Low Blood Sugar (Hypoglycemia),* p. 67.

11. Huggins, *It's All in Your Head,* p. 154.

12. Doris J. Rapp, *Is This Your Child: Discovering and Treating Unrecognized Allergies* (New York: William Morrow and Co., 1991), p. 361.

13. Bud, *Low Blood Sugar (Hypoglycemia),* p. 67.

Question 26. Are you willing to eat more of the 10 kinds of foods most likely to improve depression?

1. Herman Aihara, *Acid & Alkaline* (Oroville, CA: George Ohsawa Macrobiotic Foundation, 1986), p. 96.

2. John Parks Trowbridge and Morton Walker, *The Yeast Syndrome* (New York: Bantam Books, 1986), p. 96.

3. Marshall Mandell and Lynne Waller Scanlon, *Dr. Mandell's Five Day Allergy Relief System* (New York: Pocket Books, 1979), p. 182.

4. Justice, *Who Gets Sick?* p. 108.

5. Frances Moore Lappe, *Diet For a Small Planet* (New York: Ballantine Books, 1982), p. 159.

6. Null, *Nutrition and the Mind*, p. 156

7. Ibid., p. 199.

8. Udo Erasmus, *Fats That Heal, Fats That Kill* (Burnaby, B.C.: Alive Books, 1993), p. 21.

9. "Steroid Hormones, Clinical Correlates," Diagnos-Techs Inc. Seminar.

10. Erasmus, *Fats That Heal, Fats That Kill*, p. 360.

11. Bland, "A Functional Approach to Mental Illness," p. 1336.

12. Richard A. Kunin, *Meganutrition* (New York: New American Library, 1981), pp. 189, 190.

13. Erasmus, *Fats That Heal, Fats That Kill*, p. 360.

14. Mark Bricklin, *Prevention Magazine's Nutrition Advisor* (Emmaus, PA: Rodale Press, 1993), p. 573.

15. Vicki Glassburn, *Who Killed Candida?* (Brushton, NY: TEACH Services Inc., 1991), p. 148.

16. Jean Carper, *Food—Your Miracle Medicine* (New York: HarperCollins, 1993), p. 291.

17. Bryan Ballantyne, Timothy Marrs, and Paul Turner, eds., *General and Applied Toxicology*, Vol. 2 (New York: Stockton Press, 1993), p. 1330.

18. Hathcock, *Nutritional Toxicology*, Vol. II, p. 282.

19. Rudolph Ballentine, *Diet and Nutrition* (Honesdale, PA: Himalayan International Institute, 1978), p. 492.

Question 28. Are you willing to give up antibiotics and other additives in your food?

1. Hathcock, *Nutritional Toxicology*, Vol. I, p. 462.

2. Lewis D. Stegink and L.J. Filer, Jr., eds., *Aspartame* (New York: Marcel Dekker Inc., 1984), pp. 350, 359.

3. Ballantyne, Marrs, and Turner, *General and Applied Toxicology*, Vol. 1, p. 482.

4. Ibid.

5. Klara Miller, *Toxicological Aspects of Food* (London: Elsevier Applied Science, 1987), p. 70.

6. Glassburn, *Who Killed Candida?* p. 34.

7. Jacobson, Lefferts, and Garland, *Safe Food*, p. 91.

8. Pfeiffer, *Mental and Elemental Nutrients*, p. 37.

9. Miller, *Toxicological Aspects of Food*, p. 360.

10. Kanarek and Marks-Kaufman, *Nutrition and Behavior*, p. 131.

11. Jacobson, Lefferts, and Garland, *Safe Food*, p. 150.

12. Kanarek and Marks-Kaufman, *Nutrition and Behavior*, p. 3.

13. Lawson, *Staying Well in a Toxic World*, p. 253.

14. Susan C. Smolinske, *Handbook of Food, Drug, and Cosmetic Excipients* (Boca Raton, FL: CRC Press, 1992), p. 236.

15. George R. Schwartz, *In Bad Taste: The MSG Syndrome* (Santa Fe, NM: Health Press, 1988).

16. Leon Chaitow, *Thorson's Guide to Amino Acids* (London: Thorsons, 1991), p. 95.

17. Glassburn, *Who Killed Candida?* p. 116.

18. Hathcock, *Nutritional Toxicology, Vol. I*, p. 475.

19. Miller, *Toxicological Aspects of food*, p. 360.

20. Smolinske, *Handbook of Food, Drug, and Cosmetic Excipients*; D.M. Conning and A.B.G. Lansdown, *Toxic Hazards in Food* (New York: Raven Press, 1983), pp. 58-61.

Question 29. Do you need to rotate your diet?

1. Rochlitz, *Allergies and Candida With the Physicist's Rapid Solution*, p. 42.

2. Mandell, *Dr. Mandell's Five-Day Allergy Relief System*, p. 12.

3. Rochlitz, *Allergies and Candida With the Physicist's Rapid Solution*, pp. 43, 56.

4. Claude A. Frazier, *Coping with Food Allergy* (New York: New York Times Book Co., 1974), pp. 51-52.

5. Natalie Golos and Frances Golos Golbitz, *If This Is Tuesday, It Must Be Chicken* (New Canaan, CT: Keats Publishing, 1983).

6. "The Rotary Diversified Diet," *Mastering Food Allergies* 1, no. 6 (June 1986), p. 2.

Question 30. Do you drink enough water and eat enough salt?

1. Hannaford, *Smart Moves*, p. 91.

2. F. Batmanghelidj, *Your Body's Many Cries For Water* (Falls Church, VA: Global Health Solutions, 1992), pp. 91, 26.

3. Ibid., pp. 51-59.

4. Glassburn, *Who Killed Candida?* p. 77.

5. Mitchell Sudy, ed., *Personal Trainer Manual* (San Diego, CA: American Council on Exercise, 1991), p. 129.

6. "U.S. Tap Water Is Dirty," Associated Press Report, June 1, 1995.

7. Jacobson, Lefferts, and Garland, *Safe Food*, p. 130; "How Pure Is Your Water?" *Delicious* 11, no. 4 (April 1995), pp. 38-39.

8. Glassburn, *Who Killed Candida?* p. 76.

9. John Tintera, "Adrenal Dysfunction," *Hypoglycemia Association Bulletin* 96 (n.d.).

10. Smart Basics, Inc., "Smart Basics Minerals Glossary," http://www.smartbasic.com/glos.minerals.dir.html, 1996.

11. Tintera, "Adrenal Dysfunction."

Question 31. Does your body properly absorb vitamins?

1. Philpott and Kalita, *Brain Allergies*, p. 59.

2. Richard T. Cotton, ed., *Aerobics Instructor Manual* (San Diego, CA: American Council on Exercise, 1993), pp. 130-31.

3. Ibid., p. 131.

4. "Clinging to Their Bottles," *Taste Matters, American Council on Exercise* 3, no. 1 (Jan.-Feb. 1997), p. 2.

Question 32. Do you have symptoms that might indicate a deficiency of B vitamins?

1. Philpott and Kalita, *Brain Allergies*, p. 66.

2. H.L. Newbold, *Dr. Newbold's Nutrition for Your Nerves* (New Canaan, CT: Keats Publishing, 1993), pp. 159, 162.

3. Pauling, *How to Live Longer and Feel Better*, p. 340.

4. Newbold, *Dr. Newbold's Nutrition for Your Nerves*, p. 299.

Question 33. Are you deficient in Vitamin C?

1. Pauling, *How to Feel Better and Live Longer*, p. 308; Newbold, *Dr. Newbold's Nutrition for Your Nerves*, p. 215.

Question 34. Do you absorb a balanced ratio of calcium and magnesium?

1. "Seventy-Two Percent of Americans Are Magnesium-Deficient," *Better Nutrition for Today's Living* 57 (March 1995), p. 34.

2. Slagle, *The Way Up From Down*, p. 304.

Question 35. Do you get enough exercise?

1. Siegfried Weyerer and Brigitte Kupfer, "Physical Exercise and Psychological Health," *Sports Medicine* 17, no. 2, pp. 108-116.

2. "Mood Alteration with Yoga and Swimming: Aerobic Exercise May Not Be Necessary," *Perceptual Motor Skills* 75 (1992), pp. 1331-1343.

3. La Forge, Ralph, *Mind-Body Fitness: Encouraging Prospects for Primary and Secondary Prevention Programs* (San Diego: San Diego Cardiac Center Medical Group, 1996).

4. Moshe Feldenkrais, *Awareness Through Movement* (New York: Harper & Row, 1977), p. 31.

5. Ibid., p. 39.

6. Weyerer and Kupfer, "Physical Exercise and Psychological Health," pp. 108-116.

Question 36. Should you learn new techniques to balance your mind and body?

1. Jan Irving, "PACE Research Keeps Pace with First-Year Nursing Students," *Brain Gym Journal* 10, no. 1 (April 1996), pp. 1-2.

Question 37. Do you think positively to create the reality you want?

1. Matthew 18:29.

2. Martin E.P. Seligman, *Learned Optimism* (New York: Alfred A. Knopf, 1991), p. 70.

3. Matheny and Riordan, *Stress and Strategies for Lifestyle Management*, p. 12.

4. Ibid., p. 13.

Question 38. Have you learned what your depression has to teach you?

1. Viktor E. Frankl, *Man's Search for Meaning* (New York: Touchstone Books, 1984), p. 113.

"An Adequate Breakfast." *Hypoglycemia Association Bulletin* 95 (July-Aug. 1977).

Aihara, Herman. *Acid & Alkaline.* Oroville, CA: George Ohsawa Macrobiotic Foundation, 1986.

"Alcoholism." *Mastering Food Allergies* 5, no. 1 (Dec.-Jan. 1990).

"Americans Doing Better at Eating Their Veggies." Medical Tribune News Service, Dec. 15, 1995.

Andreani, D., P.J. Lefebvre, V. Marks, and G. Tamburrano, eds. *Recent Advances in Hypoglycemia.* New York: Raven Press, 1992.

Appleton, Nancy. *Lick the Sugar Habit.* Garden City Park, NY: Avery Publishing Group, 1988.

Arky, Ronald, ed. *Physicians' Desk Reference.* Montvale, NJ: Medical Economics Co., 1997.

Asaad, Ghazi. *Understanding Mental Disorders Due to Medical Conditions or Substance Abuse.* New York: Brunner/Mazel, 1995.

Avery, Phyllis. *Stop Your Indigestion: Causes, Remedies, Recipes.* Vista, CA: Hygeia Publishing Co., 1993.

Ballantyne, Bryan, Timothy Marrs, and Paul Turner, eds. *General and Applied Toxicology,* Vols. 1 and 2. New York: Stockton Press, 1993.

Ballentine, Rudolph. *Diet and Nutrition.* Honesdale, PA: Himalayan International Institute, 1978.

Bartlett, John, ed. *Familiar Quotations.* Boston: Little Brown and Co., 1882.

Batmanghelidj, F. *Your Body's Many Cries For Water.* Falls Church, VA: Global Health Solutions, 1992.

Baumel, Syd. *Dealing with Depression Naturally.* New Canaan, CT: Keats Publishing, 1995.

Becker, Kenneth L., ed., *Principles and Practice of Endocrinology and Metabolism,* 2d ed. Philadelphia: J.B. Lippincott & Co., 1995.

"A Beneficial Effect of Calcium Intake on Mood." *Journal of Orthomolecular Medicine* 9, no. 4, (fourth quarter 1994).

"Biodetoxification." *Mastering Food Allergies* 35 (1989).

Blakeslee, Sandra. "Brain in the Gut Makes Gut Reactions." *The New York Times,* Jan. 23, 1996.

Bland, Jeffrey S. "A Functional Approach to Mental Illness: A New Paradigm for Managing Brain Biochemical Disturbances." *Townsend Letter For Doctors*, Dec. 1994.

Bourne, Ronald F. "Serotonin: The Neurotransmitter for the '90s." *Drug Topics*, Oct. 10, 1994.

Breggins, Peter R. *Toxic Psychiatry: Why Therapy, Empathy, and Love Must Replace the Drugs, Electroshock, and Biochemical Theories of the "New Psychiatry."* New York: St. Martin's Press, 1991.

Brennan, Barbara Ann. *Hands of Light*. New York: Bantam Books, 1988.

Breneman, James C. *Basics of Food Allergy*. Springfield, IL: Charles C. Thomas Publisher, 1984.

Bricklin, Mark. *Prevention Magazine's Nutrition Advisor*. Emmaus, PA: Rodale Press, 1993.

Brostoff, Jonathan, and Linda Gamlin. *The Complete Guide To Food Allergy and Intolerance.* New York: Crown Publishers, 1989.

Brostoff, Jonathan, and Stephen J. Challacombe. *Food Allergy and Intolerance*. London: Bailliere Tindall, 1987.

Bud, Martin L. *Low Blood Sugar (Hypoglycemia): The 20th-Century Epidemic?* New York: Sterling Publishing Co., 1983.

Buffaloe, Adrienne. "Chemical Sensitivity: It's a More Serious Problem More Often Than You Think." http://www/accessnewage.com/articles/health/chemical.htm.

Calbom, Cherie, and Maureen Keane. *Juicing for Life*. Garden City Park, NY: Avery Publishing Group, 1992.

Carper, Jean. *Food—Your Miracle Medicine*. New York: HarperCollins, 1993.

Casdorph, H. Richard, and Morton Walker. *Toxic Metal Syndrome: How Metal Poisonings Can Affect Your Brain*. Garden City Park, NY: Avery Publishing, 1995.

"Cerebral Allergies," *Mastering Food Allergies* 3, no. 5 (May 1988).

Chaitow, Leon. *Thorson's Guide to Amino Acids*. London: Thorsons, 1991.

Childre, Doc Lew. *Freeze Frame: Fast Action Stress Relief.* Boulder Creek, CA: Planetary Publications, 1995.

Clinical Chemistry 40, no. 2 (1994), pp. 296-302.

"Clinging To Their Bottles." *Taste Matters, American Council on Exercise* 3, no. 1 (Jan.-Feb. 1997).

Coca, Arthur F. *The Pulse Test: Easy Allergy Detection*. New York: Arco Publishing, 1982.

Conning, D.M., and A.B.G. Lansdown. *Toxic Hazards in Food*. New York: Raven Press, 1983.

Cope, Cuthbert L. *Adrenal Steroids and Disease*, 2d ed. Philadelphia: J.B. Lippincott Co., 1972.

Cotton, Richard T., ed. *Aerobics Instructor Manual*. San Diego, CA: American Council on Exercise, 1993.

"Critical Issues in the Treatment of Affective Disorders." *Depression* 3 (1995).

Crook, William G. *The Yeast Connection*. Jackson, TN: Professional Books, 1984.

————. *The Yeast Connection and the Woman*. Jackson, TN: Professional Books, 1995.

"CSF 5-HIAA Predicts Suicide Risk After Attempted Suicide." *Suicide & Life-Threatening Behavior* 24, no. 1 (1994).

David, T.J. *Food and Food Additive Intolerance In Children*. London: Blackwell Scientific Publications, 1993.

Dennestein, Lorraine, and Ian Fraser, eds. *Hormones and Behavior*. New York: Excerpta Medica, 1986.

Dennison, Paul, and Gail Dennison. *Brain Gym Teachers' Edition, Revised*. Ventura, CA: Edu-Kinesthetics Inc., 1989.

Depue, Richard A. *The Psychobiology of the Depressive Disorders*. New York: Academic Press, 1979.

"Detoxification." *Nutritional Pearls* 24. Marietta, GA: Metagenics, n.d.

"The Detoxification Supplementation Therapy: A Shortcut to the Recovery of the Mental and Degenerative Diseases." *The Journal of Orthomolecular Medicine* 9, no. 4 (fourth quarter, 1980).

Dickey, Thomas, ed. *The Wellness Encyclopedia of Food and Nutrition*. New York: Health Letter Associates, 1992).

Duffy, William. *Sugar Blues*. New York: Warner Books, 1975.

Eliot, T.S. *The Four Quartets*. London: Faber and Faber, 1976.

"Emotions Impact on Allergies." *Mastering Food Allergies* 9, no. 4 (July-Aug. 1994).

Erasmus, Udo. *Fats That Heal, Fats That Kill*. Burnaby, B.C.: Alive Books, 1993.

Erdman, Robert. *The Amino Revolution*. New York: Simon and Schuster, 1987.

Extein, Irl, and Mark S. Gold, eds. *Medical Mimics of Psychiatric Disorders*. Washington, DC: American Psychiatric Press, 1986.

Feldenkrais, Moshe. *Awareness Through Movement*. New York: Harper & Row, 1977.

Fox, Arnold, and Barry Fox. *DLPA To End Chronic Pain and Depression*. New York: Pocket Books, 1985.

Frankl, Viktor E. *Man's Search for Meaning*. New York: Touchstone Books, 1984.

Frazier, Claude A. *Coping with Food Allergy*. New York: New York Times Book Co., 1974.

Fredericks, Carlton. *Carlton Fredericks' New Low Blood Sugar and You*. New York: Putnam Publishing, 1985.

Friend, Kathleen D., and Carol L. Alter. "T4 Therapy in Depression and Hypothyroidism." *Depression* 2 (1994/1995).

Gerber, Richard. *Vibrational Medicine: New Choices for Healing Ourselves*. Sante Fe, NM: Bear & Co., 1988.

Glassburn, Vicki. *Who Killed Candida?* Brushton, NY: TEACH Services Inc., 1991.

Golos, Natalie, and Frances Golos Golbitz. *If This Is Tuesday, It Must Be Chicken*. New Canaan, CT: Keats Publishing, 1983.

Grimmett, Charlene. *Beat the Yeast Cookbook*. Aurora, IL: Charlene Grimmett, 1985.

Hannaford, Carla. *Smart Moves: Why Learning Is Not All In Your Head*. Arlington, VA: Great Ocean Publishers, 1995.

Hathcock, John N. *Nutritional Toxicology*, Vol. I. New York: Academic Press, 1982.

———. *Nutritional Toxicology*, Vol. II. Orlando, FL: Academic Press, 1987.

Hawkins, David R. *Power Vs. Force: An Anatomy of Consciousness*. Sedona, AZ: Veritas Publishing, 1995.

Health ResponseAbility Systems, Inc., "Preventing Food-Borne Illness," HRS Health Knowledge Center, AOL Health and Medical Forum (America Online), 1995.

"Health Risks of the 21 Most Common Chemicals Found in 31 Fragrance Products by a 1991 E.P.A. Study," immune-request@weber.ucsd.edu.

Himwich, Harold Edwin. *Biochemistry, Schizophrenia and Affective Illnesses*. Baltimore: Williams and Wilkins, 1971.

Hofeldt, Fred D. *Preventing Reactive Hypoglycemia*. St. Louis: Warren H. Green, Inc., 1983.

Hoes, M.J.A.J.M. "Stress and Strain: Their Definition, Psychobiology, and Relationship to Psychosomatic Medicine." *The Journal of Orthomolecular Medicine* 1, no. 1 (first quarter 1986).

"How Much Does Depression Cost Society?" *Harvard Mental Health Letter*, Oct. 1994.

"How Pure Is your Water?" *Delicious* 11, no. 4 (April 1995).

Huggins, Hal A. *It's All in Your Head.* Garden City Park, NY: Avery Publishing Group, 1993.

Hunter, J.O. "Food Allergy or Enterometabolic Disorder?" *Lancet* 338 (Aug. 1991).

"Hypoglycemia, The Modern Holistic Approach: A Talk By Mark S. Smith." *Hypoglycemia Association Bulletin* 185 (n.d.).

"Hypothyroidism: A Missed Diagnosis." *The Felix Letter: A Commentary on Nutrition* 42 (1988).

"Investigations of the Cellular Immunity During Depression and the Free Interval: Evidence for an Immune Activation in Affective Psychosis." *Progress in Neuro-Psychopharmacology and Biological Psychiatry* 17 (1993).

Irving, Jan. "PACE Research Keeps Pace with First-Year Nursing Students." *Brain Gym Journal* 10, no. 1 (April 1996).

Jacobson, Michael F. *Eater's Digest: The Consumer's Factbook of Food Additives.* Garden City, NY: Doubleday & Co., 1972.

Jacobson, Michael F., Lisa Y. Lefferts, and Anne Witte Garland. *Safe Food: Eating Wisely in a Risky World.* New York: Berkeley Books, 1993.

Jones, Marjorie Hurt. *The Allergy Self-Help Cookbook.* Emmaus, PA: Rodale Press, 1984.

Justice, Blair. *Who Gets Sick?* New York: Tarcher, 1988.

Kanarek, Robin B., and Robin Marks-Kaufman. *Nutrition and Behavior.* New York: Van Nostrand Reinhold, 1991.

Koranyi, Erwin K., ed. *Physical Illness in the Psychiatric Patient.* Springfield, IL: Charles C. Thomas Publisher, 1982.

Kunin, Richard A. *Meganutrition.* New York: New American Library, 1981.

La Forge, Ralph. *Mind-Body Fitness: Encouraging Prospects for Primary and Secondary Prevention Programs.* San Diego, CA: San Diego Cardiac Center Medical Group, 1996.

Lazarus, Pat. *Healing the Mind the Natural Way.* New York: G.P. Putnam's Sons, 1995.

Lappe, Frances Moore. *Diet For a Small Planet.* New York: Ballantine Books, 1982.

Lawson, Lynn. *Staying Well in a Toxic World.* Chicago: Noble Press, 1993.

"Leaky Gut: A Common Problem with Food Allergies." *Mastering Food Allergies* 7, no. 5 (Sept.-Oct. 1993).

"Lithium-Thyroid Interactive Hypothesis of Neuropsychological Deficits: A Review and Proposal." *Depression* 1 (1994/1995).

MacMahon, Brian, and Takashi Sugimura. *Banbury Report: Coffee and Health.* Cold Spring Harbor, NY: Cold Spring Harbor Laboratory, 1984.

"Magnesium and Health." *Vitamin Research Products Nutritional News,* July 1993.

Mandell, Marshall, and Lynne Waller Scanlon. *Dr. Mandell's Five Day Allergy Relief System.* New York: Pocket Books, 1979.

Matheny, Kenneth B., and Richard J. Riordan. *Stress and Strategies for Lifestyle Management.* Atlanta: Georgia State University Business Press, 1992.

Miller, Klara. *Toxicological Aspects of Food.* London: Elsevier Applied Science, 1987.

Minirth, Frank B., and Paul D. Meier. *Happiness Is a Choice.* Grand Rapids, MI: Baker Book House, 1988.

"Mood Alteration with Yoga and Swimming: Aerobic Exercise May Not Be Necessary." *Perceptual Motor Skills* 75 (1992).

Nerozzi, Dina, Frederick K. Goodwin, and Erminio Costa, eds. *Hypothalamic Dysfunction in Neuropsychiatric Disorders.* New York: Raven Press, 1987.

Newbold, H.L. *Mega-Nutrients for Your Nerves.* New York: Berkeley Books, 1981.

———. *Dr. Newbold's Nutrition for Your Nerves.* New Canaan, CT: Keats Publishing, 1993.

"Nicotine Addiction and Schizophrenia." *The Journal of Orthomolecular Medicine* 5, no. 3 (1990).

Null, Gary. *No More Allergies.* New York: Villard Books, 1992.

———. *Nutrition and the Mind.* New York: Four Walls Eight Windows, 1995.

Odds, F.C. *Candida and Candidosis.* Baltimore: University Park Press, 1979.

"One Reason You May Fail To Get Well—Even On Best Diet." *Mastering Food Allergies* 42 (1990).

Palgrave, Francis T. *The Golden Treasury.* New York: MacMillan Co., 1956.

Pauling, Linus. *How To Live Longer and Feel Better.* New York: Avon Books, 1987.

Pfeiffer, Carl C. *Nutrition and Mental Illness.* Rochester, VT: Healing Arts Press, 1987.

———. *Mental and Elemental Nutrients.* New Canaan, CT: Keats Publishing, 1975.

Philpott, William H., and Dwight G. Kalita. *Brain Allergies: The Psychonutrient Connection.* New Canaan, CT: Keats Publishing, 1980.

Pierrakos, John C. *Core Energetics.* Mendocino, CA: LifeRhythms, 1990.

"Plasma Concentrations of Gamma-Aminobutyric Acid (GABA) and Mood Disorders: A Blood Test for Manic Depressive Disease?" *Clinical Chemistry* 40, no. 2 (1994).

"Plasma Ratios of Tryptophan and Tyrosine to other Large Neutral Amino Acids in Manic Depressive Patients." *Journal of Psychiatry & Neurology* 46, no. 3 (1992).

"Plasma Tryptophan Levels and Plasma Tryptophan/Neutral Amino Acids Ratio in Patients with Mood Disorder, Patients with Obsessive-Compulsive Disorder, and Normal Subjects." *Psychiatry Research* 44, no. 2 (1992).

Price, Lawrence H., and George R. Heninger, "Lithium in the Treatment of Mood Disorders." *The New England Journal of Medicine,* Sept. 1, 1994.

Randolph, Theron G., and Ralph W. Moss, *An Alternative Approach to Allergies.* Rev. ed. New York: Harper & Row, 1989.

Rapp, Doris J. *Is This Your Child: Discovering and Treating Unrecognized Allergies.* New York: William Morrow and Co., 1991.

Rea, William J. *Chemical Sensitivity: Principles and Mechanisms.* Boca Raton, FL: Lewis Publishers, 1992.

"Relationship Between Irritable Bowel Syndrome and Double Depression." *Depression* 3 (1996).

Richardson, Malcolm D., and David W. Warnock. *Fungal Infection: Diagnosis and Management.* Boston: Blackwell Scientific Publications, 1993.

"The Risks of Excessive Drinking." The Coalition for Consumer Health and Safety Web Site: Hidden Hazards, http://www.essential.org./cchs.hh.html#Alcohol.

Robinson, Robert G., and Peter V. Rabins. *Aging and Clinical Practice: Depression and Coexisting Disease.* New York: Igaku-Shoin, 1989.

Rochlitz, Steven. *Allergies and Candida With the Physicist's Rapid Solution.* New York: Human Ecology Balancing Sciences, 1989.

Rogers, Sherry. *The E.I. Syndrome.* Syracuse, NY: Prestige Publishers, 1986.

———. *You Are What You Ate: An Rx for the Resistant Diseases of the 21st Century.* Syracuse, NY: Prestige Publishing, 1988.

Rosenthal, M. Sara. *The Thyroid Sourcebook.* Los Angeles: Lowell House, 1995.

Rosenvold, Lloyd. *Can A Gluten-Free Diet Help?* New Canaan, CT: Keats Publishing, 1992.

Ross, Harvey M. *Fighting Depression.* New Canaan, CT: Keats Publishing, 1992.

Roth, June. *The Food/Depression Connection: Dietary Control of Allergy-Based Mood Swing.* Chicago: Contemporary Books, Inc., 1978.

"The Rotary Diversified Diet." *Mastering Food Allergies* 1, no. 6 (June 1986).

Salaman, Maureen. *Foods That Heal.* Menlo Park, CA: Stratford Publishing, 1989.

Sanbower, Martha. "Recognition and Treatment of Physical Factors in Psychotherapy Clients." *Journal of Orthomolecular Medicine* 5, no. 2.

———. "Manic Depression: An Alternate Treatment." *Journal of Orthomolecular Medicine* 2, no. 3.

"Schizophrenia and Bipolar Disorder May Be On a Continuum." *The Schizophrenia-Bipolar Interface: Current Research and Future Directions.* Presented at the 1995 International Stanley Foundation Satellite Symposium, organized by Dr. E. Fuller Torrey. Stanley Foundation Web Site, http://www/nami.org/about/stanley.htm.

Schulkin, Jay, ed. *Hormonally Induced Changes in Mind and Body.* New York: Academic Press, 1993.

Schultz, Dorothy. "The Information Super Highway." *Hypoglycemia Association Bulletin* 197 (Oct.-Dec. 1995).

Schwartz, George R. *In Bad Taste: The MSG Syndrome.* Santa Fe, NM: Health Press, 1988.

Seligman, Martin E.P. *Learned Optimism.* New York: Alfred A. Knopf, 1991.

Service, F. John. *Hypoglycemic Disorders.* Boston: G.K. Hall Medical Publishers, 1983.

"Seventy-Two Percent of Americans Are Magnesium-Deficient." *Better Nutrition for Today's Living* 57 (March 1995).

Shinn, Florence Scovel. *The Wisdom of Florence Scovel Shinn.* New York: Fireside, 1989.

Siegel, George J., Bernard W. Agranoff, R. Wayne Albers, and Perry B. Molinoff, eds. *Basic Neurochemistry: Molecular, Cellular, and Medical Aspects,* 4th ed. New York: Raven Press, 1989.

"Significantly Increased Expression of T-Cell Activation Markers in Depression: Further Evidence for an Inflammatory Process During That Illness." *Progress in Neuro-Psychopharmacology and Biological Psychiatry* 17 (1993).

Slagle, Priscilla. *The Way Up From Down.* New York: St. Martin's Paperbacks, 1992.

Smart Basics Inc. "Smart Basics Glossary: Amino Acids," 1996, http://www/vrcreations.com/index.html.

———. "Smart Basics Minerals Glossary," 1996, http://www.smartbasic.com/glos.minerals.dir.html.

Smith, Marge. "Feeding Yourself in All Sorts of Circumstances." *Hypoglycemia Association Bulletin* 164 (Sept. 1995).

Smolinske, Susan C. *Handbook of Food, Drug, and Cosmetic Excipients*. Boca Raton, FL: CRC Press, 1992.

Speer, Frederick. *Food Allergy.* boston: PSG Inc., 1983.

Steginck, Lewis D., and L.J. Filer Jr., eds. *Aspartame.* New York: Marcel Dekker Inc., 1984.

"Steroid Hormones, Clinical Correlates." Diagnos-Techs Inc. Seminar in Atlanta, GA, October 1995.

Sudy, Mitchell, ed. *Personal Trainer Manual.* San Diego, CA: American Council on Exercise, 1991.

Thie, John. *Touch for Health: A New Approach To Restoring Our Natural Energies.* Sherman Oaks, CA: T.H. Enterprises, 1994.

"The Treatment of Depression: Prescribing Practices of Primary Care Physicians and Psychiatrists." *The Journal of Family Practice* 35, no. 6 (1992).

Tintera, John W. "Adrenal Dysfunction." *Hypoglycemia Association Bulletin* 96 (n.d.).

Trowbridge, John Parks, and Morton Walker. *The Yeast Syndrome.* New York: Bantam Books, 1986.

Tunbridge, W.M.G. *Thyroid Disease: The Facts.* Oxford: Oxford University Press, 1991.

"Update on Mood Disorders." *The Harvard Mental Health Letter,* Dec. 1994.

"U.S. Tap Water Is Dirty." Associated Press Report, June 1, 1995.

Vagnini, Frederick J. "What's Wrong With Pasta?" *Cardiovascular Newsletter,* http://www.holistic.com/essays/insuln01.html.

Vayda, William. *Mood Foods.* Berkeley, CA: Ulysses Press, 1995.

Weyerer, Siegfried, and Brigitte Kupfer. "Physical Exercise and Psychological Health." *Sports Medicine* 17, no. 2.

Whybrow, Peter C. "Sex Differences in Thyroid Axis Function: Relevance to Affective Disorder and Its Treatment." *Depression* 3 (1995).

Wilson, Cynthia. *Chemical Exposure and Human Health.* Jefferson, NC: McFarland and Co., 1993.

Wolstenholme, G.E.W., and Ruth Porter. *The Human Adrenal Cortex: Its Function Throughout Life.* Boston: Little, Brown and Co., 1967.

Wurtman, Richard J. and Judith J. Wurtman. "Carbohydrates and Depression." *Scientific American,* Jan. 1989.

———. *Nutrition and the Brain,* Vol. 4. New York: Raven Press, 1979.
"X-Linked Dominant Manic-Depressive Illness." *The Journal of Orthomolecular Psychiatry* 8, no. 2.

Zamm, Alfred V. "Removal of Dental Mercury: Often an Effective Treatment for the Very Sensitive Patient." *The Journal of Orthomolecular Medicine* 5, no. 3 (third quarter 1990).

Ziff, Sam, and Michael F. Ziff. *Dentistry Without Mercury.* Orlando, FL: Bio-Probe Inc., 1993.

Index

About the Author

Catherine Carrigan is president of Total Fitness and honorary board chairman of the Holistic Depression Network. Her mission is to empower herself and others to achieve total fitness of mind, body, and spirit. She is certified in personal fitness training through the American Council on Exercise, in group exercise through A.C.E. and N.D.E.I.T.A, and in yoga through the White Lotus Foundation. She is a certified Brain Gym consultant and Touch for Health practitioner. Three of her twelve plays have been produced in New York.

A Phi Beta Kappa graduate of Brown University, Ms. Carrigan spent three years researching depression at the Emory University Medical Library in Atlanta, and twenty years working with a variety of practitioners to bring about her own healing. She lives in Atlanta, Georgia, with her husband, Henry Edmunds.

She can be reached via her website, www.totalfitness.net.